D1234679

Evolutionary Concepts in Contemporary Economics

Economics, Cognition, and Society
This series provides a forum for theoretical and empirical investigations of social phenomena. It promotes works that focus on the interactions among cognitive processes, individual behavior, and social outcomes. It is especially open to interdisciplinary books that are genuinely integrative.

Editor: Timur Kuran

Editorial Board: Ronald Heiner
Sheila Ryan Johansson

Advisory Board: James M. Buchanan
Albert O. Hirschman
Mancur Olson

Titles in the Series

Ulrich Witt, Editor. *Explaining Process and Change: Approaches to Evolutionary Economics*

Young Back Choi. *Paradigms and Conventions: Uncertainty, Decision Making, and Entrepreneurship*

Geoffrey M. Hodgson. *Economics and Evolution: Bringing Life Back into Economics*

Richard W. England, Editor. *Evolutionary Concepts in Contemporary Economics*

Evolutionary Concepts in Contemporary Economics

Richard W. England, Editor

Ann Arbor

THE UNIVERSITY OF MICHIGAN PRESS

330
E933

Copyright © by the University of Michigan 1994
All rights reserved
Published in the United States of America by
The University of Michigan Press
Manufactured in the United States of America

1997   1996   1995   1994   4   3   2   1

A CIP catalogue record for this book is available from the British Library.

Library of Congress Cataloging-in-Publication Data

Evolutionary concepts in economics / Richard W. England, editor.
        p.   cm. — (Economics, cognition, and society)
    Includes bibliographical references.
    ISBN 0-472-10483-7 (alk. paper)
    1. Evolutionary economics.   I. England, Richard W.   II. Series.
HB97.3.E93   1994
330—dc20   93-42743
                                                               CIP

This book is dedicated to the memory of Kenneth E. Boulding, who challenged us to imagine a peaceful, just, and sustainable society.

Preface

This book has an evolutionary history, as do all other artifacts of human culture. In 1967, I was fortunate to attend a graduate seminar on conflict resolution and general systems theory offered by Kenneth E. Boulding, who was then in Ann Arbor. A few years later, I was exhilarated when I first encountered Nicholas Georgescu-Roegen's *The Entropy Law and the Economic Process*.

Those two experiences had an important impact on my intellectual development, but that influence was not evident until recently. It's difficult to say what rekindled my interest in evolutionary economics, but witnessing the large and enthusiastic audience at the 1990 American Economic Association (AEA) session on path-dependence in economics certainly played a role.

It seemed to me that the economics profession might be more receptive to fresh perspectives than it had been for a number of decades, and I resolved to organize an AEA panel on evolutionary concepts in contemporary economics. William Vickrey was kind enough to place my proposed session on the 1992 meeting schedule (even though his initial reaction was that the topic was "a little kooky"). Once again, a large and lively audience appeared to hear the panelists' message that history matters in economics and that economies evolve as history unfolds.

Because of these encouraging events, I decided to invite the panelists and several additional authors to contribute to this anthology. In my opinion, the collection of essays that follows is something to savor and to enjoy. I hope that you, the reader, will agree.

Acknowledgments

The editor of this anthology gratefully acknowledges the editorial guidance of Colin Day (University of Michigan Press), the secretarial help of Sinthy Kounlasa (Whittemore School of Business and Economics), and the financial support of the Faculty Scholars Program (University of New Hampshire). All successful projects require cooperative efforts: This book is no exception.

Contents

Part 1. Introduction to Evolutionary Economics

Time and Economics: An Introductory Perspective 3
  Richard W. England

Precursors of Modern Evolutionary Economics:
Marx, Marshall, Veblen, and Schumpeter 9
  Karl Marx
  Alfred Marshall
  Thorstein Veblen
  Joseph Schumpeter
  The New Wave
  Geoffrey M. Hodgson

Part 2. Evolution and Economic Methodology

Rethinking Complexity in Economic Theory: The Challenge
of Overdetermination 39
  Conceiving Existence and Causation
  Dialectics, Change, and Evolution
  Operationalizing Overdetermination
  Overdetermination and Economics
  Overdetermination and Consumer Sovereignty
  Conclusion
  Appendix: The Overdetermination of Economic Theories
  Stephen A. Resnick and Richard D. Wolff

Evolutionary Economics and System Dynamics 61
  What Exactly *Is* Evolutionary Economics?
  What Exactly Is Evolutionary Economics *Modeling*?
  Characteristics of System Dynamics Models
  An Illustration: Learning Curves, Imperfect
    Appropriability, and Evolving Industry Structure
  Software and Other Resources for System Dynamics
    Modeling

Conclusions
Michael J. Radzicki and John D. Sterman

Part 3. Evolution and Social Institutions

An Evolutionary Approach to Law and Economics   93
General Characteristics of an Evolutionary Approach
The Neoclassical Approach in Contrast
The Principal Elements of Developmental Analysis
Conclusion
*Warren J. Samuels, A. Allan Schmid,
and James D. Shaffer*

Communication in Economic Evolution: The Case of Money   111
Changing the Primary Distinction: From Observer
to Observation
Economy and Money
Conditions of Evolutionary Economic Change
The Evolution of Money during the Seventh Century B.C.
Final Remarks
Michael Hutter

Part 4. Innovation and the Firm

The Coevolution of Technologies and Institutions   139
Recent Research Bearing on the Coevolution of Technology
and Institutions
Implications for Economic Analysis
Reprise
Richard R. Nelson

Some Elements of an Evolutionary Theory
of Organizational Competences   157
The Notion of Competence
Competence and Decision Making
Competence, Learning, and Organization
Exploitation vs. Exploration in Organizational Learning
Conclusions: Patterns of Learning and Selection
Giovanni Dosi and Luigi Marengo

Entrepreneurial Imagination, Information, and the Evolution
of the Firm   179
Information Systems and the Creative Self-Constitution
of the Firm

Optimization and the Informational Constitution
  of the Firm
Prelude to a Theory of the Informational Constitution
  of the Firm
  Randall Bausor

Part 5. Nature and Economic Evolution

On Economic Growth and Resource Scarcity: Lessons
from Nonequilibrium Thermodynamics   193
  On Physics and Economics
  Thermodynamics and Resource Scarcity
  Dissipative Structures and Evolution
  Evolutionary Futures: A Simple Model
    Richard W. England

The Coevolution of Economic and Environmental Systems
and the Emergence of Unsustainability   213
  Dominant Premises of Western Thought
  Development as a Coevolutionary Process
  The Coevolution of Unsustainability
  Conclusions
    Richard B. Norgaard

Bibliography   227

Contributors   253

Part 1
Introduction to Evolutionary Economics

Evolutionary elements predominate in every concrete economic phenomenon of some significance—to a greater extent than even in biology. If our scientific net lets these elements slip through it, we are left only with a shadow of the concrete phenomenon.

—Nicholas Georgescu-Roegen (1971)

Time and Economics: An Introductory Perspective

Richard W. England

Time, it seems, "is one of the great sources of mystery to mankind. Throughout history, human beings have restlessly puzzled over time's profound yet inscrutable nature" (Coveney and Highfield 1990, 23). Economists have frequently encountered this temporal puzzle and are still wrestling with the implications of history for economic thought (Currie and Steedman 1990). This anthology reports on several promising attempts to introduce historical time into economic reasoning in a serious fashion.

Human efforts to grasp the nature of time have traditionally produced a number of proposed solutions. Observation of the tides, solstices, seasons, and celestial motions led many primitive cultures and the ancient Greeks to perceive time as a cycle of rebirth and renewal (Coveney and Highfield 1990, 25). This cyclic conception has survived up to the modern era, e.g., in Keynes's circular flow of aggregate expenditure or in Sraffa's production of commodities by means of commodities.

More commonly, however, modern science has simply denied any significant role for time in its theoretical representations of the empirical world. As Prigogine (1990, 16–17) has remarked, "[T]he research programme of classical science . . . focused on a description in terms of deterministic, time-reversible laws . . . . Laws were associated [with] . . . deterministic predictions and ultimately . . . the very negation of time." This characterization applies equally well to Newton's mechanics, Einstein's relativity theory, and the quantum mechanics of Heisenberg and Schrödinger, "all [of which] appear to work equally well with time running in reverse" (Coveney and Highfield 1990, 23). As Robinson (1978, 138) pointed out in a delightful lecture at Oxford, neoclassical economics adopts a similar logic in its use of "a metaphor based on [reversible motions in] space to explain a process which takes place in time."

During the past century, however, research in such fields as evolutionary biology, cosmology, and thermodynamics has begun to weaken the "mechanistic epistemology" (Georgescu-Roegen 1971) that has gripped the scientific imagination for several centuries. "Indeed, science *is* rediscovering time, and

3

in a sense this marks an end to the classical conception of science. . . . Actually, this programme was never completed as, in addition to laws, we need also events, which introduce an arrow of time into our description of nature. . . . Events imply an element of arbitrariness as they involve discontinuities, probabilities and irreversible evolution" (Prigogine 1990, 16–17).

This notion that time flows irreversibly from the past to the future, that there is an "arrow of time" (Eddington 1943), is a temporal perspective that has appealed to a number of prominent economists. As Geoffrey M. Hodgson documents in the next chapter, Marx, Marshall, Veblen, and Schumpeter all wrestled with evolutionary concepts as they addressed economic questions. However, in contrast with several contemporary economists (Hanusch 1988; Nelson and Winter 1974) who have looked to Schumpeter for inspiration, Hodgson argues that Veblen offered a more coherent vision of what an evolutionary economics might be.

During the past two decades, evolutionary approaches have displayed increasing influence within academic economics. Examples include Georgescu-Roegen (1971); Day and Groves (1975); David (1975); Boulding (1981); Nelson and Winter (1982); Solow (1985); Anderson, Arrow, and Pines (1988); and Faber and Proops (1990). This growing impact is perhaps not surprising, since, as Rosser (1992) has argued, the influence of evolutionary concepts originating in natural science on economic reasoning has been a longstanding one. Hence, a growing respect for "the arrow of time" among contemporary biologists, chemists, and physicists has helped to create an audience for evolutionary messages within economics.

At the same time, however, the ahistorical approach preferred by neoclassical theorists continues to dominate economic discourse, especially in the United States. How are we to explain this persistent and widespread resistance to evolutionary concepts within the economics profession? One reason, perhaps, is "the lamentable past association of biological thought [evolution in particular] with 'social Darwinism' . . ." (Hodgson 1991b, 520). An unfounded fear that evolutionary concepts inevitably imply reactionary and even racist ideologies may deter some economists from thinking such thoughts.

Of far greater importance, however, is the type of graduate education that several generations of economists have received since World War II. Under the influence of Samuelson (1947) and Friedman (1953), budding economists have learned that they should build simple mathematical models to represent complex social processes and then, using equilibrium and optimization postulates, logically deduce behavioral predictions that can be checked for their degree of empirical accuracy. More recently, Becker (1976) and Hirshleifer (1985) have promised fellow economists that this neoclassical brand of positivism will produce an ever wider domain for economic research, presumably thereby expanding employment opportunities within the profession as a whole.

Once one entertains an evolutionary approach to economics, however, it becomes difficult, if not impossible, to retain neoclassical positivism as a methodology. One reason mentioned by Boulding (1968, 162) and by Faber and Proops (1990) is that *novel events* repeatedly alter the systems whose behavior the economic forecaster seeks to predict. This observation that economies repeatedly generate surprises can lead one down either of two methodological paths. One option is to continue pursuing prediction as the only worthy scientific goal, thereby denying evidence of historical novelties. The alternative path, which Charles Darwin squarely faced, requires one to "confront history, where complex events occur but once in detailed glory . . ." (Gould 1986, 64). This methodological approach eschews equilibrium theories built on universal axioms and downplays prediction as a scientific goal. Instead, the evolutionary approach directs one to inspect the historical record in a patient search for homologous patterns. Taxonomy, not deduction, is the primary tool with which to expose and grasp the past (Gould 1986).

Until recently, another obstacle to the emergence of evolutionary economics has been a shortage of tools with which to *formally model* evolutionary processes. As Colander and Brenner (1992, 6–7) point out, modern economists have been taught to admire econometric and mathematical technique. However, as Boulding (1981, 86) has recognized, the differential calculus and dynamic optimization methods that have served neoclassical theorists so well are not suitable tools with which to formally represent evolutionary processes. Thus, it has seemed as though economists must choose between formal rigor and realistic description as they try to analyze complex, evolving economies.

Fortunately, modeling tools that are more in the spirit of Darwin than Newton have begun to emerge. As Michael J. Radzicki and John D. Sterman point out in part 2 of this book, advances in computer technology permit the evolutionary analyst to simulate complex systems with numerous dynamic feedback loops and complicated lag structures. These system-dynamics models are able to mimic evolutionary processes, as the authors' simulation of competition for market shares demonstrates. Bifurcation analysis (Brøns and Sturis 1991) and nonlinear stochastic models (Arthur, Ermoliev, and Kaniovski 1987) also show promise as tools with which one can model path-dependent processes.

Perhaps the greatest obstacle of all to the widespread acceptance of evolutionary economics, however, is its message that economic processes seldom display *optimality*. The claims that economic agents seek maxima or minima (or at least behave "as if" they do), and that, under appropriate conditions, optimal social outcomes will be realized, are cherished postulates of neoclassical economics. In a widely cited essay, Alchian (1950) speculated that Darwinian selection processes within the economic realm result in optimal outcomes. However, as Samuelson (1978) later pointed out, evolutionary processes cannot, in general, be characterized as extremum problems.

A careful reading of recent debates among evolutionary biologists suggests why this is so. As Lewontin (1982, 159) affirms, there is a

> central problem in the metaphor of trial-and-error adaptation. . . . [It] begins with a world in which an organism's environment is somehow defined without reference to the organism itself. . . . This is the notion that the world is divided up into pre-existent ecological niches and that evolution consists of the progressive fitting of organisms into these niches.

The claim that relatively fit organisms are selected to fill preexisting niches and that an optimal outcome results can be rejected for a number of reasons. First, even if such environmental niches were to exist, an infinite sequence of trials and errors would be necessary to identify the optimal match of organism and environment (Allen and McGlade 1989, 4). Second, since an organism's environment consists of populations of other organisms, the ecological niches themselves evolve. "This [coevolutionary process] means that as a population climbs a hill in the evolutionary landscape, so the hill and the evolutionary landscape move" (Allen and McGlade 1989, 18). Third, "organism-environmental interactions . . . almost never involve the organism in a purely passive role. . . . [O]rganisms actively choose their environment so as to give themselves the greatest chance of survival" (Ho and Saunders 1982, 355). That is to say, "Organisms . . . do not *adapt* to environments; they *construct* them" (Lewontin 1982, 163). Arguments such as these have resulted in a far more complex conception of evolution than the neo-Darwinism that dominated biology several decades ago, and which seems to have influenced Alchian (1950).

Although apparently remote from economic theory, these recent developments in evolutionary biology offer important lessons for the economist. Perhaps the most fundamental lesson is that empirical phenomena cannot be viewed as the direct effects of a compact set of essential causes. As Wesson (1991, 26) concluded after his exhaustive survey of evolutionary research:

> The ladder of natural systems consists of elementary particles, atoms, molecules, macromolecules, cell parts, cells, organs, organisms, populations, species, and ecosystems. . . . Each level has its own reality, as real as any other; and more complex systems require appropriate levels of

explanation and display regularities, or laws, that cannot be deduced from simpler components. . . . In wholes, new properties "emerge.". . .

In a similar vein, Stephen A. Resnick and Richard D. Wolff argue in this volume that neoclassical economics has been misguided in its effort to theorize all economic phenomena as the direct consequences of a few essences like subjective preferences, technology, and factor endowments. Resnick and Wolff propose an evolutionary methodology that partitions reality into economic, political, cultural, and natural processes that interact in complex and contradictory ways. Their concept of *overdetermination* entails a systematic rejection of all essentialist (i.e., determinist or reductive) linkages among discrete phenomena in economics.

Should mainstream economists, then, reject their neoclassical roots and abandon concepts of equilibrium, optimality, and essential causation? The answer to that question can be hammered out during future methodological debates. But "the case for methodological pluralism" (Norgaard 1989) within economics is already strong and compelling.

The essays that follow support this case for intellectual tolerance and methodological pluralism within the economics profession. Warren J. Samuels, A. Allan Schmid, and James D. Shaffer, for example, demonstrate that an evolutionary approach to law and economics illuminates the open-ended, historical character of the law and of the distinction between the public and private domains. In another chapter that addresses the institutional environment of the market economy, Michael Hutter argues that money is not only a quantity that increases in magnitude but also an evolving means of communication among economic agents, a social construction that mutates and diffuses with far-ranging consequences.

In part 4, a trio of chapters points to the deepening influence of evolutionary concepts on the theory of the firm. Richard R. Nelson surveys recent research on technological innovation and concludes that institutions such as universities, professional societies, and government agencies provide a crucial context for the technological developments implemented by business firms. In their chapter, Giovanni Dosi and Luigi Marengo suggest that firms should be seen as organizations in which information-processing capabilities and decision rules coevolve in a process of learning and adaptation. In a complementary chapter, Randall Bausor argues that the formation and evolution of a firm cannot be reduced to optimization decisions. Entrepreneurial imagination is required to design and redesign the information systems that guide "normal" business operations.

In the final section, the evolving relationship between the economic system and its natural environment is addressed. Richard W. England discusses why the classical thermodynamic arguments of Georgescu-Roegen

(1971) failed to convert most economists to an evolutionary perspective and why far-from-equilibrium thermodynamics offers a better framework for analyzing economic and environmental interactions. In the last chapter, Richard B. Norgaard argues that knowledge, values, technology, social organization, and nature coevolve in a complex fashion. The coevolution of the modern economy with fossil hydrocarbons poses questions about its long-term sustainability, questions that must be faced in the coming decades.

What all of these chapters reflect is their authors' firm commitment to take history seriously. If economics is to be both properly scientific and also practically useful, then ahistorical models of economies gliding along frictionless orbits are not good enough. We shall have to face the mysteries of time and wrestle with their consequences.

Precursors of Modern Evolutionary Economics: Marx, Marshall, Veblen, and Schumpeter

Geoffrey M. Hodgson

The term *evolution* is used casually in public and academic circles, vaguely connoting "development," and often with the unwarranted confidence and assurance that everyone knows what it means. Nothing is more guaranteed to generate confusion and to stultify intellectual progress than to raise a muddled term to the centerpiece of economic research, while simultaneously suggesting that a clear and well-defined approach to scientific enquiry is implied. "Evolution" can be used to describe a varied group of approaches in contemporary economics, perhaps in contrast to the exclusive focus on equilibrium in neoclassical theory, but it does not indicate a well-defined type of analysis.

In order to disentangle several of the different meanings of "evolutionary" it is useful to examine the "evolutionary" or "biological" ideas of Marx, Marshall, Veblen, and Schumpeter. That is the purpose of this chapter, which devotes one section to each of the four economists. There is also some discussion of other relevant and related thinkers. For instance, the section on Marshall provides an opportunity to introduce the conceptions of evolution found in the work of Lamarck and Spencer. In the section on Veblen, the distinction between phylogenetic and ontogenetic evolution is outlined. The final section, on Schumpeter, concludes that much modern work in evolutionary economics may be more "Veblenian" than "Schumpeterian" in character, despite the almost universal use of the latter description.

Karl Marx

Karl Marx (1818–83) and Charles Darwin (1809–82) were close contemporaries. It is well known that Marx was impressed by Darwin's *Origin of*

The author wishes to thank Stephan Boehm, Dale Bush, John Foster, Christian Knudsen, Richard Nelson, Pavel Pelikan, and many others for discussions on the subject matter of this chapter and Richard England for editorial assistance. This chapter uses material from my book *Economics and Evolution* (1993), by permission of Polity Press, Cambridge.

9

Species, although the idea that he went so far as to ask permission from Darwin to dedicate a volume of *Capital* to him turns out to be a myth (Colp 1982). While praising Darwin's theory as "a natural-scientific basis for the class struggle in history," Marx (1977, 525–26) also hinted, as early as 1862, at the possibility of apologetic and procapitalist interpretations: "It is remarkable how Darwin recognises among beasts and plants his English society with its division of labour, competition, opening-up of new markets, 'inventions' and the Malthusian 'struggle for existence.'" Thus Marx correctly foresaw the Panglossian ideological uses to which Darwinism would later be put.[1]

It is probable that Marx and Engels lauded Darwinism because they welcomed this breakthrough in natural science and because they were attracted to Darwin's covert atheism and materialism (Gould 1978, 23–28). However, it is clear from a close examination of their writings that Marx and Engels did not actually take Darwin's theory of natural selection on board. Consequently, if their theory of socioeconomic change is evolutionary, it is not so in a Darwinian sense. This section considers the different sense in which the economics of Marx can be regarded as "evolutionary" and the distance between Darwinian and Marxian conceptions of natural or social change.

Marx mentions Darwin in a few places in *Capital*, but normally he left his friend Frederick Engels (1820–95) to deal with controversies in the natural sciences. The most extensive treatment of Darwin and Darwinism by Marx or Engels is in the latter's *Dialectics of Nature*. Therein Engels incorporates a brief critical discussion of the Darwinian idea of the "struggle for existence" or "struggle for life" (Engels 1964, 311–14). This particular notion is associated by Engels with Malthus and rejected as a weak ideological buttress for capitalist competition. Hence Engels writes of the possibility of evolution "without need for selection and Malthusianism." Although Engels's *Dialectics of Nature* is not without its merits, the reader will search there in vain for a clear and adequate account of Darwin's theory of natural selection.

On close examination there is much in the Marxian theoretical system that is antagonistic to Darwinian evolutionary ideas. The idea of change resulting from a process of natural selection among a population of individual entities exhibiting great diversity and variety is markedly different from the conception of history as the clash of collectives engaged in class struggle.

In Marx's economics it is assumed that value calculations pertain to the most profitable technique that has become established at a given time. Value quantities thereby relate to the amount of "socially necessary" labor time involved with this technique. By this theoretical device, the essential function of variety in the economic process is expunged. Without ever-present variety, however, there is no raw material for natural selection.

---

1. Notably, modern evolutionary theory does not sustain such a Panglossian approach. See Hodgson (1991b).

Some commentators have highlighted the famous footnote in *Capital* where Marx (1976, 493n) relates technological development to Darwin's account of "the formation of the organs in plants and animals." Here Marx is not drawing a direct analogy between technological and biological evolution. He is simply making the point that the development of technology should not be regarded solely as the inspiration of single individuals, but as a complex historical process.[2]

Although Marx's extensive discussion of machinery and technological change remains unparalleled among economists, the mechanisms leading to the expansion and development of the productive forces are not sufficiently clear. A prominent and celebrated feature of Marx's analysis is the idea of the "forces of production" straining against and eventually breaking the "relations of production" in some revolutionary convulsion. Whatever the veracity of such a vision, it leaves the nature of those very "productive forces" and the energies impelling them to be explained. Although he made a major contribution to the theory of technological change, the account of how productive forces themselves evolve is left vague.

The Marxian conception of history has much more in common with evolution's Latin etymology as *evolvere*, or "unrolling," than with Darwinian natural selection. However, a clear limitation of the analogy with the unrolling of a parchment is that it does not encompass a key idea that Marx inherited from Hegel, that of internal contradiction and conflict leading to disruptive change. For Marx and Engels, of course, the class struggle is the motor of history, with change occurring in leaps of a revolutionary, and possibly violent, nature.

Also, as Hegel did before, Marx and Engels regard history as a series of developmental stages. For them, historical progress is represented by a sequence of social formations, from "primitive communism," through to communism in the "higher" form. Note, first, that with the supposed development from "primitive" to "full" communism, there is precisely a suggestion of a revolving movement, returning to the original position but at a "higher" level. Clearly the Marxian view of history is more revolutionary, in that sense, than evolutionary.

Second, and more importantly, communism refers to a unified social order in a state of harmony. Not only is the basis and actuality of social struggle presumed to have disappeared, but also there is no variety in the forms of ownership and of productive institutions. It is assumed that under communism there is neither conflict between classes nor a diversity of material interests and socioeconomic forms. Marx and Engels suggest that such a

---

2. One of the few explicit references to "natural selection" in Marxian writings is in another footnote in *Capital* (Marx 1976, 461n). Here, however, the phrase appears within a direct quotation from the *Origin of Species*.

system could be technologically dynamic, but insofar as human motivation depends upon some degree of social variety and disruption, in such a system there is no fuel for further change.

Karl Marx and Herbert Spencer are usually regarded as being at the opposite ends of the political spectrum, the former believing in common ownership, the latter in markets and laissez-faire. However, they both believed in the perfectibility of society, and both on the basis of a single and ubiquitous type of economic arrangement. In this respect at least, Marx's evolutionism has more in common with Spencer's ideas than with the Darwinian emphasis on variety.

Notably, Malthus had opposed the idea of the perfectibility of society. Malthus (1926, 379) saw "the infinite variety of nature" that "cannot exist without inferior parts, or apparent blemishes." The function of such diversity and struggle was to enable the development of the improved forms. Without such a contest, no species would be impelled to improve itself. The existence of diversity, with its blemishes and impurities, was seen by Malthus as essential. (See Young 1969.)

While Marx and Engels admired Darwin, they clearly abhorred Malthus. For them, Malthus was a plagiarist, a bought advocate, and a shameless sycophant of the ruling classes (Marx and Engels 1953, 22–23). Wishing to associate their theory with the Darwinian scientific revolution, they attempted to force Darwin and Malthus apart, professing the view that Darwinism would be more scientific without its Malthusian content.[3]

Malthus contrasts with Marx in that he emphasizes diversity and pluralism. In this vein a Malthusian critique of perfectibility applies to the modern proponents of a "pure" economic system based entirely on markets and private property, just as it does to advocates of 100 percent central planning.[4]

In a pioneering comparison of institutional and Marxian conceptions of economic evolution, Harris (1934, 56) makes a perceptive assessment of the differences between Marxian and Darwinian theory:

It is not strange that Marx and Engels, preoccupied with the arduous labours of propagating heterodox ideas in a hostile intellectual environ-

---

3. Although Marx and Engels accepted that Darwin had been strongly influenced by Malthus, the extent of the influence has become controversial. Although Darwin (1904, 120) himself explains how his own theory was inspired by the picture of "the struggle for existence" in the *Essay on the Principle of Population* by Malthus, this autobiographical statement has been belittled by some, particularly by those (e.g., Schumpeter 1954, 445–46) with some kind of allergy to the reverend. However, detailed examination of Darwin's notebooks (Gruber 1974) suggests that the great biologist found crucial stimulation in Malthus's *Essay*, even if some of the elements in Darwin's thinking had already been formed and were indeed inspired by other theorists (Schweber 1977; Jones 1989).

4. See Hodgson (1984; 1988, 252–74) for a further discussion of this issue.

ment, overlooked the stark differences between their own preconceptions and those of Darwin. Except for superficial resemblances in terminology, there is hardly any connection between class conflict and Darwin's principles of "struggle for existence" and "natural selection." For when the dialectics of historical movement is made to proceed in terms of Darwin's biological principles it is impossible to predict the character and form of social change. On the basis of Darwinism change would occur as chance variations, unpredictable phenomena, highly uncertain in outcome, and tending to no predetermined goal.

As Schumpeter (1954, 445) remarks: "Marx may have experienced satisfaction at the emergence of Darwinist evolutionism. But his own had nothing whatever to do with it, and neither lends any support to the other." In a similar vein, Giddens (1984, 243) notes that "in Marx there is an inverted Hegelian dialectic, tortured into a particular developmental shape, that has no direct analogue in more orthodox evolutionary theories."

It is not to belittle Marx's great contribution to economics to discover that he did not take on board much of Darwin's theoretical revolution in biology. Marx and Engels did not assimilate Darwinian theory because it was incompatible with the mechanistic zeitgeist within which they were still entrapped. To escape, much of their theoretical system would have had to change. As Clark and Juma (1987, 48) argue:

> The main problem with Marx is that he recognized the significance of evolutionary factors but returned to a classical Newtonian world-view, especially in his prognosis for future social systems. In Marx's world, the socioeconomic system tends to move from moments of extreme fluctuations, of class struggles, towards social equilibria governed by socialist principles—classless societies in which the sources of fluctuations and struggle are eliminated. Like Newton's cosmology, society settles into an equilibrium, as the underlying social laws that Marx sought to lay bare, prevail over individual action.

Thus, although Darwin's *Origin* shattered many ancient ideas concerning the creation of species in general and humanity in particular, the full scientific force of his theory was not widely appreciated in Marx's day. Indeed, the ontological and methodological implications of Darwinian biology have yet to be spun out in full.

Alfred Marshall

Alfred Marshall is known for his repeated invocation of biological analogies. However, the specific influence of the social and biological theorist Herbert

Spencer on Marshall is often ignored. When Marshall turned for inspiration to biology it was to Spencer rather than to the author of the *Origin of Species*. Also, it is not widely acknowledged that the discussion of biological ideas by Marshall is concentrated very much into just one chapter of his *Principles*. In sum, the extent of Marshall's failure to move beyond the equilibrating and static theoretical system is often unappreciated.

Marshall is often quoted for his statement that "the Mecca of the economist lies in economic biology rather than in economic dynamics," but we are less often reminded of what immediately follows: "But biological conceptions are more complex than those of mechanics; a volume on Foundations must therefore give a relatively large place to mechanical analogies; and frequent use is made of the term 'equilibrium,' which suggests something of a statical analogy" (Marshall 1961, xiv).

Marshall saw the limitations of mechanical reasoning, and turned to biology in his search for inspiration and metaphor. However, the science was then young and the mechanisms of evolution were not fully understood. At the time, many biologists questioned or misunderstood the Darwinian approach. As Bowler (1988, 5) argues: "Darwin's theory should be seen not as the central theme in nineteenth-century evolutionism but as a catalyst that helped bring about the transition to an evolutionary viewpoint within an essentially non-Darwinian conceptual framework."

In fact, there was an even bolder synthesis to Darwinism on offer. For Marshall, as for many of his contemporaries, "the writings of Herbert Spencer were even more significant than those of Darwin" (Thomas 1991, 3). Marshall (1975, 1:109) recollected how "a saying of Spencer sent the blood rushing through the veins of those who a generation ago looked eagerly for each volume of his as it issued from the press." Keynes (1924, 313) quoted Mary Marshall's account of how her husband would read volumes of Spencer on their walking holidays in the Alps. In the preface to the first edition of the *Principles*, Marshall singled out for mention the writings of Spencer and Hegel.

Early on in his career, Marshall began to see the limitations of mechanistic reasoning in economics. In particular, in his investigations of increasing returns, it became clear to him that a movement up or down the long-period supply curve is irreversible.[5] He was nagged by the problems of increasing returns and time irreversibility for the remainder of his life. Although the *Principles* deals primarily with economic statics, Marshall planned another volume to deal with dynamics and the elusive element of time (Whitaker

---

5. See Appendix H of the *Principles*. For discussions of Marshall's treatment of time and increasing returns, see Currie and Steedman (1990, chap. 2), Loasby (1978), Shackle (1972, 244, 286–96), Sraffa (1926), and Thomas (1991, 4–5).

1990). This companion work would address irreversible changes and organic development, drawing its inspiration more from biology than from physics. Some of these issues are briefly addressed in the *Principles*, but, contrary to the suggestions of some interpreters, they are not integrated into his analysis in a systematic way. Although that work is peppered with the occasional biological metaphor, the essence of the analysis is mechanical, addressing equilibrium outcomes, as Marshall himself admits.

Boulding (1981, 17), Reisman (1987, 338–57), Niman (1991), and others have noted the extent to which Marshall depicts economic development as being "organic" in quality. However, this does not necessarily imply an organicist ontology, in which relations between entities are internal rather than external, and the essential characteristics of any element are outcomes of relations with other entities. Such organicism is incompatible with the metaphor of nineteenth-century mechanics, which is based on an atomist ontology.

The acknowledged influence of Hegel on Marshall would seem to provide a prima facie case for imputing to the economist an organicist view. This does not, however, stand up to closer examination. The influence of Hegel, at least on Marshall's mature writings, is rather limited (Groenewegen 1990; Whitaker 1977). As Parsons (1932, 319) put it: "He took from Hegel only what suited his own preconceptions, and used it only to round off the sharp edges of his own tradition—as in his idea of the 'organic' nature of social change."

Although Marshall often discussed the way in which an economic entity may depend on its relations with others, he was unable to proceed in his *Principles* without considering each element as an atomistic unit. The "organic" reasoning in the *Principles* was indeed of a limited and Spencerian kind, impoverished in comparison with the richer organicism of philosophers such as Alfred North Whitehead.

Consider, for example, Marshall's treatment of the "representative firm." Although he associates this notion with a vague idea of "organic development," it is essentially a theoretical device to deal with organic variety by entrapping and ignoring it, rather than by encompassing diversity within an idea of an ongoing process of competition and change. This largely heuristic concept deals with the varied population of firms by identifying a single set of distinct characteristics that are deemed to represent the essential qualities of the population—i.e., the industry—as a whole. It is not a single firm, nor even a typical firm. Rather it is an imaginary firm that exhibits, in microcosm, the "representative" features of the entire industry.

Not only is the substance of the "representative firm" inorganic, its application is mechanical. It is a reductive method of depicting a long-period equilibrium for the industry as a whole, by means of a theory of the firm. As Thomas (1991, 7) remarks: "If the 'representative firm' is a biological concept, is it not strange that two-thirds of the references to it in the *Principles* are in Book 5, which is devoted to mechanical equilibrium analysis?"

Although Marshall's mode of reasoning in regard to the industry diminishes the role of variety, he occasionally recognizes its function elsewhere —for instance, in terms of entrepreneurial activity leading to variations in organization and innovation. Marshall (1961, 355) writes: "The tendency to variation is a chief cause of progress." He also considers some kind of selection for profitability in the competitive process, but without any extended reference to the selectionist metaphor of Darwinian evolution. These important insights represent signposts to a truly evolutionary economics, but they are overshadowed in the *Principles* by the mechanical concept of equilibrium and the representative firm.

By abstracting from diversity within an industry, the concept of the representative firm is more an example of "typological essentialism" rather than "population thinking." The latter concept is emphasized by the modern biologists such as Ernst Mayr. In "population thinking" variety and diversity are all-important: "There is no 'typical' individual" (Mayr 1982, 46). This mode of thought contrasts with the Platonic notion of "typological essentialism," in which entities are regarded as identifiable in terms of a few distinct characteristics that represent their essential qualities. Accordingly, all variations around the ideal type are regarded as accidental aberrations.

By contrast, in population thinking, species are described in terms of a distribution of characteristics. "The heart of population thinking," as Sober (1985, 880) writes, "consists in the idea that theories may be stated relating the interactions of population properties and magnitudes." It is precisely these population and relational properties that the concept of the representative firm ignores. Whereas in typological thinking variation is a classificatory inconvenience, in population thinking it is of paramount interest because it is precisely the variety of the system that fuels the evolutionary process.

Importantly, the maintenance of variety in the Darwinian scheme involves constant error making, as well as the continuous selection of the more adapted forms. For selection to work there must be rejection, and the process must thus involve ceaseless mistakes as well as refinements. A key question concerning any theory or model of economic evolution is whether or not it encompasses a renewable source of variety and change.

The relevance of "population thinking" to economics has been stressed by Metcalfe (1988) and others. It suggests the importance of the examination of frequencies and their distribution, rather than ideal cases. Hence, instead of the Marshallian "representative firm," the evolutionary economist should address the specific population of firms and the variation of key characteristics within that population.

As in the case of Marshall, the functional role of diversity was also played down by Spencer. Although, like Darwin, Spencer saw diversity and variety as part of evolution, these concepts played different roles in their theories. For Darwin, diversity was the essential fuel for the process of natural selection. Although Spencer also saw selection at work, for him diversity was more significant as the teleological result of the evolutionary process, rather than its crucial starting point. Instead of a full exposition of the processes of selection, Spencer's writings contain an overriding emphasis on the supreme law of progress, the transformation "from homogeneity to heterogeneity" and the evolution to evermore complex systems. Spencer mentions struggle, but he gives it no special stress. Instead, he adopts the Lamarckian idea of "use and disuse." As we shall see below, identical conceptions of both diversity and "use and disuse" are found in the works of Marshall.

The most penetrating and analytical remarks from Marshall concerning the application of evolutionary ideas to economics are in chapter 8 of book 4 of the *Principles*, which "reads like a blueprint of a book on economic biology" (Thomas 1991, 8–9). Its eight pages indicate substantial appreciation and understanding, both of the biology of his time and of the difficulties that would be faced if the full volume on economic dynamics were ever to be written.

In the chapter, Marshall sees an analogy between the subdivision of functions and organic differentiation in nature and similar phenomena in industry. Here the influence of Spencer is abundantly clear. For instance, Marshall (1961, 241) postulates

a fundamental unity of action between the laws of nature of the physical and in the moral world. This central unity is set forth in the general rule, to which there are not very many exceptions, that the development of the organism, whether social or physical, involves an increasing subdivision of functions between its separate parts on the one hand, and on the other a more intimate connection between them.

Marshall is clearly evoking Spencer's central idea that evolutionary progress involves a combination of differentiation and integration. Like Spencer and Adam Smith, but unlike Darwin, variety is seen as a result of social, economic, or biological development, not its major cause. Furthermore, Marshall is clearly replicating Spencer's idea of the unity of the natural and the social sciences.

Consider the Spencerian precedent in more detail. Following Karl Ernst von Baer, Spencer formulated two significant principles that recurred in his writings. The first, the "change from the homogeneous to the heterogeneous, is displayed equally in the progress of civilization as a whole, and in the progress of every tribe or nation; and is still going on with increasing rapidity" (Spencer 1890, 342–43). The second concerned a simultaneous tendency toward integration: "In every more or less separate part of every aggregate, integration has been, or is, in progress" (Spencer 1890, 307).

Marshall (1961, 241) goes on to argue:

> This increased subdivision of functions, or "differentiation," as it is called, manifests itself with regard to industry in such forms as the division of labour, and the development of specialized skill, knowledge and machinery: while "integration," that is, a growing intimacy and firmness of the connections between the separate parts of the industrial organism, shows itself in such forms as the increase of security of commercial credit, and of the means and habits of communication by sea and road, by railway and telegraph, by post and printing-press.

Once again, this is clear evidence of the influence on Marshall of Spencer's belief in the progressive combination of differentiation and integration. Accordingly, Spencer (1892, 10) defined evolution as "a change from an indefinite, incoherent homogeneity, to a definite, coherent heterogeneity through continuous differentiations." Such Spencerian ideas have frequently recurred, well into the twentieth century, and often without reference to, or apparent knowledge of, their precedent (Turner 1985).

Again invoking Spencer, Marshall (1961, 246) makes the important point that

> the doctrine took no account of the manner in which organs are strengthened by being used. Herbert Spencer has insisted with much force on the rule that, if any physical or mental exercise gives pleasure and is therefore frequent, those physical or mental organs which are used in it are likely to grow rapidly.

This is a clear recognition of the significance of a Lamarckian doctrine of evolutionary change. Lamarck argued that environmental circumstances lead to the differential use and disuse of organs. High levels of use encourage the strengthening and development of the organ, while low levels lead to deterioration and eventual disappearance. Such Lamarckian ideas were adopted by Spencer wholesale, and through him they found their way to Marshall.[6]

---

6. Not only does Marshall argue that skills are developed by use, but he also sides with Babbage (1846, 175–76), in contrast to Adam Smith, in presuming that the division of labor must itself be founded on differences of skill (Marshall 1961, 265).

Similarly, Marshall elsewhere argues that activities may give rise to new wants, just as wants may give rise to new activities.[7]

However, Marshall's support for Spencer is not uncritical. He perceptively suggests that the "law" of the "survival of the fittest" addresses survival not in an absolute sense but in relation to the environment.[8] He considers the possibility of selection processes that are detrimental rather than optimal. Accordingly, and again in some contrast with Spencer, Marshall (1961, 242) resists the temptation to paint the evolutionary analogy in Panglossian tones.

After Marshall's prescient chapter on industrial organization, and apart from the occasional organic metaphor, we journey through a static and mechanical world, leaving the dynamic promises of evolution long behind.

After 1890, Marshall continued to express further disillusionment with static analysis based on competitive equilibrium. He wrote that "all sciences of life are akin to one another, and are unlike physical sciences. And therefore in the later stages of economics, when we are approaching nearly to the conditions of life, biological analogies are to be preferred to the mechanical, other things being equal" (Marshall 1898, 42–43). He saw, with increasing clarity, the relevance of biological analogies for this project. Yet, as Thomas (1991, 11) regretfully concludes: "Economic biology remained promise rather than substance."[9]

Ironically, far from instigating an interdisciplinary research program on economic dynamics, Marshall's evolutionary insights were subsequently ignored. As Foss (1991) and Niman (1991, 32) point out, later Marshallians neglected the biological aspects of Marshall's thinking and abandoned the attempt to recast economics along biological and evolutionary lines. Thus, for instance, Marshall's influential follower, Pigou (1922), turned instead to physics for inspiration, and in his hands the representative firm became the firm in mechanical equilibrium (Pigou 1928). Furthermore, as Moss (1984) shows, equilibrium concepts were developed that were no longer consistent

---

7. Marshall (1961, 1) suggested that "character is being formed" during employment and that "each new step upwards is to be regarded as the development of new activities giving rise to new wants" (Marshall 1961, 89). This assumption of changeable preferences is in contrast to much of economic orthodoxy (Chasse 1984; Hodgson 1988; Parsons 1937, chap. 4).

8. Marshall (1961, 242). Notably, it was Spencer, not Darwin, who invented the slogan "survival of the fittest." It was not until 1866 that Darwin was persuaded by Wallace to use the phrase in subsequent editions of the *Origin of Species*.

9. Marshall repeated his qualified sentence on "the Mecca of the economist" in every preface to the *Principles* from the fifth edition on. However, he delayed and procrastinated over the planned volume on economic dynamics. In effect, Marshall's statements in the prefaces and in the chapter on industrial organization were together a farewell to the biological analogy for mainstream economic science, for most of his followers did not share his reservations concerning mechanical modeling, nor his concern still to turn to the biological Mecca for inspiration and guidance.

with nonhomogeneous economic agents. The ease with which biology was later purged from the Marshallian system, to be replaced by a fortified metaphor from mechanics, suggests the highly limited degree to which truly Darwinian evolutionary ideas had been originally implanted by Marshall in his *Principles*.

By the time of Marshall's death in 1924, the dialogue between economics and biology had virtually ceased. It lived on in the United States, but only with the periodic recitation of Veblen's contribution by a minority of economists. Interdisciplinary work became less fashionable. Biology no longer claimed much intercourse with economics, and the evocation of biology by economists was left to a small minority of mavericks.

Accordingly, biology was virtually excluded from orthodox economics from the late 1920s until the middle of this century, when the evolutionary analogy was rediscovered in the famous article by Alchian (1950). But it was not until the 1980s that evolutionary ideas gathered wider attention among economists, particularly after the publication of Nelson and Winter's pioneering work in 1982.

Thorstein Veblen

Just before the end of the nineteenth century, Thorstein Veblen (1919, 56) asked in a famous article: "Why is economics not an evolutionary science?" The term *evolutionary* was subsequently adopted by institutional economists, but often with little attention to the more precise mechanisms of natural selection as developed in biology. Veblen made a direct appeal to biological science for inspiration; but subsequently, and until very recently, this example has rarely been replicated.

Like Marshall, Veblen saw that the ideal metaphor for economics was to be found in the biology, rather than the physics, of his time. In particular, Veblen saw the evolutionary metaphor as crucial to the understanding of the processes of technological development in a capitalist economy. But unlike his English counterpart, he did not care to develop a static, equilibrium analysis as a prelude to the dynamic. He characterized his own economics as post-Darwinian and argued that economics should embrace the metaphor of evolution and change, rather than the static ideas of equilibrium that had been borrowed from physics by the neoclassical economists.

Veblen had two primary reasons for the adoption of a Darwinian and evolutionary metaphor. One relates to the idea of cumulative causation and an opposition to depictions of the economic process that are consummated in equilibrium. The other is based on the formation of analogies to both the gene and the processes of natural selection in the social world.

However, Veblen was faced with a biology at a stage of development at which the mechanisms of evolution were only partly understood. Consequently, and given his own personal aversion to intellectual "symmetry and system-making" (Veblen 1919, 68), there was little chance that Veblen would be able to build an economic theory on the Marshallian scale. Instead, he leaves us with plentiful hints and insights, many that are brilliant, several contradictory. He writes in a style that is often dazzling and illuminating, but also sometimes evasive or unclear. Partly for this reason, and partly because he did not provide us with a systematic theoretical legacy, his significance for evolutionary economics still remains underestimated to this day.

As Veblen attempted to found an economics closely inspired by Darwinian biology, it is thus worth reflecting on the main principles of Darwinian evolutionary theory. First, there must be sustained variation among the members of a species or population. Variations may be blind, random, or purposive in character, but without them, as Darwin insisted, natural selection cannot operate. Second, there must be some principle of heredity or continuity, through which offspring have to resemble their parents more than they resemble other members of their species. In other words, there has to be some mechanism through which individual characteristics are "passed on" through the generations. Third, natural selection itself operates either because better-adapted organisms leave increased numbers of offspring, or because the variations or gene combinations that are preserved are those bestowing advantage in the struggle to survive. The latter is the principle of the struggle for existence. It is important to note that evolutionary selection in biology occurs both by differential rates of death and differential rates of birth; it is a matter of procreation as well as destruction.

The application of the metaphor of Darwinian natural selection to economics must be on the basis of analogous principles. It is argued here that Veblen was relatively successful in this regard.

Under the sway of thinkers such as Charles Sanders Peirce, William McDougall, Herbert Spencer, and William Graham Sumner, Veblen attempted to develop a theory of socioeconomic evolution (Edgell and Tilman 1989). Presuming that human behavior is dominated by habits of thought, Veblen inquired as to the causes of these habits. Veblen took the view that habits were partly rooted in instincts; they were seen to represent evolutionary adaptations to changing environmental conditions. However, Veblen identified instincts of both a progressive and regressive kind, and stressed the conflict between them in the modern world. From the concept of habits of thought, it was a short step for Veblen to a definition of institutions. According to him, institutions are "settled habits of thought common to the generality of men" (Veblen 1919, 239). In other words, they are seen as an outgrowth of the routinized thought processes that are shared by a number of persons in a given society.

Veblen's account of the relationship between instincts, habits of thought, and social institutions is not entirely coherent. He may have originally entertained a reductionist position in which explanations of human behavior can be reduced to instinctive drives. However, he quickly moved away from it when he realized that institutions could be seen as not only being formed by, but formative of, such elements.

This development and change in his thought accounts for some of its contradictory aspects. Veblen often repeats that habits of thought are molded or even inculcated by culture, practice, or technology. For example: "A habitual line of action constitutes a habitual line of thought, and gives the point of view from which facts and events are apprehended and reduced to a body of knowledge" (Veblen 1934, 88). Thus, for Veblen, habits of thought are founded not simply on biological instincts but on human culture and habitual action.

In at least one place Veblen (1914, 2, 7) made it clear that instincts are not purely biological, nor genetically transmitted. Indeed, not only were instincts seen to give rise to habits of thought but in some places they were regarded as being formed by them. Instinct is thereby "a matter of tradition out of the past, a legacy of habits of thought accumulated through the experience of past generations." It "falls into conventional lines, acquires the consistency of custom and prescription, and so takes on an institutional character and force."

Notwithstanding this, and as Leathers (1990, 166) notes, Veblen still failed to explain how instincts "became and remain heredity elements of human nature." Although Darwin, Spencer, and Sumner put Veblen on this path, his "use of instinct theory declined markedly in his later work, and for most of his positive theory of institutions and institutional change his instinct theory has only minor significance" (Rutherford 1984, 331).

Nevertheless, the incomplete move against biological or genetic reductionism in Veblen's work is of enormous significance. It distinguishes him from the prevailing biologism of the late nineteenth century as well as from the ubiquitous evolutionary theory of Spencer. Veblen (1899, 188) clearly saw institutions as well as individuals as units of evolutionary selection. With modern hindsight, this suggests the notion that the information transmitted through learning or imitation to institutions or individuals was analogous, but different from, the transmission of genetic information in the process of biological evolution. Consequently, institutions are both replicators and the units of selection in socioeconomic evolution.

Veblen's adoption of institutions as units of selection clearly demarcates his theory from that of Spencer, and several criticisms of Spencer's theory are noted in his works. (See Veblen 1919, 192n, 402–5.) Veblen had a much more adequate explanation of the sources of creativity and variety in socio-economic evolution than Spencer. In some passages he relied on biological mutation. Elsewhere, Veblen (1914, 86–89) devised the concept of "idle curiosity" and this can serve as a genesis for diversity and variation. He suggested that the human tendency towards experimentation and creative innovation could generate novelty in an ongoing manner.[10] This could lead to new and improved ways of thinking and doing, and consequently the generation of the greater variety upon which evolutionary selection would operate. For Veblen, in particular, "idle curiosity" is a major source of technological change.

As in his criticisms of Marx, Veblen rejected the notion of the perfectibility of society. The same critique applied to Spencer's ideal state of laissez-faire. Being more a Darwinian than Spencer, Veblen inclined to the Malthusian critique of the notion that society could be perfected or human happiness could be optimized. As Young (1969) argues, Spencer's belief in progress and perfectibility was fundamentally anti-Malthusian, and on this point Veblen is closer to Malthus than to Spencer. Although Veblen had socialist leanings, he argued, contra Marx, against the idea of finality or consummation in economic development. Variety and cumulative causation mean that history has "no final term" (Veblen 1919, 37).

Notably, Malthus saw diversity as both prior to change and renewed through time, and hinted at a process of selection that was to inspire Darwin. Like Lamarck, Spencer saw the source of variety in the adaptation of individuals to their environment (Burkhardt 1977). Organisms adjust continuously as if attempting to reach harmony with their surroundings. For Lamarck and Spencer, the environment was the key agent of change. It was for Darwin, too, but for him "variation was present first, and the ordering activity of the environment ('natural selection') followed afterwards" (Mayr 1982, 354). For Darwin, change resulted from a combination of variation and environmental selection. It was this insight—which Darwin had taken and modified from Malthus—that Veblen followed.

Hence Veblen and Spencer had different conceptions of the place and function of variety in the evolutionary process. Lamarck and Spencer saw the pressure of adaptation by individual organisms to their environment as the main source of variety and change. In contrast, for Darwin and Veblen,

---

10. Dyer (1986, 31–38) argues convincingly that in deriving the idea of creative "idle curiosity," Veblen was influenced by Peirce's notion of "musement." Note that a similar idea was also put forward by Hobson (1914, 240–41, 336), the closest contemporary English thinker to the American institutionalists, who saw the role of human error and playful inventiveness as decisive in creating mutations in behavioral patterns, and thereby a source of continuous evolutionary innovation.

change also resulted from selection upon preexisting variety in a population. In sum, there is a considerable divergence between the ideas of Veblen and Spencer.

Veblen (1919, 37) argued that pre-Darwinian science was "taxonomic," mistakenly focusing on how things

> "naturally" stood to one another before causal disturbance took place between them, the orderly unfolding of the complement of causes involved in the transition over this interval of transient activity, and the settled relations that would supervene when the disturbance had passed and the transition from cause to effect had been consummated—the emphasis falling on the consummation.

In opposition to this "taxonomic" view, Veblen (1919, 37) saw "post-Darwinian" science as "substantially a theory of the process of consecutive change, realized to be self-continuing or self-propagating and to have no final term." For Veblen, a key attraction of Darwinian ideas had to do with the examination of causal processes, of a never-ending and cumulative nature.

The emphasis on cumulative change is a persistent theme in Veblen's work, signaling a source of fundamental divergence between his type of thinking and the equilibria-oriented conceptions of both neoclassical economics and of Spencerian evolutionary theory. Criticisms in this vein are raised, for example, against the work of Marshall, who ignored "the conditions of variational growth" (Veblen 1919, 176–77).

Similarly, Veblen (1919, 70) criticizes the economics of Menger and the Austrian school: The "Austrian group struck out on a theory of process, but presently came to a full stop because the process about which they busied themselves was not, in their apprehension of it, a cumulative or unfolding sequence." In the work of such economists, Veblen argues, the process stops for a simple reason: a "faulty conception of human nature." He elaborates:

> In all received formulations of economic theory, whether at the hands of English economists or those of the Continent, the human material with which the inquiry is concerned is conceived in hedonistic terms; that is to say, in terms of a passive and substantially inert and immutably given human nature. (Veblen 1919, 73)

Hence the cumulative quality of evolutionary thinking rests precisely on the fact that it does not take human nature or preference functions as given. Both the circumstances and temperament of an individual are part of the cumulative processes of change:

They are the products of his hereditary traits and his past experience, cumulatively wrought out under a given body of traditions, conventionalities, and material circumstances; and they afford the point of departure for the next step in the process. (Veblen 1919, 74)

What Veblen was seeking was precisely a theory as to why change and transformation take place, not a theory that muses over equilibrium conditions after individual preferences and technological possibilities are established. "The question," he wrote, "is not how things stabilize themselves in a 'static state,' but how they endlessly grow and change" (Veblen 1934, 8). In sum, as Veblen (1919, 77) asserts:

An evolutionary economics must be a theory of a process of cultural growth as determined by the economic interest, a theory of a cumulative sequence of economic institutions stated in terms of the process itself.

This passage is one of many where Veblen presents the idea of cumulative causation. Veblen's work in this area is thus an important precursor to that of Young (1928), Myrdal (1939, 1944, 1957), Kaldor (1972), and Kapp (1976).

Veblen (1919, 241) argues that "institutions are an outgrowth of habit" and the "growth of culture is a cumulative sequence of habituation." Also:

The situation of today shapes the institutions of tomorrow through a selective, coercive process, by acting upon men's habitual view of things, and so altering or fortifying a point of view or a mental attitude handed down from the past. . . . At the same time, men's present habits of thought tend to persist indefinitely, except as circumstances enforce a change. . . . This is the factor of social inertia, psychological inertia, conservatism. (Veblen 1899, 190–91)

It would seem that the cumulative and self-reinforcing aspect of institutions and routines relates to some kind of process of positive feedback. Positive feedback can engender lock-in phenomena—to use the modern parlance— where outcomes become frozen because of their self-reinforcing attributes (Arthur 1989, 1990a). Such locked-in phenomena can thus be regarded as sufficiently stable units of selection in an evolutionary process.

However, cumulative reinforcement of a number of parallel institutions can eventually lead to conflict and disruption. Edgell (1975, 272–73) summarizes Veblen's view in these terms: "Institutions that emerge during one era may persist into another, and the resulting cultural lag is likely to give rise to 'friction' between the habits of thought generated by the new material conditions and the habits and institutions more appropriate to an earlier period of cultural development." The processes underlying institutional change can be likened to strata that shift slowly at different rates but occasionally cause seismic disturbance and discontinuities.

Furthermore, by recognizing the durable character of institutions, Veblen discovered an equivalent to the gene in the socioeconomic world. This is the second main reason for his adoption of the metaphor of Darwinian evolution. Socioeconomic evolution is regarded as a selection process, working on institutions as replicators and units of selection, combined with the simultaneous processes of adaptation of both individuals and institutions to their mutual environment:

> The life of man in society, just as the life of other species, is a struggle for existence, and therefore it is a process of selective adaptation. The evolution of social structure has been a process of natural selection of institutions. The progress which has been and is being made in human institutions and in human character may be set down, broadly, to a natural selection of the fittest habits of thought and to a process of enforced adaptation of individuals to an environment which has progressively changed with the growth of community and with the changing institutions under which men have lived. Institutions are not only themselves the result of a selective and adaptive process which shapes the prevailing or dominant types of spiritual attitude and aptitudes; they are at the same time special methods of life and human relations, and are therefore in their turn efficient factors of selection. So that the changing institutions in their turn make for a further selection of individuals endowed with the fittest temperament, and a further adaptation of individual temperament and habits to the changing environment through the formation of new institutions. (Veblen 1899, 188)

What is most interesting here is Veblen's suggestion that institutions and habits of thought are units of selection in an evolutionary process. While these are more malleable and do not mutate in the same way as their analogue in biology, institutions and settled habits do have a sufficient degree of durability to regard them as having quasigenetic qualities. Veblen thus implied that biology and economics were on different ontological levels but were united by some broad and common evolutionary themes.[11]

Not only does this idea provide Veblen with a biological metaphor, it also becomes a basis for analysis of fundamental economic activities. Work, for

---

11. The question is raised here of the appropriate unit(s) of selection in socioeconomic evolution. On this, see Hodgson (1991a) and the references therein.

instance, is seen as involving a degree of practical knowledge that is both acquired and routinized over time. Indeed, the industrial skill of a nation consists of a set of relevant habits, acquired over a long time, widely dispersed through the employable work force, reflective of its culture, and deeply embedded in its practices (Veblen 1914; Dyer 1984). This idea has been rediscovered by Nelson and Winter (1982) and applied to their evolutionary theory of the firm.

To some extent, the degree of imprecision with which Veblen's evolutionary ideas were formed became an impediment to their theoretical development. In part, this imprecision and incompleteness stems from the limited development of evolutionary theory in biology during his time. However, despite some problems and inadequacies, on the whole, Veblen was relatively successful in establishing the basis of a Darwinian economics. First, the principle of "idle curiosity" became the ongoing source of variety or mutation in the evolutionary process. Second, the institution became the unit of relative stability and continuity through time, ensuring that much of the pattern and variety is passed on from one period to the next, so that selection has relatively stable units upon which to operate. Third, mechanisms are identified through which well-adapted institutions are imitated and replicated and the less-adapted become extinct, analogous to the "struggle for existence."

Hence a principal component of this achievement is its embodiment of the idea of the cumulatively self-reinforcing institution as a unit of evolutionary selection, subject to the procedures of mutation and selection. The nature of the evolutionary process governing these elements is selective rather than purely developmental, and phylogenetic rather than simply ontogenetic. This distinction between ontogeny and phylogeny is borrowed from biology. Ontogeny involves the development of a particular organism from a set of given and unchanging genes. Its environment will also affect this development, but nevertheless the growth of the organism is the result of genetic instructions. Hence the genes represent a given set of (environmentally dependent) developmental possibilities. In contrast, phylogeny is the complete and ongoing evolution of a population, including changes in its composition and that of the gene pool. It involves changes in the genetic potentialities of the population, as well as the phenotypic development of individuals.[12]

Veblenian economic evolution is not confined to the development of the organism from its genetic rules.[13] It is phylogenetic in that the ongoing processes of selection and development of the whole population of institutions

---

12. The distinction between ontogenetic and phylogenetic is applied for the purposes of analogy, not to imply that human behavior is necessarily determined by the genes.

13. The fact that the Veblenian cumulative process of evolutionary change of, say, consumer tastes, is phylogenetic, and not ontogenetic, was perhaps first noted by Copeland (1958, 64, 67).

is considered. Veblen's evolutionary theory is thus more extensive than that of Smith or Menger, and it does not share the exclusive biological reductionism to be found in the works of Spencer. Hence, despite their limitations, Veblen's writings stand out as the most successful attempts, at least until the 1970s, to incorporate post-Darwinian biological thinking into economics and social science.[14]

In his relative success with the evolutionary metaphor, Veblen speaks more loudly and clearly than Marx, although his theoretical system as a whole lacked the latter's symphonic grandeur. It is argued below that Veblen's use of evolutionary thinking from biology was much more extensive than that of Schumpeter. Veblen should thus be placed among the founding figures of modern evolutionary economics: perhaps even the greatest of them all.

Joseph Schumpeter

Joseph Schumpeter is celebrated today as a mentor of evolutionary economics, and his name is explicitly connected with its modern developments.[15] He admired Darwin and appreciated the importance of Darwinian biology for science. Notably, Schumpeter's (1976, 82) own adoption of an evolutionary metaphor was particularly enthusiastic and sustained: "The essential point to grasp is that in dealing with capitalism we are dealing with an evolutionary process. It may seem strange that anyone can fail to see so obvious a fact which moreover was long ago emphasized by Karl Marx."

So it may be surprising to discover that Schumpeter's own notion of economic evolution is distanced explicitly from evolution of a biological kind and excludes any suggestion of a Darwinian or a Lamarckian process of selection. Aware that Marx's evolutionism had nothing whatever to do with Darwinism, Schumpeter (1954, 445) remarked: "Marx may have experienced satisfaction at the emergence of Darwinist evolutionism. But his own had nothing whatever to do with it, and neither lends any support to the other." Thus when he praised Marx's conception of capitalist development as an evolutionary process, Schumpeter was knowingly employing the word *evolutionary* in a sense much closer to Marx than to either Darwin or Lamarck.

---

14. A particular relevance of Veblen's evolutionary theory is his analysis of science and technology in modern capitalism. It is clear from Veblen's writings that he regarded science and technology as one of the major motors of economic and social advance. The relevance of evolutionary principles from biology to the theory of technological change has again been recognized in recent years, with the consequence that many of Veblen's insights are being repeated and rediscovered, often without recognition of their precedent.

15. See, for example, Dosi et al. (1988), Futia (1980), Hanusch (1988), Heertje and Perlman (1990), Iwai (1984a, 1984b), Nelson and Winter (1982), and Silverberg, Dosi, and Orsenigo (1988).

Schumpeter's ideas on "economic evolution" are scattered through a number of his works. What gives his theory an apparently schizophrenic quality is his simultaneous admiration for the general equilibrium analysis of Walras. Today, Walras is widely regarded as the antithesis of a fully dynamic or "evolutionary" approach in economics. Not so for Schumpeter (1954, 827), who wrote:

So far as pure theory is concerned, Walras is in my opinion the greatest of all economists. His system of economic equilibrium, uniting, as it does, the quality of "revolutionary" creativeness with the quality of classic synthesis, is the only work by an economist that will stand comparison with the achievements of theoretical physics.

This was not a theoretical lapse or a bout of infatuation with formalism. Neither is it correct to follow Oakley (1990, 19) and describe Schumpeter's admiration for Walras's general equilibrium model as "a blind-spot in Schumpeter's intellectual make-up." Not only is the homage to the neoclassical theorist repeated elsewhere (Schumpeter 1952, 76, 79), but these words were, significantly, written in Schumpeter's mature years.

I would argue that it is highly misleading to assert, as Hanusch (1988, 1) does, that Schumpeter "is not at all interested in optimization and pure equilibrium economics." Indeed, the contrasting statement of Mises (1978, 37) that "Schumpeter's *Theory of Economic Development* is a typical product of the equilibrium theory" is indeed closer to the truth. In fact, Schumpeter's work derived directly and immediately from the theory of Walras. But rather than it being a "typical product," it is an extraordinary but ultimately unsuccessful attempt to reconcile statics with dynamics.

Schumpeter consistently pointed to a problem in Walrasian theory concerning its portrayal of the entrepreneur. In the circular-flow model of general equilibrium theory, perfect competition means that entrepreneurs "operate without profit" (Schumpeter 1934, 31). Accordingly, Schumpeter introduced a pertinent discussion of Walras's model:

In most minds, the idea of economic evolution will call up the associated idea of enterprise. Here again analytic advance, though substantial, proceeded mainly along the old lines . . . the source of entrepreneurs' profits was the fact that things do not work out as planned, and persistence of positive profits in a firm was due to better-than-normal judgement . . . the obvious common sense of this explanation may easily cover up its inadequacy. Walras's contribution was important though negative. He introduced into his system the figure of the entrepreneur who neither makes nor loses. . . . And since this system is essentially a static theory . . . he thereby indicated a belief to the effect that entrepreneurs' profits can arise only in conditions that fail to fulfil the requirements of static equilibrium and that, with perfect competition prevailing, firms would break even in an equilibrium state—the proposition from which one starts all clear thinking on profits. (Schumpeter 1954, 893)

Thus, for Schumpeter and Marshall, but unlike Veblen, the excursion into economic dynamics started from a static system of economic equilibrium. Furthermore, in the case of both authors, the one was seen to complement, rather than to negate, the other. The "theoretical norm" of general equilibrium, "however distant it may be from actual life, is what renders to the theorist the service which to the businessman is rendered by the idea of a normal business situation" (Schumpeter 1939, 1:45). Having his feet on this apparently firm ground, Schumpeter went on to consider dynamics. As Clark and Juma (1987, 57) put it: he starts "his analysis by assuming an equilibrium state but devotes much time to the analysis of the manner in which the equilibrium is destabilized."

For Schumpeter, the theoretical starting point was provided by the general equilibrium system of Walras. This is not quite as anomalous as it might sound, for Walras's conception of reality is that of "a process in which there are equilibriating forces at work but where the attainment of equilibrium is invariably frustrated by both endogenous changes and exogenous disturbances" (Currie and Steedman 1990, 69).

Indeed, as Morishima and Catephores (1988, 37–38n) point out, "it is not unreasonable to suggest that Schumpeter's view of the development of the capitalist economy might have been suggested by Walras's descriptions." In support of this interpretation they quote the following passage from Walras's (1954, 380–81) work:

Such is the continuous market, which is perpetually tending towards equilibrium without ever actually attaining it, because the market has no other way of approaching equilibrium except by groping, and, before the goal is reached, it has to renew its efforts and start over again, all the basic data . . . [including] the utilities of goods and services, [and] the technical coefficients . . . having changed in the meanwhile. . . . For, just as a lake is, at times, stirred to its very depths by a storm, so also the market is sometimes thrown into violent confusion by *crises*, which are sudden and general disturbances of equilibrium.

Here Walras went beyond the bounds of much of neoclassical theory by considering changes in both technology and tastes. Note also his particular mention of crises and technological change, and the similarity with some of

Schumpeter's statements. For instance, in Walras, as well as in Schumpeter (1934, 64), there is the conception of "change arising from within the system which so displaces its equilibrium point that the new one cannot be reached from the old one by infinitesimal steps" [emphasis removed]. In Walras, as well as in Schumpeter (1939, 1:64), we find a discussion of changing consumer tastes.[16]

This does not mean that Schumpeter was entirely satisfied with Walras's theory. For instance, his conception of the source of entrepreneurial profit was different from that of Walras. It is known that when Schumpeter met his aging mentor in Switzerland in 1909, he was told by Walras that the theory of the stationary process constitutes the whole of theoretical economics and that economists cannot say anything about historical changes. Schumpeter was profoundly dissatisfied with this remark (Swedberg 1991, 22, 31–32). Yet throughout the remainder of his life, "again and again he talked about the need to dynamize the Walrasian system" (März 1991, 167). His dissatisfaction with Walras was not sufficient to lead him to adopt a quite different starting point.

From the Walrasian system, which evidently does contain a kind of limited dynamism, Schumpeter indeed took his cue. He wrote: "What matters to us is precisely the presence or absence of an actual tendency in the system to move toward a state of equilibrium." Furthermore, "this mechanism for establishing or reestablishing equilibrium is not a figment devised as an exercise in the pure logic of economics but actually operative in the reality around us" (Schumpeter 1939, 1:47).

Schumpeter repeatedly emphasized Walras's point that entrepreneurial profit can arise only out of equilibrium. He saw static equilibrium conditions as "a limiting state" (Schumpeter 1954, 893n). By "statics," Schumpeter (1934, 83n) generally means the "theory of the circular flow," and by "dynamics," he means economic development in the full, qualitative sense. But the combination of these two quite different modes of reasoning is highly problematic.

This can be illustrated by considering the role of the entrepreneur. As both Day and Boehm have independently remarked, Schumpeter did not show why the entrepreneur should intrude into or emerge from the "limiting state"

---

16. A number of other studies have confirmed this appraisal of the relationship between Walras and Schumpeter. Thus, Schefold (1986) identifies the indispensable Walrasian starting point of Schumpeter's analysis. Walker (1986) notes Schumpeter's indebtedness to Walras for his conception of the entrepreneur. Shionoya (1986) insists that Schumpeter's admiration for Walras was no mere affectation or passing phase but was an integral part of his entire theory, as it developed over his life. And Santarelli and Pesciarelli (1990, 680) argue convincingly that "the homage paid by Schumpeter to general equilibrium theory is far from being lip service and that it is not entirely due to his admiration for the formal coherence of the theory." Indeed, Schumpeter was far from hostile to equilibrium analysis. His hallmark is the idea of innovation; as in the case of Walras this can be placed in an equilibrium framework.

of the smooth circular flow. These writers point out that the entrepreneurs thrive in a disequilibrium "with the fundamental function of creating the mechanisms that allow the economy to work" (Day 1984, 73). Consequently: "Instead of regarding entrepreneurship as an exogenous push thrust upon the economy, it should be seen as part and parcel of the market process" (Boehm 1990, 230).

Given the time during which he wrote, when developments in both the presentation and the criticism of the Walrasian approach were at an early stage, Schumpeter was understandably unaware of all the difficulties involved in attempting to "dynamize" that system. For instance, he paid no heed to the fact that Walras excluded out-of-equilibrium trading from his model, and that its inclusion leads to severe problems such as path-dependency (Bertrand 1883; Fisher 1983). Furthermore, Schumpeter made great play of innovation and the introduction of new products. But subsequent attempts to encompass such "future" phenomena within the general equilibrium model, by Debreu (1959) and his followers, have run into severe difficulties. We now know that it is impossible to specify a full list of futures markets, partly because of the escalating complexity and information problems that are involved (Radner 1968). As Arrow (1986, S393) sums it up: "A complete general equilibrium system . . . requires markets for all contingencies in all future periods. Such a system could not exist."

Despite these analytical problems, Schumpeter continuously tried to reconcile the equilibrating or static with the dynamic theoretical schema. On the one hand is his idea of a stationary state. This refers to "an economic process that goes on at even rates or, more precisely, an economic process that merely reproduces itself." This, being "nothing but a methodological fiction," nevertheless gives us an insight into which real phenomena "are lacking" (Schumpeter 1954, 964). But Schumpeter did not tell us how we can identify what is missing from a picture without a more adequate depiction with which to compare.

Schumpeter was never able to remove the inconsistencies that resulted from his juxtaposition of equilibriating and disequilibriating mechanisms. As Freeman (1990, 28) observes:

> It is, of course, essential in any theory of cycles to account for the "glue" that holds the system together and keeps it on a growth path despite its fluctuations. It is essential to account for continuities as well as discontinuities. Walrasian equilibrium theory explains neither, and it was Schumpeter's misfortune that he attempted to marry it with his own theory of dynamic destabilizing entrepreneurship.

Schumpeter's definition of economic evolution is evident from the following passage, where he sees evolution in its "wider sense" as comprising all the phenomena that make an economic process non-stationary. In the narrower sense it comprises these phenomena minus those that may be described in terms of continuous variations of rates within an unchanging framework of institutions, tastes, or technological horizons, and will be included in the concept of growth. (Schumpeter 1954, 964)

Thus for Schumpeter, "evolution" in the broader sense meant little more than general "change." In the narrower—but still spacious—sense it was equivalent to the richer notion of economic development.

Development, for Schumpeter, is distinguished from aggregative growth. He wrote that if "the phenomenon that we call economic development is in practice simply founded upon the fact that the data changed and that the economy continuously adapts itself to them, then we shall say that there is no economic development." In contrast, the true development of an economy involves "changes in economic life as are not forced upon it from without but arise by its own initiative, from within" (Schumpeter 1934, 63). Although this idea of development clearly embraces structural, qualitative, and cultural change, it is too vague to give the concept of evolution a sharp or precise meaning. Throughout his works, Schumpeter most frequently employed the term "evolution" in this broad, developmental sense, but excluded a Lamarckian or Darwinian process of evolutionary selection.

For Schumpeter, evolution meant the denial that equilibrium can be attained as a permanent state of rest, and the assertion of unceasing novelty and change. Entrepreneurial activity and technological transformations meant that theory should treat the economy as a process: as ever-changing in historical time. Accordingly, Schumpeter's conception of evolution was closer to that of Hegel and Marx, rather than to that of Darwin or Lamarck. Economic development, as Schumpeter (1934, 63) often emphasized, is "development from within," the dynamic role of the entrepreneur being one example. Here one finds a sense of innovation and the rational spirit pitted against rigid institutions and the established order.

Schumpeter belittled the value of biological theory for social science:

It may be . . . that certain aspects of the individual-enterprise system are correctly described as a struggle for existence, and that a concept of survival of the fittest in this struggle can be defined in a non-tautological manner. But if this be so, then these aspects would have to be analyzed with reference to economic facts alone and no appeal to biology would be of the slightest use. (Schumpeter 1954, 789)

In his work on competitive processes there is no clear analogy made with biological inheritance or evolutionary selection.

In sum, it appears that while Schumpeter conceived of "economic evolution" in a wide and developmental sense, it was not sufficiently wide to incorporate an analogy with natural selection. Schumpeter's own conception of evolution was less selectionist and much more Marxian in character: more *evolvere* than natural selection; more economic revolution than economic evolution. It also forms an adjunct of Walrasian equilibrium and represents an ostensible but ultimately unsatisfactory attempt to reconcile general equilibrium theory with notions of variety and change.[17]

Overall, despite the manifest limitations, internal problems, and logical conflicts within Schumpeter's theoretical system, he does surely rank as an outstanding economic theorist. In spite of his doomed attempt to grow a fully dynamic theoretical system in a Walrasian soil, Schumpeter remains a worthy inspiration for theorists of dynamic economic systems, and he is full of insight and potential for further development. Contrary to many admirers, however, Schumpeter provides neither a systematic theory nor an ideal epitome for a new evolutionary economics, if that is to be a precise and meaningful term.

The New Wave

The invocation of Schumpeter's name by the new wave of evolutionary theorists in the 1980s and 1990s is both misleading and mistaken. Note, for instance, the evolutionary modeling in the vein of Iwai (1984a, 1984b), Nelson and Winter (1982), Rahmeyer (1989), Silverberg (1988), and Silverberg, Dosi, and Orsenigo (1988). These authors make repeated claims that their work is in a "Schumpeterian" or "neo-Schumpeterian" mold. There are superficial similarities, of course, such as an emphasis, in common with Schumpeter, on invention and innovation, and perhaps even on imitation. But at a deeper theoretical level there is a complete divergence.

In contrast to Schumpeter, the work of the new evolutionary modelers is based on a "natural selection" analogy, of a Darwinian or of a Lamarckian kind. Nelson and Winter (1982), for example, see routines in firms as being analogous to genes, adopt the idea from Lamarckian biology of the inheritance of acquired characters, draw an analogy to mutation in economic systems, and set up selection mechanisms in their evolutionary models. Despite their current diplomatic convenience and positive ambience, the "Schumpeterian" or "neo-Schumpeterian" (Nelson and Winter 1982, 39) labels are thus inappropriate for theoretical work of this type.

Instead, the exciting evolutionary ideas that have emerged with the "new

---

17. Schumpeter's name is also widely invoked as the father of a theoretical school addressing technological change, despite the fact that he had very little to say about the latter in his work. Indeed, as Heertje (1988, 82) concludes, "technical change, in the strict sense of the development of new technical knowledge and possibilities, and the diffusion of knowledge are almost wholly absent from his exposition."

wave" have much more to do with Veblen and the "old" institutionalism than with Schumpeter himself. In contrast to Schumpeter, Veblen did embrace the evolutionary analogy from biology. There are clear analogies to both the gene and natural selection in his work. He is a clear predecessor of the idea advanced by Nelson and Winter that routines within the firm are similar to genes.

Using the microcomputer to model evolving complex systems, the wave of evolutionary theorists who have followed Nelson and Winter have brought rigor to a modern version of evolutionary economics, but one more in the spirit of the "post-Darwinian" economics of the Veblenians. As yet, the closer resemblance of this contemporary work to that of Veblen rather than Schumpeter has not clearly surfaced either in the academic journals or in the proceedings of the academic associations. But, then, the evolution of economic theory itself has far from ceased.

Part 2
Evolution and Economic Methodology

[I]n economic analysis there are to be found suggestions of nonlinear dynamics. However, the formal difficulties of solution are so great that very much remains to be done. . . . This is a fact to inspire humility in both literary and mathematical investigators, but should prove discouraging to neither.

—Paul A. Samuelson (1947)

Rethinking Complexity in Economic Theory: The Challenge of Overdetermination

Stephen A. Resnick and Richard D. Wolff

Suppose the following kind of representation of complexity: any entity—for example, a human subject, a social institution, a body of knowledge, a particle in space, or a word in a sentence—is understood to be the combined result, quite literally the site, of diverse effects emanating from all other entities. This notion of an entity's existence or causation, called overdetermination, is radically different from that which informs much of human knowledge inside and outside the tradition of economics.[1] It carries profound epistemological implications for the status of our claims about the world as well as ontological consequences for how we conceive of change and development in the world.

In many ways, overdetermination is an insidious idea, one that undermines the foundationalist theories of causation long dominant in philosophy (Rorty 1979, 1991), discourse theory (Norris 1982), the natural sciences generally (Prigogine and Stengers 1984), biology (Levins and Lewontin 1985), particle physics (Bohm 1988; Zukav 1979), Marxism (Althusser 1969), and non-Marxian economics (McCloskey 1985), among other fields. Like other convention-disrupting ideas, overdetermination carries a cost that many otherwise willing adherents may not want to pay, once they see how far it extends: accepting relativism, uncertainty, chaos, and radicalism. The notion of overdetermination entails rejecting singular truth for multiple, irreducibly different truths; determination for determinations; certainty for uncertainty; necessity for contingency; order for disorder; and conservatism for deep change. It is a completely antiessentialist theory: there are no essential causes or dimensions of being. There is no escape from this conclusion.

---

1. Initial formulations of overdetermination in the sense used here may be found in Freud (1950, 174–205) and Althusser (1969, 100–101); its application to economics appears in Resnick and Wolff (1987). The difference in economics between this form of reasoning and determinist logic is discussed further in Resnick and Wolff (1988) and Amariglio, Resnick, and Wolff (1990).

Conceiving Existence and Causation

Because so much seems to follow from overdetermination, let us carefully set out this kind of representation, using as our illustrative example the causation of a human subject. This seems an appropriate choice because of the central importance placed on how one conceives of the human subject in social theory, including, of course, economic theory. Any particular human being is here understood to be the locus of qualitatively distinct influences produced by an immense array of other people and objects in that person's environment. These different influences quite literally constitute that individual as the site of their combined effects. The fusion of these effects creates something entirely new and different from each and every one of them: the unique complexity called a particular human subject, and that subject's social and natural behavior, i.e., his or her particular evolutionary path.

Indeed, overdetermination implies that every object, constituted as the site of endlessly diverse influences emanating from all other objects, is correspondingly pushed and pulled in endlessly diverse ways and directions and is therefore endlessly changing. Overdetermination thus means that all objects are conceived to exist *in change*. To underscore this point, we refer to all possible objects of an overdeterminist analysis as *processes*, rather than objects. The "being is becoming" notion is thus woven into the basic contours of overdeterminist economic analysis.

Dividing, for analytical purposes, all processes (rather than objects) in the world into four broad categories, we may say that any individual's existence and, hence, behavior, is produced by the influences upon her or him that emanate from economic processes (the production and distribution of wealth), political processes (the distribution of authority or control), cultural processes (the production and dissemination of meanings), and natural processes (biological, chemical, and physical transformations). The three different sets of social processes and the set of natural processes combine to give birth to the human subject, to any "I." They complexly constitute (overdetermine) the behavior of that particular individual as a unique physical and mental body. It follows from such a conception that no subject could be considered a product *only* of his/her genes or of economic or political or cultural influences *alone*. Such a reductive search for an ultimately determining cause (essence) of life and its evolution is not sensible from an overdeterminist perspective.[2]

---

2. There are other consequences of rejecting reductionist analyses in favor of recognizing the literally infinite, qualitatively distinct influences ("causes") overdetermining any possible object of analysis. For example, converting qualitatively distinct influences into quantitatively greater or lesser determinant factors of some economic variable, as regularly occurs in many usages of econometrics, is a reductionism ruled out by overdetermination. Thus, the stricture against converting correlations into causations becomes a serious ban on precisely the sorts of

Logically, what is true for any one subject is true for all.[3] In addition, overdetermination means that each and thus all of these determining processes are themselves the complex sites of overdeterminations. Hence for any particular process to exist—for example, the process of commodity exchange—it too requires that all of its concrete social and natural conditions be in place: all of those other economic, political, cultural, and natural processes whose combined force creates (and whose combined effects constitute) the process of trade in produced wealth.[4]

Taken together, human subjects and the processes in which they participate are caught in this swirl of interacting influences. It follows that no individual or process can exist alone, for each must exist in interactive, constitutive relationships with that which it is not: its Hegelian "other," all the other processes in the socionatural totality. Accordingly, *autonomous* individuals or processes or those clusters of specific processes designated as "institutions"—whether the latter take the form of households, enterprises, or states—cannot exist. In contrast, autonomy for such entities can and does exist in and for those different theoretical perspectives that presume that autonomy.

This rejection of independence among social and natural processes means that it is not possible to rank determinations in regard to their qualitative or quantitative importance. Put simply, one cannot affirm a notion of overdetermination and simultaneously hold onto some kind of last-instance economic or noneconomic determinism.[5] Logically, these are inconsistent positions. The ordering of influences—some ranked as more or less important than others—depends on an a priori assumption: the independence of entities to be ordered. Once independence is asserted, then one has the necessary basis to ascertain which entity comes first (that which is ranked more impor-

---

conclusions about causative *weights* of different factors that such econometric usages regularly produce. Instead of justifying their focus on a subset of the overdeterminants of any object—and a subset is all any analyst can or ever could accomplish—by reductionist claims about that subset's "great or greater explanatory weight," other grounds for the focus will have to be admitted, described, and justified.

3. By "logically," we mean to refer only to the consistency in our argument. Nonetheless, a caveat is in order: we recognize that such terms are rhetorical devices, metaphors intended to persuade. For us, there is no absolute standard of what is logical or consistent, no standard that transcends the discourse in which it functions. One of the epistemological consequences of overdetermination is that all standards of logic (or consistency, truth, *etc.*) remain intratheoretical (relative) rather than, as in determinist epistemologies, intertheoretical (absolute).

4. The prefix *over-* was added to the word *determination* to capture this kind of notion of mutual, many-sided constitutivity among all processes.

5. *Determinism* means reducing a complexity to a simplicity, i.e., discovering some final governing cause of the totality's behavior. It attaches to the adjective *economic* or *noneconomic* depending on whether the originating process in question involves, respectively, the production or distribution of wealth, or the political, cultural, and natural processes of life.

tant), which comes second (less important), and so on; or, possibly, to see that they are equally important. In contrast, because overdetermination means that each of these considered entities—whether human subject, social or natural process, or institution—only exists in a constitutive relationship to that which is outside of it, there can be no independence of entities one from another. Thus, this different prior assumption—one of mutual constitution or dependence—rules out the basis for any kind of ranking of effectivities.

What can be affirmed, however, is that process A produces its particular effectivity on all others, but that its effectivity is always *relative* to the constitution of process A itself, for it is that precise constitution that creates the unique effectivity of process A. This reasoning returns us to our initial premise: the influence of any entity on the others is irrevocably caught up in this web of interacting influences. In this sense of a complete and total mutual interaction among all entities, each becomes, via its constituent role on the others, a partial cause of its own being. Each entity (process, human subject, or institution) is both a cause and an effect of every entity.[6]

The concept of overdetermination thus negates and rejects the two classical ways of conceiving of social order, the two classical ontologies of social science. On the one hand, it stands as the alternative to humanism with its given or predetermined (i.e., autonomous) human agents—the historic and current basis of most microeconomic theorizing. On the other hand, overdetermination stands as well against structuralism with its given or predetermined (autonomous) laws, rules, and propensities—the basis of so much of macroeconomic theorizing.[7] From this standpoint, both Marxian and non-Marxian searches for ultimately determinant causes (essences) of economic life are as logically inappropriate as are physicists' searches for a final, determining particle; or literary theorists' searches for the ultimate meanings of texts; or philosophers' quests for a singular truth or analytical rule of falsification.[8]

---

6. Here our approach touches that of the group of economists who have been stressing the unacceptable reduction of most modern economics to an essential dependence on logical rather than "historical" time (see the review and extension of their approach in Bausor 1986). If, as we presume, every social process is both overdetermined by, and participates in, the overdetermination of every other, then the flow of "historical time" is embedded in each and every proposition of our economic analysis. Our approach is, however, rather more general and all-inclusive than theirs. For us, not only is each moment in economic life unique, unrepeatable, and irrevocable, but we also argue that the multiple, different conceptions of time (logical, historical, etc.)—existing and changing in any population—are also themselves always among the constituent processes shaping the uniqueness of all moments and hence of the structure and dynamic of economic life.

7. For further discussion within the radical economics tradition, see Resnick and Wolff (1992); and for discussion comparing neoclassical, Keynesian, and Marxian traditions, see Wolff and Resnick (1987) and Amariglio, Resnick, and Wolff (1990).

8. On the theoretical role of Cartesian and Hegelian reasoning in economics, see Cullenberg (1988).

As standing against traditional Marxian theory, we cannot accept the special status assigned to some particular economic process—whether forces or relations of production—as the final, governing cause of societal behavior. Similarly, we cannot accept neoclassical theory's parallel assignation of such status to indifference curves or endowments. And the same applies to Keynesian theory's assignment of determinance to aggregate psychological propensities to consume or hold money. From an overdeterminist perspective, each of these designated determinants is a complexity, a site of distinctly different influences, and, as such, is determined in unique ways by each of all the other entities, at the same time as it partly constitutes each of them.

Dialectics, Change, and Evolution

The term *overdetermination* embodies a particular interpretation of the concept of dialectics. This may be shown by returning briefly to the overdetermination of our human subject. Now, however, let us reverse the logic by stripping away, one by one, the various determinations that combined to produce the subject. In this manner, we eventually would be left with a site that is lifeless and empty, for we have abstracted from the very conditions of its existence. Let us now proceed in the other direction: to the empty site of the human subject, we add successive determinations, starting, for example, with that emanating from an economic process of wealth production. We might then consider various other determinations stemming, for example, from a class process of surplus labor production, a political process of being relatively powerless on the job, a natural process of chemical and biological transformations, and a cultural process of making sense of (theorizing) all of these other processes. Making use of Hegelian imagery, we conclude that it is these diverse economic, political, natural, and cultural determinations that have transformed our individual from an autonomous (i.e., empty and lifeless) entity into one that is now socialized (i.e., alive and "full" of constitutive determinations).

As each of these social and natural determinations adds its unique dimension, the subject successively becomes transformed, changed from what it was, to what it is, to what it shall be.[9] At any moment, the subject, as the site of the determinations, is propelled in different directions. For example, the momentum of the above political process may push the subject to perform the work ordered, while the impact of that cultural process may make that subject

---

9. Note again how this idea precludes us from excluding any particular effectivity in considering its unique impact on the existence and behavior of the subject. The "I" as a complex result of all of them will be radically altered by removing any one. This means, of course, that the way we comb our hair adds its particular determination to who we are, what we do, and how we do it. Its effectivity is merely different from, but no less or more important than, the effectivity emanating from any other process.

conscious of involvement in an exploitative class process, and thus not anxious to work at all. As their combined site, the individual is pushed in different directions at the same moment: to work and not to work. His or her behavior is deeply contradictory. The addition of all the other determinations from all the other processes of a socionatural totality adds all the more to the multiple, diverse contradictions that comprise any human subject. Change in this subject, as we noted above, is the expression or result of these contradictions. Since each subject changes (that is the mode of its being), its influence on all other entities changes; this changes them and their influences back upon the subject and so on.

Existing in contradiction or ceaseless change becomes an apt way to describe this condition, for it captures nicely how these different determinations propel any subject in contrary behavioral directions at any one moment. Evolution—the complex movement of behavior—becomes then a product of any subject's unique set of overdetermined contradictions (that result from these diverse, constituent effects).[10]

To conclude: human subjects and, by logical extension, processes and institutions exist in contradiction, in change, for their origin (constitution) as contradictory sites means that they always are becoming that which they are not. An overdetermined, contradictory existence implies that the resulting changes are never reducible to any subset of the constituent overdeterminants of that existence. It also implies an evolution that is inevitably jumpy, nonsmooth, and generally deeply uneven in character.[11] From this overdeterminist perspective then, it is never surprising to discover radically new entities emerging, for that is precisely the state in which all entities exist.

Operationalizing Overdetermination

As an ontological perspective, overdetermination poses an immediate problem. How is analysis to proceed when every possible object for it is constitutively connected to every other? How can anything be explained? How, in short, can we operationalize the notion of overdetermination in the sense of making it a workable ontological presupposition of theoretical and empirical investigations?

The solution we have found to this problem is to extend the reach of overdetermination, to make it epistemological as well as ontological (Resnick and Wolff 1987). That is, an overdeterminist concept of thought as a process (and forms of knowledge as its products) yields a consistent and workable

---

10. This implies that no *telos* guides or governs such evolution, for that would entail a determinism: some ultimate pull (essence) which alone dominated the evolutionary movement.

11. For a discussion of the theoretical link between overdetermination and uneven development in particular, see McIntyre (1989).

way to do social and economic analysis on the basis of an overdeterminist ontology. As we propose to show, it offers a way to do analyses of complexities without ignoring or reducing them to one simplicity or another.

Since any subject's thinking (or sensory experience) can only exist in relation to that subject's sensory experience (or thinking), neither can exist independent of the other. Parallel to all other entities, they constitute one another. Thus, different ways of thinking (theories) influence sensory experiences in correspondingly different ways. We all "see," in part, what our theoretical commitments point us toward, while theorizing is also shaped, in part, by observations. But neither is the determinant, alone, of the other; both are overdetermined.

Hence neither sensory data nor thought can serve alone as an independent, final, absolute standard or foundation to determine the truth (singular) of its "other." Yet the conventionally dominant epistemologies are all absolutist and determinist in just these ways: empiricism (establishing its standard of sensory experience), rationalism (establishing its standard of thought and reason), and positivism (producing its composite standard of thought and reason). They all presume thought and being to be independent and then argue over which determines the other and which provides the truth of the other. Their truth is always singular—*the* adequate or best possible explanation of how any object of thought actually exists.[12]

An overdeterminist approach must reject these determinist epistemologies and the singular, absolute truth they all aim to establish. Quite parallel to the ontological conclusion of the relative, but never absolute, effectivity of a subject or process, this overdeterminist epistemology implies relative truths. Truth claims are irrevocably relative to the differing theories and sensory experiences that produce them. There can be no intertheoretic truth, for without the prior assumption of a dichotomy between thought and reality, there is no way to establish it. All we ever can have are differing and contending truth-claims within different theoretical representations of "the" world, each of which is bound up in a diverse array of social and natural effectivities that overdetermine it. Whatever entity exists in the world does so *in part* because

---

12. Thus, to take the classic and still-influential argument of Milton Friedman (1953) as an example, a theory's adequacy or "significance" depends chiefly on its predictive value, on whether "experience" proves the predictions it generates. This approach must, of course, presume that while theories differ among people, "experience" is accessed singularly (identically) by all. The different theories need not and should not, in Friedman's mind, exert any influence upon how we all experience life. His positivist method, or "methodological instrumentalism" (Caldwell 1986, 173–88), depend totally on that presumption. Since we make a very different presumption, that theories and observations or experiences participate in each other's overdetermination, Friedman's methodological prescriptions have no relevance to us and to our formulation of economic arguments. His prescriptions are particular to his theoretical agenda; they are not universals (Resnick and Wolff 1987, 1–37).

we have, via our sense and our reason, posited it there. Facts are overdetermined in part by us; we are active constituents, not merely passive observers, of them.[13]

We may now answer the question invariably put to epistemological positions such as ours—often labeled "relativist" or "idealist" as if these were precise designations and/or sufficient grounds for dismissal. First, the question: If one accepts this overdeterminist notion of causation and complexity, then how, at least on this earth, could any theorist make sense of anything at any time? To explain anything seems to require explaining everything; thus, the impossibility of the latter renders all particular explanatory efforts absurd in principle.

Our answer is that any analyst picks one or more of the aforementioned processes out of the totality of all processes, and from that choice begins to unravel the totality, to construct thereby a meaning or understanding of that totality. We have called such choices conceptual "entry points" into analysis.[14] They represent any analyst's specifically focused theoretical intervention to bring a correspondingly specific kind of order to the infinity of complexly interacting processes comprising the totality of socionatural life. Entry points imply ordering by impelling any theorist initially to divide that life into two sets of processes: the entry point and all others. Once accomplished, all other processes may be theorized from the perspective, the standpoint, of those chosen as entry points. This ordering of the complexity remains, however, a *theoretical* act performed by each analyst.

Analysts differ not only in terms of which social and natural processes they single out as their respective entry point, but also in terms of how they connect their entry point processes to all the others that comprise the complex objects of their analyses. Overdetermination implies that the world of theory is a world of difference: differently socialized schools of analysis constructing different understandings that influence and contest with one another. No one theory says or captures it all; none analyzes "best"; none ever has.

Theories are ways in which humans interact with (or appropriate) their world; in that they are like different modes of dress, prayer, dancing, and speaking. We can be, and surely are, as passionately committed to some, and opposed to other, modes of thinking as we are to alternative modes of most other human activities. Theorizing in one particular way needs no more justification that it grasps the absolutely right way to do it than one way of dancing or praying or speaking does. An overdeterminist epistemology recognizes difference among theories in this sense. It accepts that each theory is one glimpse, unavoidably partial and open-ended, into the ceaselessly changing

---

13. For further discussion of how facts in scientific research can be understood to be socially contrived, see Latour and Woolgar (1979).

14. See, for example, Resnick and Wolff (1987, 1992).

complexities that are its objects. Instead of reducing the complexities into simplicities—by collapsing the complexity into the effect of one particular set of entry points—an overdeterminist epistemology enables the partiality of each theory to proceed and interact with alternative partialities via mutually critical comparisons and contrasts rather than by dismissals and condemnations premised upon absolutist criteria of some singular truth and protocols of falsification.

Once chosen, the entry points tend to become more than merely a partial beginning to theorizing about the world. Psychologically, they become for many of us valued and special friends, personal guides to untangling that web of interconnectedness, difference, and alienation constituting and haunting our lives. We know who these friends are in economics: preferences, endowments, and the production function in neoclassical theory; aggregate psychological propensities, uncertainty, and the power of trade unions to bargain for money wages in Keynesian theory; the production and appropriation of surplus labor in Marxian theory; technology and the wage rate in neo-Ricardian theory; and corporate or state power in institutional theory. Moreover, composites of these, as well as new theories, continually appear, heralding the birth of still new economic theories.

Yet, in contrast to overdeterminist epistemology, in conventional, determinist epistemologies, a bizarre and magical event often occurs in the use of a particular set of entry points to construct a social analysis. That which was merely a personal choice and bias, a friend or guide that momentarily transformed disorder into order for the analyst (*relative* to the analyst), becomes instead an *absolute*, a God. The chosen entry point no longer only points the way to one understanding of the world, it also becomes essentialized, transformed into the ultimate, final cause and truth of that world. The infinity of other processes now become merely effects caused by the chosen entry points, while the latter approximate ever more to the status of pure origins.

Consequently, one forgets how socially contrived is the entry-point choice of one subset out of an infinity of socionatural processes. One forgets that this particular choice—just like *all* choices—is itself an overdetermined site, constituted by a diverse totality of social and natural determinations (see the appendix to this chapter, where this point is applied to the history of economic thought). One forgets how different groups within societies make different entry-point choices and thereby construct different theories, meanings, or understandings of social life. This lapse of memory is expressed by absolutist assertions that one's entry points are valid for everyone, that they are the only way to understand what is "really" happening; the corollary is that other people's overdetermined entry points and analyses are absolutely wrong (and hence to be dismissed) rather than relatively different (and hence to be learned from and engaged).

However, invariably something quite discomforting challenges those who have essentialized their entry points in this way. Critics appear (i.e., those who deploy other points of entry) who argue that what some affirm to be the ultimate causes of behavior are not that at all. In economics, for example, there have been the critical claims that preferences are constituted by prices and incomes; that the value of capital is constituted by the income distribution; that class exploitation is constituted by consciousness; that value is constituted by price; that power is constituted by class exploitation; and so forth in an endless questioning and critique of those entry-point processes that essentialists have endowed with the status of being absolute origins.

In reaction to such criticisms, the essentialists may take a defensive step backward, giving fulsome lip service to the idea of endogeneity. Of course, they say, their entry point is not an essence; obviously the effects of other processes constitute it. Yet, more often than not, these turn out to be empty words used to defend an impossible position. For example, in economics, the essentialist role of the entry point may well be dropped, when the prose half of the story is told, but when the modeling begins, the essence looms every bit as causally powerful as ever.[15] To fully embrace endogeneity—the complexities of the evolving socionatural totality—means precisely the ontological and epistemological commitment to overdetermination argued above. We will attempt to demonstrate this vis-à-vis economic theories below.

Overdetermination and Economics

Any event in economics, chosen for analytical scrutiny, presents an age-old analytical problem. Even cursory examination reveals an immense diversity of occurrences preceding the event in question, a different but comparably immense diversity of succeeding events, and finally an immense array of other events occurring at about the same time in the surrounding social and natural totality. Depending upon how each analyst connects the chosen event to the others that precede, coexist with, or follow it, distinctive notions of the evolution of events emerge.

Each analyst, in constructing his or her particular evolution, is deciding, implicitly or explicitly, self-consciously or otherwise, how to cope with these immense diversities, this overwhelming and daunting complexity. The prevalent mode of coping in economics has long been determinist reasoning. This amounts to procedures for dissolving complexity into simplicity, for excavating some basic simplicity presumed to underlie and hence determine the apparent complexity. In the various forms of determinist reasoning, certain key (i.e., determinant) factors are argued to be self-evident or logically necessary or empirically "found" via some presumably reliable investigatory proto-

---

15. An excellent example of this can be found in Roemer's work (1986, 1988).

col. Research and exposition then focus on tracing out the lines and mechanisms of determination flowing from the key factors (causative essences) to determined effects (concrete, actual, complex phenomena).

The twin results of such procedures are, in economic *theory*, abstract "models" of the relationships among the key factors, and, in economic *analysis* ("applied work"), empirically elaborated refinements and demonstrations of the predictive powers of the models. The maximum simplicity and explanatory power of the models and demonstrations are presumed to be the twin goals of all analysts' research into complexity. The greater the simplicity and predictive power, the closer economics has approximated the (presumably singular) truth of the actual economic evolution in which the event participates.

In contrast, our alternative mode of coping with complexity begins by refusing to reduce it to any simplicity. The results of proceeding in an overdeterminist manner are the following: a radically different analytical accommodation to complexity, different economic theories with different policy implications, and a different concept of economic evolution. What follows is a brief sketch of some of these differences.[16]

In neoclassical theories, determinist reasoning has been exhaustively elaborated across the twentieth century. The causative essences have been condensed down to individual preferences and rationality, endowments, and technologies. All economic events at the micro and macro levels have been reduced to effects of those essences.[17] Models display the mechanisms of determination (above all, but not exclusively, constrained optimizations). Applied work endlessly refines the models and displays their predictive powers.[18] The entire enterprise is justified and legitimated as building the discipline of economics on its proper political and moral foundations: a humanism in which the sovereignty and liberty of the individual govern all else in society. Economic evolution is then the grand narrative of the human discovery of how the trinity of free markets, private property, and capitalist enterprises maximize economic well-being for all.

Yet, some neoclassical economists have known and expressed reservations about constructing too complete and closed a determinist theoretical edifice on this individualist foundation. Thus, the Walrasian auctioneer, while

---

16. For a fuller exposition, see our *Knowledge and Class* (Resnick and Wolff 1987, chap. 2).

17. Perhaps the ultimate and fully complete extension of this neoclassical system appears in the work of the Nobel Prize winner R. H. Coase (especially his famous 1960 article).

18. Econometrics is the preferred "tool" for the applied work. As mentioned in footnote 2, this set of arithmetic procedures proceeds, of course, from two thoroughly determinist (i.e., reductionist) presumptions: (1) that among the myriad possible causes of any economic event, some determine more, in *quantitative* terms, than others; and (2) that we can meaningfully rank the effectivities of the causes within any such subset by means of correlational tests juxtaposing the variations of those causes and the variations of the event thereby "to be explained."

indispensable to the neoclassical edifice, cannot quite be reduced to preferences, endowments, and technology.[19] Is the auctioneer then a necessary and irreducible (to individuals' preferences or actions) social structure or institution?

Then there are those more or less neoclassical economists who stress questions such as the following: Do bounded rationality and uncertainty guarantee that institutions such as particular kinds of firms, markets, and trade unions exist more or less independently alongside individuals?[20] Do such institutions explain and determine structural propensities (customary behaviors) to consume and invest? Do institutions and structural propensities then become codeterminants alongside individuals of all economic events, or may they be determinants of the individuals themselves? And what then determines the institutions; is it back to determination in the last instance by the individual agents, as seems to be the prevalent trend in the "new institutional economics"?[21] Or may institutions as well as individual agents shape institutions? Where and why do we stop in this *reduction* of the tracing out of determinants of determinants of determinants? In short, how should economics cope with the full extent of endogeneity?

Institutional economists ("old" as well as "new"), Keynesians, neo-Ricardians, and Marxists—the "others" of modern economics—have variously and continuously plagued neoclassicals by insisting upon the economic effectivities of social structures and institutions separate from and/or determinant of individuals (Resnick and Wolff 1992; Amariglio, Resnick, and Wolff 1990). Economic evolution here becomes the grand narrative of institutions arising, changing, and dying, and thereby periodizing human history (including individual behaviors, economic and otherwise) by their distinguishing characteristics. Yet some structuralists have also recognized the limits upon their structuralisms. How are they to explain the existence and changes in the structures whose economic effectivities they stress? How are they to take account of the effectivities of individuals upon structures?

Among both humanists and structuralists of all stripes, some reacted to the limits they recognized in their positions by espousing some sort of endo-

---

19. Hahn (1987) has clearly admitted this: "But the auctioneer's pricing rules are not derived from any consideration of the rational actions of agents on which the theory is supposed to rest. Thus the equilibrium notion becomes arbitrary and unfounded."

20. See the classic formulations of such ideas in, for example, the works of Hayek (1945), Simon (1957), Keynes (1937), and Williamson (1975).

21. The so-called New Institutional Economics (NIE) focuses both on (1) the role of institutions alongside agents in determining economic processes, and (2) a theory of such institutions' origins and effectivities. However, as Langlois (1986, chap. 1) demonstrates in his introduction to NIE, after insisting that institutions are codeterminant with agents, NIE seeks, in effect, to make its peace with the neoclassical tradition by tending toward an individualist theory of the formation and functioning of institutions.

geneity assumptions connecting individuals and structures or institutions. That is, they affirmed some causal effectivity upon the economy of both individuals and institutions and some mutual effectivity upon one another. Individuals shape institutions while, and as well as, being shaped by them. In playing ("optimizing") by the rules of the game, players and games change each other; each is a function of the other.

Yet those relative few among the humanist neoclassicals and structuralist "others" who did recognize the limitations of their respective determinisms still lacked any theoretical strategy to synthesize and go beyond the two perspectives in a way that might overcome the one-sidedness of each. They did not deploy the notions of dialectic inherited from Hegel and Marx to outgrow determinist reasoning as such. They either do not know or can not utilize the fruits of the last fifty years of discussions, debates, and developments in dialectical reasoning, one of whose products is the notion of over-determination, sketched above.[22]

Some of its other products are the new dialectical biology (Levins and Lewontin 1985), the psychological decentering of the subject (Clement 1983; Coward and Ellis 1977), dialectical discourse theory (Foucault 1976), deconstructive literary and philosophic theory (Derrida 1981; Bakhtin 1981; Norris 1983), and the various tendencies of the diffuse movement known as postmodernism (Lyotard 1984).

In this light, we may consider the economists Bowles and Gintis (1986, 1990) and Gintis (1992) the latest to proclaim a new synthesis of neoclassical, Keynesian, and Marxian economics that they believe surpasses them all. Distancing their "post-Walrasian" synthesis from both the structuralists (typically macroeconomists) and the humanists (typically microeconomists), they aim to "jointly deploy" both perspectives rather than opt for one "by methodological fiat" (Bowles and Gintis 1990). However, what they do is to oscillate from one determinism to the other, now privileging structure (relatively rarely), now individuals (usually). They justify their deterministic privileging of individuals (their "case for microfoundations") on two grounds: (1) it is merely a "descriptive statement" about virtually all economic systems, and (2) "it is a normative commitment guiding democratic theory" (ibid.).

Whatever else one might say about this approach, it does not overcome the determinism of both humanism and structuralism. It recognizes, but cannot overcome, their one-sidedness. Instead, Bowles and Gintis simply com-

---

22. See Resnick and Wolff (1987, chaps. 1 and 2). Another discussion of this point—formulated in the related terms of the modernist, as against postmodernist, biases infusing the dominant modes of economic reasoning—is available in Amariglio (1990). His discussion illustrates the systematic refusal, even among neoclassical economics' major critics (structuralist and otherwise), to imagine systematic alternatives to, let alone make a break from, determinist modes of economic theory and analysis.

bine humanism and structuralism additively and according to their particular, idiosyncratic definitions of democracy and their equally particular "descriptions" of something *they* see as common to all economic systems. Thus Gintis (1992, 112) has most recently denounced structuralism (*"there is no such thing as socialization,"* emphasis in original) because individuals are "autonomous" and "act strategically." He concludes that a "game theoretic model is perfectly constructed to handle this insight and draw out its macrosocial implications."

Game theory has been rediscovered and refitted—by a sizeable group of economists of very diverse persuasions—to enable analyst and analysis to oscillate from individualism (autonomous individuals optimizing) to structuralism (rules of the game controlling) as the mood suits. Notwithstanding lip service paid to the notion that individuals and rules change one another, the actual analysis of Bowles and Gintis (as of many others in this group) remains trapped within the oscillating either/or of humanism and structuralism. That the rules of the economics game entail taking one or the other position or combinations of both is not a rule that these autonomous individuals recognize or challenge or change in their work. Their "post-Walrasian political economy" pastes the humanist determinism of the first term together with the structuralism associated with political economy. It does not surpass either of them. Instead, common to both radical and nonradical endeavors to overcome the determinism presented by one or the other logics (structuralism-macro or humanism-micro), there is a tendency to combine both within the same discourse.[23]

In simplest terms, Bowles and Gintis and others who theorize that neither structures nor individuals should be reduced to mere effects of the other, nonetheless recoil at the immense vista of interactions and transformations that such theorizing opens up. They hesitate and turn away from the pandora's box of possibilities when determinisms per se are rejected, when economic complexities cannot be reduced to individuals, structures, or games. Thus, they neither inquire about nor theoretically accommodate the possibility that individuals transform one another in continuous, countless ways—in and by market exchanges as well as in and by the myriad other processes of interaction in which they engage. They do not acknowledge, let alone integrate, the comparable transformations among interacting structures and institutions. Most importantly, they remain unaware of the progress in dialectical reasoning that suggests the need to disaggregate analysis below the *macro*levels of both individual and structure to a microfoundation they never imagined: processes (Resnick and Wolff 1987). They could not or would not question the theoretical rules of the game that limit play (research and debate in eco-

---

23. See our discussion in Resnick and Wolff (1992, 32–34) of several such attempts within the radical economics tradition.

nomics) to oscillations between individualism and structuralism. Thus their individuals are all "centered selves," theorized as though there had not been fifty years of Freud, Lacan, and a multidisciplinary postmodernist deconstruction ("decentering") of such simplistic aggregates into their overdetermined, contradictory, and ever-changing constituent processes (P. Smith 1988). Likewise, their institutions are comparably "centered," aggregates that act as singular entities rather than unstable clusters of very different and contradictory social processes.

Overdetermination and Consumer Sovereignty

Let us consider consumer sovereignty, an idea central to neoclassical thought. Recall how this theory structures its discourse: for any given resource endowment and technology, the economic behavior of each individual, and, a fortiori, the aggregation of them all, is constructed on the basis of certain axioms of choice, typically represented by a set of indifference curves. These contours of human choice are taken to be rooted in human nature. Hence, given the technical side of the economy, society's production and distribution of wealth become the phenomenal expression of this underlying human essence. In this context, sovereignty means that this foundational characteristic of human nature rules production and distribution, while *it* remains forever immune from the impact of that which it determines.

Suppose we begin to deconstruct this predetermined human nature with its gene or God-given axioms of choice. Instead, we replace it with our overdetermined notion of a human being. What would this change imply for this key notion of consumer sovereignty?

It disappears. Each individual agent and each socially contrived institution become active participants in the (over)determination of the nature of all agents and institutions. In this regard, the very existence of each individual's indifference map, including the shape of the involved contours, becomes constituted by diverse effects stemming from all social and natural processes. In other words, each individual map is overdetermined by the clusters of such processes that comprise the different institutional forms—individual, corporation, state, church, household, etc.—in society.

There are profoundly unsettling consequences for neoclassical theory in admitting that the economic processes of exchange and production, occurring respectively between and within such institutions, participate in determining the preferences of each individual in society. For example, the value and quantity of wealth in a society can then no longer be conceived as merely the epiphenomena of such preferences. Hence human nature, and its inherent characteristic of choice, is no longer sovereign over, and thus immune from, these and still other economic and social processes occurring in society.

Consider briefly a concrete illustration of this overdeterminist view. For savers and workers, their preferences, respectively, for present and future consumption and for leisure and real income would depend upon, among other things, their own and others' received income, wealth, class position, power wielded, conscious and unconscious thoughts. Further, each one of these overdeterminants of preferences is itself understood to be a site of influences emanating from all the others and also from the set of preferences themselves. From this perspective, it becomes impossible to discover an ultimate origin for the determination of prices and individual's incomes, for the real costs of labor power and capital, partly shaped by these preferences, themselves help to determine such determining preferences.

This recognition of human preferences as a complex site of social forces actually has had a long tradition in the history of economic thought. At the turn of the nineteenth century Veblen (1899) offered a notion of a socialized individual, one whose preferences were interconnected to those of his or her neighbors at home and partners at work. Almost four decades later, Dobb (1937, chap. 5) argued that individuals' preferences were shaped by the production relations into which they entered. More recently, Galbraith (1960) analyzed the citizens of a modern industrial society as molded by the culture of advertising, produced in and by giant corporations and financed by their distributions from profits.

Their writings enable an understanding of how types and prices of commodities help to create who we are in society, including our own and others' conceptions of our relative status and standing in life, and, hence, our preferences for wealth, work, and capital to help secure our relative standing in society. These writings recognize how class positions help to determine what we think consciously and unconsciously of ourselves, both as individuals and as social beings; what level and kind of consumption we perceive to be necessary for our social survival; which trade-offs we can conceive and how willing we are to trade off one thing for another. We confront a relationship: individual preferences variously create, transform, and destroy the institutions of modern society even as those institutions exert parallel influences over our preferences for one particular kind of good or resource over another.

This notion of overdetermined agents presents a major problem for those social theorists who at one and the same time want to claim a kind of postmodern notion of decentered agents, while holding onto the different and contending modernist assumption of autonomously determined indifference curves in mathematical models supposed to represent agent behaviors. A rejection of consumer sovereignty seems to be the rule in such theorists' prose, but its acceptance is the rule in their mathematical models.

To explore this inconsistency for a moment, consider the existence of any individual's set of indifference curves, if indeed one has abstracted from their constituent overdeterminants in posing any kind of behavior model. What remains is a set of preferences totally empty of content, for one would have abstracted from their very conditions of existence, from the diverse determinants of whatever they are. And without the latter, they have no content or meaning whatsoever.

Such theorists are faced with a conundrum: either such conditions do matter to the human condition, in which case no model can be specified that treats preferences as autonomously determined; or such conditions do not matter, in which case the entire edifice of microeconomic theory, as it currently exists, rests on an empty idea, that is, one that is without content *from the perspective of overdetermination*. If the latter proves to be as persuasive an idea in economics as it has in other fields, then the theoretical research agenda would be set: the specification of a new kind of complexity for the human agent in economic reasoning.

Conclusion

The evolutionary paths of economic change resulting from humanist, structuralist, or combinatory determinisms display a "coherency" of which their authors are proud.[24] This coherency consists of an ordering—that is, a stark simplification—of the manifold complexity of economic events accomplished by organizing them around the particular determinist schemes the theorists variously champion.

The alternative, an overdeterminist notion of complexity and evolution, refuses the coherency of reducing, via determinism, the complex to the simple. Instead, evolution is seen as the utterly open-ended, endless play of contradiction and change among social processes generating and generated by individuals, groups, structures, and institutions.[25] No ordering exists within all this. Ordering is rather a theoretical act performed upon a complexity as an intervention designed to add yet another determination to that complexity, hopefully to move it this way instead of that.

Theorists can never be anything but partial in their orderings. All they can do—all that they ever have done—is to focus their minds upon tiny portions of complex realities and construct partial glimpses into a few of the interconnections within those portions, connections changing during and partly because of their constructions. No megalomania need or should attach to these glimpses; they are not God-like "truths about what is really going on out there." Yet they are noble, powerful human acts in their own right.

---

24. Bowles and Gintis (1990) refer to most microfoundationalists (other than themselves) as "intellectually incoherent."

25. Since no game or set of games captures or limits this play, game theory is just another determinist attempt to order (i.e., reduce) economic evolution to some determinate pattern preferred by the theorist.

Theories are one of the ways in which human beings act in and upon their worlds, changing them, which has always been their purpose, their achievement, and all the justification they need.

Overdetermination implies that economic evolution is an agonistic field, one arena of theory alongside all the others. Economic complexity or evolution is above all a site about whose every dimension there are alternative, contesting theories that struggle for attention and adherence (Ruccio 1991). The contesting theories counterpose their partial glimpses at fleeting aspects of social change; the theories are simply forms in which thinking people appropriate and transform the world in directions they deem desirable. Thus, determinists advance their goals and values by locating a reductive order in economic evolution. This order proceeds from what they take to be an ultimate cause of economic life. That cause is their focal point, their particular object of thought and action as players within the world they seek to change.

We, of course, are no different in this regard. Our rejection of reductive, determinist theories of economic complexity and evolution reflects our own goals and values, which are inimical to monotheoreticism (the latest form of monotheism). We prefer to acknowledge the unavoidably partial perspectives of any theory of economic evolution (as of any other possible topic or object of theorizing). Let's put all the cards on the table; whether we order and how we order economic evolution is an active, partisan, current intervention in social life.

APPENDIX: THE OVERDETERMINATION OF ECONOMIC THEORIES

The history of economic thought records differing and contending entry points overdetermined by one another and by the economic, political, cultural, and natural circumstances unique to each. Any particular point of entry is anything but an inevitable result of such events. Instead, its birth always is understood as contingent, reflecting those peculiar interactions of personal, societal, and natural forces that occur in specific times and spaces. Focusing on but a few of these forces, we may begin to sketch such a history for the three entry points that have dominated economic reasoning for the last two hundred years.

The years of classical and neoclassical economic thought coincided with the development of capitalism and the economic questions it produced. That developing capitalism and those questions helped to provoke in Adam Smith a new idea that formed the basis—the discursive entry point—of classical and neoclassical economic thought for the next two hundred years: the essence of society and its evolution lies in each of us, in our own inherited human nature. Classical thought ordered its societal vision from the standpoint of an inherent self-interested struggle of each individual to produce and accumulate wealth. Neoclassical thought added to that vision each individual's inherent ability and tendency to make rational choices as to means as well as ends. Hence a new economic theory's entry point of rational self-interest was born, partly out of the very capitalism that it would soon help to alter.

By the 1890s a maturing capitalism required a new idea to explain how its intense competition among producers and the resulting inequalities of income and consumption among its citizens would produce harmony in society rather than political turmoil and socialist revolution. The economic and intellectual stage beckoned Pareto to demonstrate how a combination of Smith's and Mill's entry points—the two selfish sides of our human nature— could be dialectically combined to form the opposite of selfishness, a perfect capitalist harmony of mutual interests. The capitalist Utopia of Pareto optimality had arrived, an idea fostered in part by capitalism's own, deeply contradictory development.

The birth of a humanist entry point in Smith and its further development and refinement in the writings of Jevons, Walras, and then Pareto bore the imprint not only of the newly emerging and then rapidly changing and threatening capitalist order but of an intellectual tradition that had its complex origins centuries before in the Renaissance. The emergence out of feudalism in Western Europe signaled an intellectual transition to an entirely new way to order society: the placing of the human agent at the center of explanation. This idea of individualism and the liberation of the self was molded further in the Scottish Enlightenment, methodologically sharpened under the impact of Cartesian thought, and given concrete form by Bentham. Whether or not writers in this tradition are conscious of this particular cultural history, its philosophic legacy nonetheless shapes their choice to center their analysis of economic society on the foundation of a predetermined human subject.

Partly influenced by, as well as reacting against, this humanism and how it had evolved in the hands of Smith, Malthus, and Ricardo, Marx strove to produce a new way to understand society. Forged in the emergence of what he saw as class exploitation in the rapidly developing capitalism of his day, Marx's entry point of the production and appropriation of surplus labor answered different questions, those asked by critics disillusioned by capitalism and individualism alike: how can we begin to explain capitalism's macro inefficiencies, the economic unfreedom of workers, and the crippling alienation of each from all? His answer, class exploitation—the difference between labor and labor power—was thus a response to the set of economic conditions of his day, but these were conditions that he saw very differently from the images of the followers of Smith, Ricardo, and Malthus.

His newly conceived entry point also bore the imprint of an intellectual tradition, but in his case, it was shaped far more by the notion of Hegelian dialectics than by Cartesian deductive reasoning. It was indebted far more to French socialist theory rather than to the Scottish Enlightenment. This product of German dialectical philosophy and French radical political theory helped to displace the autonomous and determining human agent of classical/ neoclassical economic thought. The newly conceived individual was now to be set adrift, his or her behavior deeply contradictory, buffeted here and there by social relationships. An opening was created to the future's postmodernist view of a decentered human agent.

A radically different kind of utopian view also emerged to contest that soon to be presented by the neoclassicist Pareto. For Marx, it was a communism, presented as a society in which class exploitation had been eliminated. His entry point thus helped to shape a new societal objective, one that soon would be taken up concretely and then modified again by the Bolsheviks.

Less than fifty years after Marx's death, the third major entry point of economic reasoning emerged. Parallel to the others, its birth too cannot be separated from the concrete economic environment of its time. Keynes's choice of a still new way to organize economic theory was provoked in part by what he saw as the changing capitalist order of his day, from its international troubles after World War I, through the boom of the 1920s, to its collapse in the Great Depression. In these circumstances, the chaos of capitalism was traced partly to a basic human limitation: our inability to foresee the future. Hence economic events helped to produce that part of Keynes's entry point that focused on the complete uncertainty of each and all agents' economic decisions. Its implication was that the economy, like the individual, always was at risk.

The Keynesian choice of a new way to organize economic thought also responded to, and reacted against, neoclassical humanism and, for Keynes, the dangerously feeble policy alternatives it suggested for a troubled capitalism. Rejecting the neoclassical vision of individualist utility calculations by consumers and workers, Keynes offered instead new causal determinants: mass psychology, his marginal propensity to consume, for the consumer group, and the power of trade unions to set money wages for the workers. Shaped both by capitalist crises and also by what he perceived as the blindness of the then-dominant neoclassical thought, Keynes's discourse ordered its societal vision from the standpoint of these combined, essential characteristics of capitalist society: human uncertainty, mass psychology, and institutional power.

A structuralist vision of society emerged, one that likely owed a heavier debt to French structuralist thought than to the British individualist tradition. The well-known result of such an approach was to place hope for economic salvation in the collective hands of the state rather than in those of each private, individual decision maker. Keynes's position marked a break from the classical/neoclassical entry point and its vision of a Paretian Utopia.

These three contending entry points demarcate the broad contours of economic thought. They also created within it the conflicts and compromises of generations of economists. Periodically, attempts emerge to reconcile any two, or even all three, by offering up grand economic syntheses of them. At still other times, first one and then another entry point is championed over all others, typically accompanied by righteous claims of the others' death because of their inherent illogic and/or obvious empirical foolishness. As the history of economic thought attests, however, such choices and claims always are relative to the cultural, economic, political, and personal circumstances that help to overdetermine them.

Evolutionary Economics and System Dynamics

Michael J. Radzicki and John D. Sterman

Time is a device to prevent everything from happening at once.

The evolutionary perspective has a long and distinguished history in the field of economics. Indeed, it was adopted by economists such as Marx (1967) and Veblen (1898) as early as the nineteenth century, and Schumpeter (1934, 1939), Myrdal (1944), and Boulding (1981, 1991) during the twentieth. Unfortunately, although provocative and insightful, the writings of the early evolutionary economists were unable to catapult the evolutionary perspective to the forefront of the economics profession. Two common explanations for this failure are that: (1) the evolutionary approach is at odds with the corpus of nonevolutionary theory that dominates economic thinking, and (2) evolutionary economics has traditionally been seen as unamenable to mathematical formalization.

With regard to its incompatibility with mainstream economic theory, there is a great deal of evidence (e.g., Mirowski 1988; England, "On Economic Growth and Resource Scarcity," in this volume) indicating that the economics profession grew up trying to imitate classical mechanics. As a result, the body of theory that emerged and still largely dominates economic analysis (i.e., neoclassical economics) is based upon the notion of conserved or Hamiltonian systems and hence on a Newtonian or time reversible view of the world (Hamilton 1953). Theories that are out of harmony with this view are, at best, treated with suspicion and, at worst, rejected or relegated to less-visible scholarly outlets by the invisible college of economists.

In terms of the historical lack of mathematical formalization in evolutionary economics, it is clear that most of the classic evolutionary theories were

John Sterman acknowledges the financial support of the sponsors of the System Dynamics National Model.

Epigraph from Joan Robinson (1962, epigraph), who attributes this quote to Henri Bergson (1944).

61

created by economists who wrote at a time when formal modeling was not practiced, who lacked the necessary training in mathematics, or who felt that the mathematical tools of the day were insufficient for representing evolutionary change. Goodwin (1991, 30), for example, remembers Schumpeter's "sadly deficient mathematical capability," and both Myrdal (1944, 1069) and Boulding (1962) expressed their pessimism regarding the possibility of mathematically representing evolutionary change.[1]

Of the two explanations for the failure of the evolutionary perspective to become the normal science of the economics profession, the first—its incompatibility with neoclassical theory—is of primary importance. The second—its presumed inability to be mathematically formalized—is really something of a historical stereotype and clearly incorrect. Nonlinear dynamic computer-simulation modeling has made the building of mathematical evolutionary economic models possible since the 1950s. These tools led to work including that of Forrester (1961), Winter (1964), Day (1975), and Nelson and Winter (1982), which formed the basis for the present resurgence of evolutionary economics.

The purpose of this chapter is to discuss the types of structure and behavior associated with mathematical models that are typically categorized as evolutionary and show that a particular type of computer simulation modeling—system dynamics—can be used to create models that possess these characteristics. To support this claim, a number of evolutionary system dynamics models will be discussed and an original evolutionary system dynamics model will be presented. Software and other resources that are available for the creation of evolutionary system dynamics models will also be discussed.

What Exactly *Is* Evolutionary Economics?

In order to review the fundamentals of evolutionary economic modeling, the characteristics of evolutionary economic change must, arguably, first be identified and understood. Although a survey of the literature would seem to indicate that no single, comprehensive definition of the phenomenon exists, it is possible to identify a number of recurring themes.

According to Hamilton (1953), evolutionary or "Darwinian" change is

---

1. More precisely, Boulding argued that dynamic economic models created with ordinary differential equations are deterministic and hence nonevolutionary, while Myrdal expressed doubt that the process of "circular and cumulative causation"—his engine of evolutionary economic and social change—could be represented mathematically. Similar positions have been taken by Kapp (1968, 13) and Gruchy (1972, 305). As is shown below, however, Boulding was incorrect, unless one takes a very narrow view of differential equations. Recent developments in nonlinear dynamics, moreover, happily reveal that Myrdal was unduly pessimistic.

caused by changes in system structure, while nonevolutionary or "Newtonian" change represents change within a given structure. He used this distinction, as did Veblen (1898), to show the nonevolutionary nature of neoclassical microeconomic theory. On the macroeconomic side, the distinction between structural and nonstructural change has been used by Johansson, Batten, and Casti (1987, 4) and Boulding (1981) to draw a distinction between economic growth and economic development. In their view, the former implies "more of the same" while the latter implies structural change.

Perelman's (1980) view of evolutionary change emphasizes the idea of time irreversibility—i.e., the notion that it is impossible to reverse time and make events undo themselves. England ("On Economic Growth and Resource Scarcity," in this volume) points out that most modern growth theoretic models violate this canon because their time paths can be reversed by switching the signs of their parameters.

The concepts of time irreversibility and structural change are closely related to the second law of thermodynamics, which shows that dissipative dynamical systems generate increased entropy or disorder over time, which prevents them from returning to their previous states. Georgescu-Roegen (1971, 1980) and Boulding (1981, 1991) have applied the second law to the analysis of economic systems.[2] Time irreversibility, structural change, and the second law of thermodynamics are themselves closely related to the idea of hysteresis, or the inability of a system that has been changed by an external force to return to its original state after the external force is removed. Blanchard and Summers (1986) have used this concept to explain European unemployment; Dixit (1992) has used it to explain the failure of firms to withdraw from investment projects after the conditions that initially made them appear profitable disappear; and Evans and Ramey (1992) have used it to create a Phillips curve that embodies rational expectations with explicit calculation costs.[3]

The view that economic systems evolve toward increased levels of disorder and entropy has sometimes been referred to as the "engineering view" of evolution. Such thermodynamic accounts cannot explain the evolution of life. Note, however, that the evolution of complex organisms does not imply teleological views that evolution is purposeful, that life "progresses" from "lower" to "higher" forms. "Coevolutionary economists" such as Chase (1985) and Swaney (1985) have developed theories that enable this conflict to be reconciled. In these theories, dissipative economic systems generate increased levels of entropy and disorder that motivate humans to develop increasingly complex entropy-skirting technical innovations and social institutions.[4]

2. See the discussion in Radzicki (1988a).
3. An overview of hysteresis effects in economics is contained in Cross and Allan (1988).
4. For a further discussion of these ideas see Radzicki (1990b).

Ilya Prigogine's original work on far-from-equilibrium thermodynamic systems is similar to the theories of the coevolutionary economists.[5] Prigogine has shown how thermodynamically open, dissipative, entropy-generating systems, operating in a far-from-equilibrium state, can reorganize themselves into more complex temporal and/or spatial structures when they are pushed against their nonlinear constraints. This view is thus able to reconcile the engineering and biological views of evolution.

What Exactly Is Evolutionary Economics *Modeling*?

An examination of the types of mathematical models that are commonly classified as "evolutionary" indicates that they are constructed in both discrete and continuous time, utilize a variety of mathematical techniques, exhibit different types of dynamical behaviors, and, in some cases, can be solved without the aid of a computer. This lack of uniformity, however, does not preclude the identification of some common characteristics. In addition to being dynamic and able to exhibit some form of disequilibrium behavior, evolutionary economic models tend to possess one or more of the following traits: (1) path-dependency; (2) the ability to self-organize; (3) multiple equilibria; and (4) chaotic behavior.

Path-dependency is a characteristic of models that can get locked into the particular dynamical path they initially "choose" (usually by chance). David (1985) and Arthur (1988, 1989, 1990b) have described numerous real-life instances of this behavior involving the adoption of new technologies and the location decisions of firms, while Arthur (1989, 1990a), Arthur, Ermoliev, and Kaniovski (1987), and Krugman (1991) have developed formal models of the phenomenon. Economic models exhibiting hysteresis (e.g., Blanchard and Summers 1986; Dixit 1992; Evans and Ramey 1992) can also be considered path-dependent, as can system-dynamics models possessing floating goal structures.

Floating goal structures are aspiration levels used by agents in decision making that adapt to past experience and hence cause present goals and activities to be influenced by past results (Forrester 1968; Meadows 1982). In a floating goal structure system, the future course of a system depends upon the cumulative impact of the potholes, actions, and obstacles it meets along the way and not solely on its current physical state. Thus, random events become critical determinants of the system's path and even of its qualitative character, as when the chance formation of a few businesses in a region causes the growth of a cluster of related industries (e.g., the Silicon Valley, the New York diamond district).

---

5. See Nicolis and Prigogine (1977), Jantsch (1980), Prigogine and Stengers (1984), Laszlo (1987), Allen and McGlade (1987), and Allen (1988).

Self-organization is exhibited by models that undergo abrupt changes in their temporal or spatial structures through changes in their parameters or via the amplification of random, microscopic fluctuations. Self-organizations of the former type include models that can exhibit bifurcations and catastrophes, such as those developed by May (1976), Varian (1979), Stutzer (1980), Mosekilde, Aracil, and Allen (1988), Andersen and Sturis (1988), Sterman (1988b, 1989b), and Lorenz (1989). Day (1983) has described bifurcations and catastrophes as being akin to a marching band suddenly breaking formation, scrambling around, and regrouping in another formation.

Examples of self-organization that occur due to the amplification of microscopic fluctuations can be found in the behavior of many nonlinear dynamic models residing within and outside the fields of economics and system dynamics. Of particular note is the work of Forrester (1961, appendix N), Nicolis and Prigogine (1977), Jantsch (1980), Moñtano and Ebeling (1980), Mosekilde, Rasmussen, and Sørensen (1983), Prigogine and Stengers (1984), Mosekilde and Rasmussen (1986), Laszlo (1987), Arthur, Ermoliev, and Kaniovski (1987), Allen and McGlade (1987), Allen (1988), Dosi (1988), Silverberg (1988), Arthur (1989), Radzicki (1990b), Moxnes (1992), and Wittenberg and Sterman (1992). In these models, random fluctuations, often representing the idiosyncratic actions of individual economic agents, become amplified by positive feedback processes and grow to dominate the macroscopic behavior of the systems.

Yet another way to identify models that are typically classified as evolutionary is via the presence of multiple equilibria. The particular equilibrium "chosen" by these models usually reflects the effects of random shocks that direct it down a particular path. Models with multiple equilibria can also be path-dependent and exhibit time irreversibility and the ability to self-organize. Diamond (1987) has shown that multiple equilibria can arise in economic models that explicitly represent market imperfections.

Deterministic chaos is an irregular oscillatory behavior that arises in nonstochastic, nonlinear feedback systems. Although it is generated by models that are completely devoid of exogenous randomness, its period and amplitude never repeat and it functions much like the idealized random variates of probability theory, generating variety and causing deviations from "average" behavior. A small sample of economic models that can exhibit chaos includes those created by Stutzer (1980), Day and Shafer (1986), and Goodwin (1991).[6] A small sample of system dynamics models that can generate chaos includes those developed by Andersen and Sturis (1988), Sterman (1988b, 1989b), and Mosekilde et al. (1992). An excellent overview of the issues associated with chaotic dynamics is presented by Mosekilde, Aracil, and Allen (1988).

---

6. See also the collection of economic models contained in Lorenz (1989).

The tie between evolutionary behavior and models that can produce chaos involves the notion of an attractor. An attractor is the set of points that defines the steady state behavior or "temporal structure" of a dynamical system. A fixed point (defining an equilibrium steady state) is the only type of attractor possible in linear systems, while fixed points, saddle loops, limit cycles, tori, higher dimensional orbits of some complexity, and chaotic attractors are possible in nonlinear systems. Of note is that many nonlinear systems exhibit bifurcations by which they switch their trajectories from one attractor to another via a small change in one of their parameters. Such switches are examples of system self-organization and hence of model-based evolutionary change.

An important characteristic of a model whose motion is defined by a chaotic attractor is that its behavior is sensitive to its initial conditions. This means that a minute change, ϵ, in its vector of state variables will cause it to travel down a time path that is significantly different (i.e., much greater than ϵ) from its previous trajectory. In fact, the chaotic attractor will stretch and fold the motion of the system so severely that it will cause an *exponential* divergence of the two time paths. As a result, models that produce chaos can also be said to produce path-dependent behavior.

One last point concerning dynamical models whose steady state behaviors are defined by attractors and whose time paths have transient components: it is *not* possible to reverse the signs of their parameters and "backward predict" their trajectories, unless their initial values are known with exact certainty (Lorenz 1989, 61–63). In this sense, then, they are time irreversible and hence evolutionary.

Characteristics of System Dynamics Models

System dynamics was originally created in the 1950s to address problems encountered by managers in corporate systems (Forrester 1961). Its use was extended during more recent decades to include economic, social, biological, and physical systems (Forrester 1969, 1972; Roberts 1978; Sturis et al. 1991). Today system dynamics is applied to diverse problems in the behavioral, economic, and natural sciences. It is used as a modeling methodology in academic research (Sterman 1989a, 1989b), as a method to stimulate learning among corporate executives (Senge 1990; Morecroft and Sterman 1992), and as a tool for teaching at the precollege level (Hopkins 1992; Gould 1993).

The intellectual roots of system dynamics lie in control engineering and the theory of servomechanisms developed in the early part of the twentieth century. Richardson (1991) has traced the history of system dynamics and the concept of feedback in the social sciences from the use of feedback in ancient mechanical devices, through the theory of feedback control systems in steam engine governors and servomechanisms, to its diffusion into the social and behavioral sciences beginning in the 1940s. Over the years, system dynamicists have developed a distinct set of guidelines for helping them build dynamic models.[7] Among the most important are that: (1) the dynamic behavior of any system emerges from its structure; (2) the modeling, and subsequent understanding, of any system requires the identification and representation of that structure; (3) decision making in human systems is boundedly rational; and (4) discovery of the decision rules that people actually use requires empirical work, including field observation of decision-making behavior.

System dynamics models, from a mathematical point of view, consist of systems of ordinary nonlinear differential equations. Typically, system dynamics models are formulated in continuous time and assume continuous variables, though the use of simulation to solve the models means continuity is not essential to the method. Indeed, where necessary for fidelity to the problem being modeled, a good system dynamics model will contain discrete elements such as queues, quantized flows (e.g., integer flows of people), probabilistic decision rules, and other departures from deterministic lumped models.[8]

System dynamics models can be characterized as structural, disequilibrium, behavioral models. They differ, therefore, from the familiar econometric models, general equilibrium models, and rational expectations models in a variety of ways.

One fundamental difference is that the concept of feedback is central to system dynamics. Feedback exists whenever decisions made by agents in a system alter the state of the system, thereby giving rise to new information that conditions future decisions. The dynamics of a system emerge out of the interaction of the multiple feedback loops in its structure. Feedback loops may be self-reinforcing (positive feedback) or self-correcting (negative feedback). Positive loops are self-reinforcing processes, such as the compounding of interest or the growth of a population. Negative loops define goal-seeking processes, such as the regulation of inventory by adjustments of production, the equilibration of demand and supply via changes in price, or the adjustment of a firm's capital stock to appropriate levels via changes in investment. A system dynamics model is an explicit mapping of a system's positive and negative feedback loops.

System dynamics models seek to portray the microstructure of a system

---

7. Day (1987) has developed a similar set of guidelines. See also the discussion in Radzicki (1988b, 1990a).

8. Software tools such as STELLA (Richmond and Peterson 1992) support both continuous and discrete elements, so it is a simple matter to simulate any system of mixed continuous-discrete elements, systems of difference equations, delay-differential models, Markov models, and so on.

at an operational level. The feedback loop structure of any dynamic system consists of the physical structure of the system, the flows of information characterizing the state of the system, and the decision rules of the agents in the system, including the behavioral decision rules people use to manage their affairs.

The physical structure of any system is represented by networks of stocks and flows. Stocks characterize the states of a system, while flows represent the rates of change of the stocks. A model of a firm, industry, or national economy, for example, would explicitly portray the stocks and flows of people, resources, money, goods, capital, information, and so on. The stock-flow representation, which is familiar to economists, is a very general idea that can be applied to the dynamics of any system. Sturis et al. (1991), for example, have created a system dynamics model of human glucose-insulin interaction that includes stocks of glucose, insulin, and glucagon, and flows that represent the synthesis, transport, and metabolism of these compounds. A system's stocks accumulate or integrate its rates of flow and determine its state at any point in time. As a result, each stock represents the accumulated history of its flows and serves as a source of system inertia and as part of its memory.

A second characteristic of stocks is that they decouple a system's inflows from its outflows. In equilibrium, the net inflows to all stocks are zero, and the stocks are thus unchanging. For example, in equilibrium orders for products must equal shipments, which must equal production (ignoring cancellations and scrappage). Since the stocks in traditional equilibrium models are unchanging, they are often omitted. To capture disequilibria in a system, however, stocks must be explicitly represented since they accumulate the imbalances between inflows and outflows. In reality, orders for products need not, and usually do not, equal shipments: the difference between these flows accumulates in order backlogs. Likewise, differences between production and shipments accumulate in inventories. Explicit representation of stocks also enables their inflows and outflows to respond to the decisions of the distinct economic agents who, in the real system, control these separate flows (e.g., buyers and sellers may place orders and produce goods at different rates, according to the separate decision rules and constraints they each face).

As a system's stocks rise and fall, agents take various actions to alter the rates of flow, thus closing the feedback loops that may bring the system into equilibrium or reinforce current trends. For example, excessive inventories may cause a firm to lay off some workers to reduce production, or to cut prices to stimulate orders, in the process reducing inventories to desired levels. Whether such corrective actions in fact bring the system into equilibrium is determined by the interaction of all the feedback processes in the system, as are the characteristics of the adjustment path itself. However, the interaction of multiple feedback processes in complex nonlinear systems often causes disequilibria to persist. For example, in the case of a speculative bubble, it has been repeatedly demonstrated empirically (e.g., Andreassen 1990; Sterman 1987) that people tend to form expectations of future asset prices (e.g., real estate prices, the price of gold, the price of tulips) by extrapolating recent price trends. An exogenous price rise may thus cause new buyers to enter the market and reduce offerings by current holders, so that the price in fact rises in a self-fulfilling prophecy, as described by Mill (1848, 2:45ff.), Merton (1936), and Kindleberger (1978).[9] Here the intendedly rational decisions of individuals create and reinforce disequilibrium.

Another important component of any system's structure is its nonlinear relationships. Every significant economic process and institution involves nonlinearities (Forrester 1987a), though much of the history of economic theory in general, and business cycle theory in particular, has been an attempt to work around nonlinearity for reasons of analytic tractability (Richardson 1991; Zarnowitz 1985, 540). Nonlinearities are responsible for a system's robustness or ability to stay within certain boundaries. For example: output suffers diminishing returns as individual factors of production are increased relative to others; gross investment remains nonnegative no matter how much a firm's capacity exceeds its orders; shipments are determined primarily by orders when warehouses are full but must drop to zero as inventories are depleted; the cash position of a firm has little influence on its capital investment or employment decisions unless a severe liquidity crisis appears and dominates all other considerations; nominal interest rates do not become negative, no matter how rapid deflation may be; and so on.

In addition, and perhaps most important, nonlinearities contribute significantly to a system's evolutionary behavior because they cause the strength of its feedback loops, and hence its "active structure," to change over time (Richardson 1991). Returning to the example of the speculative bubble, it is clear that the positive feedbacks of extrapolative expectations are opposed by the negative feedbacks created by substitution to other products, increases in production of the commodity, declining real incomes as prices rise, and arbitrage opportunities. However, if the lure of speculative profit is strong enough, the positive feedback loops created by extrapolative expectations can overwhelm the negative feedbacks that might restore equilibrium—at least for a time. As prices are bid higher and higher relative to fundamental value, however, the credibility of projections of further increases falls, weakening the positive loops. At the same time, the negative loops gain in strength. That is, the relative strength of the different loops is nonlinearly dependent on the balance between current prices and fundamental value. Eventually, the nega-

---

9. See the discussion in Richardson (1991, 77ff).

tive loops become dominant and price increases slow. As soon as this occurs, of course, some seek to liquidate their holdings, and prices begin to fall. Now the same positive feedback loops dominate again as falling prices lead to panic selling. Eventually, the negative feedback loops reassert themselves once prices are low relative to fundamental value, halting price declines. Of note in this account is the shifting dominance of the positive and negative feedbacks due to nonlinearities. The nonlinearities cause the active feedback loops—those primarily responsible for the dynamics at any given time—to change endogenously, that is, to evolve. Nonlinearities also limit unstable processes, for example, constraining variables such as inventories to remain nonnegative, thus ensuring the global robustness of the system. No linear model can capture such shifts in the relative importance of different feedback processes.

Together, these elements of structure (stocks and flows, information feedbacks, decision rules, and nonlinearities) define the feedback loops in any system. By modeling decision-making behavior and the physical structure of the system at the microlevel, the macrolevel dynamics emerge naturally out of the interactions of the system components. Because such models provide a behavioral description firmly rooted in managerial practice, they are well suited to an examination of the dynamic effects of policy initiatives.

Another fundamental feature of system dynamics models is that they are disequilibrium models. It is not assumed that economic systems are always (or ever) in equilibrium, nor that they move smoothly from one equilibrium to the next. To model dynamics (including evolution) properly, the stability of the system must not be assumed. Rather, the decision processes of the agents in the system must be modeled, including the way people perceive and react to imbalances, as well as the delays, constraints, inadequate information, and side-effects that often confound them. Stability, adjustment paths, the response to shocks, and the nature of equilibria are viewed as behavioral outcomes of a model. They are properties that emerge from the underlying assumptions about system structure and the interaction of the feedback loops created by the stock and flow networks, information flows, and decision rules of the actors in the system. Thus system dynamics models are well suited to modeling evolutionary environments where path-dependent behavior and multiple and changing equilibria often arise.

Still another fundamental feature of system dynamics models is that they rest on the theory of bounded rationality (Cyert and March 1963; Merton 1936; Nelson and Winter 1982; Simon 1947, 1957, 1979). The essence of the theory is summarized in Herbert Simon's principle of bounded rationality (1957, 198):

The capacity of the human mind for formulating and solving complex problems is very small compared to the size of the problem whose solution is required for objectively rational behavior in the real world or even for a reasonable approximation to such objective rationality.

Boundedly rational decision making means that agents at each decision point in a system must use heuristics to select among the available information cues, process and combine those cues, and make a decision. These decisions then alter the rates of flow in the system, altering its stocks and giving rise to new information—thus closing various feedback loops as the decision makers perceive and react to the new information. Though there is often a rationale, or intended rationality, to the decision-making heuristics of the agents, there is no presumption in system dynamics that these heuristics are optimal, or even consistent. Nor is it assumed that decision making is based only on rational cognitive factors.[10] The theory of bounded rationality provides both theoretical underpinnings and a rich data base for the development and testing of behavioral models of decision making in economics. Psychological, contextual, cultural, and other social and economic forces may all influence the heuristics that people use. For example, cognitive and social psychology provide a rich data base of theory and experimental results documenting numerous cognitive limitations on human information perception and processing, errors and biases in heuristics commonly used in judgment and decision making, and other deviations from the axioms of rationality (Tversky and Kahneman 1974; Hogarth 1987; Kahneman, Slovic, and Tversky 1982).

These features of system dynamics lead to its claim that a good model of economic dynamics must be descriptive. To simulate, in the root sense of "mimic," the behavior of a system accurately, decision making must be portrayed as it is, and not as it might be if people conformed to the axioms of economic rationality. Discovering, representing, and testing models of decision-making heuristics is intrinsically an empirical task. Because the focus is on the process by which people make decisions, good system dynamics modeling involves fieldwork and direct observation of the system under study as well as the traditional tools of statistical estimation.[11] The modeler must often use ethnographic and anthropological methods to elicit the decision rules of the actors (Forrester 1961; Morecroft and Sterman 1992). Additional techniques to elicit decision-making behavior include laboratory experiments (Sterman 1988b, 1988c, 1989a, 1989b) and cognitive mapping (Axelrod 1976; Checkland 1981; Vennix and Gubbels 1992; Reagan-Cirincione et al. 1991). When well done, complementary field-based, labora-

---

10. For example, emotions, habit, rules of thumb, and culture often play roles in decision making. Homer (1985), Shantzis and Behrens (1973), Levin, Hirsch, and Roberts (1975), and Homer (1993) provide examples including worker burnout, tribal rituals, and drug use.

11. See Senge (1980) for an example of econometric tools applied to system dynamics models. Validation is discussed in Forrester and Senge (1980), Sterman (1984), and Radzicki (1988b, 1990a).

tory, and statistical methods yield a rich representation, grounded in multiple data sources, of the decision-making heuristics of agents and how these rules might change over time. Evolutionary models need to be grounded in such direct observation of decision making, lest the axioms of individual profit and utility maximization be replaced by equally whimsical and arbitrary assumptions about decision-making behavior.

The attributes described above make system dynamics modeling well suited to the study of evolutionary dynamics in human systems. The flexibility of the modeling method and emphasis on empirical assessment of the decision rules of the actors means the microstructure of a system can be represented with great fidelity. The resulting high-order, nonlinear systems typically contain dozens, or even more, interacting positive and negative feedback loops. The nonlinearities in dynamic systems mean the active structure or dominant feedback loops can change endogenously. As a result, system dynamics models may possess multiple equilibria. The equilibria in a system dynamics model may or may not be stable. The models can (and do) exhibit path-dependent, irreversible dynamics. They can learn and evolve. For example, one of the earliest system dynamics models (Forrester 1961, appendix N) represents a manufacturing firm that "learns" to detect seasonal cycles in incoming orders, then adjusts production accordingly. The customer order rate has no exogenous seasonality but does contain random disturbances. As the firm responds to these random fluctuations, the resulting changes in price and product availability, in turn, induce the simulated customers to alter their ordering patterns until the system generates strong seasonal patterns, when none existed before. Other examples of evolution and learning in system dynamics models are provided by Merten, Löffler, and Wiedmann's (1987) model of a multinational firm that learns to reorganize itself as it grows; Roberts's (1974) model of elementary schools, in which each student's achievement is dependent on teacher, student, and parent expectations, which in turn are dependent on student achievement; and Levin et al.'s (1976) models of human service organizations, in which service-provider standards and client expectations are conditioned by the quality of services received, thus creating path-dependent dynamics.

There are really two ways in which system dynamics modeling can be considered evolutionary. The first is in terms of the behavior of a *particular* system dynamics model. System dynamics models can possess multiple equilibria and exhibit path-dependency, self-organization, chaos, time irreversibility, and evolution to increased levels of complexity and entropy. Moreover, their nonlinear relationships can cause their "active structures" to change as a simulation unfolds. In terms of a number of criteria, therefore, individual system dynamics models can be classified as evolutionary.

A second way in which system dynamics models can be considered evolutionary comes from the notion that the true value of modeling arises from the modeling *process*, rather than from any particular model (Forrester 1985). In other words, system dynamicists believe that it is the iterative process of making one's perceptions explicit and then testing their adequacy via simulation that generates insight into the phenomena being studied. As a result, system dynamicists never consider a model as being complete, but as being only in its latest stage of development. Moreover, they note that as new insights and ideas are generated from the modeler's participation in the process, the structure of the model will change to accommodate them. Given this perspective, the system dynamics modeling *process* can clearly be classified as evolutionary. Of note is that evolutionary economists have put forth essentially the same argument vis-à-vis their pattern-modeling process since the time of John Dewey (1910, 1938).[12]

An Illustration: Learning Curves, Imperfect Appropriability, and Evolving Industry Structure

To illustrate some of these ideas, a simple evolutionary system dynamics model will now be presented. The model depicts the competition for market share between firms where each benefits from a significant learning curve. For clarity of exposition and considerations of space, the model is highly simplified compared to typical theories of industry and firm structure in the system dynamics literature (e.g., Forrester 1961; Mass 1975; Lyneis 1980; Beinhocker et al. 1993), yet it illustrates the path-dependent, self-organizing dynamics typical of evolutionary models. Further, for brevity, empirical tests of the model are not described. The reader interested in empirical testing is referred to Paich and Sterman (1993) for an experimental study of decision-making behavior in a setting similar to the one assumed below.

Figure 1 shows the system dynamics stock-flow diagram for the learning curve model. The model's stocks are represented by the rectangles (e.g., Firm 1 Cumulative Experience), and its flows are represented by the pipe- and valvelike icons that appear to be filling and draining the tubs (e.g., Firm 1 Production). The solid arrows in figure 1 represent flows of information, while the circular icons depict constants, behavioral relationships, or decision points where the simulated agents transform flows of information into decisions (e.g., Firm 1 Price is determined by Firm 1 Unit Costs and Firm 1 Margin).

There is a one-to-one correspondence between the structural diagram and the equations. The diagram and equations are the actual output from STELLA, the software program used to develop the model (Richmond and

---

12. See also Wilber and Harrison (1978) and Gruchy (1972).

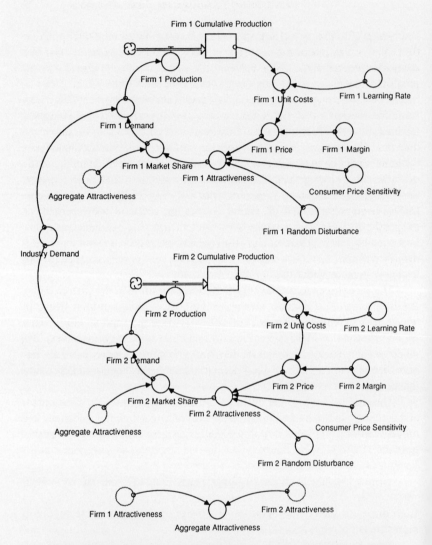

Fig. 1. System dynamics model of duopoly under a learning curve. The diagram is reproduced exactly from the simulation model in STELLA. The dashed circles are "ghosts," or copies of variables defined elsewhere in the diagram (to avoid cluttering the diagram with crossed lines).

Peterson 1992). The model was created by drawing the structural diagram on the screen of a microcomputer, then specifying the form of the equations. The software enforces consistency between the diagram and the equations and provides numerous built-in functions to assist the model builder. Experience has shown that modelers ranging from grade-school students to CEOs can learn the mechanics of the software in a few hours. A caveat, however: learning the software mechanics is easy, learning how to build good models is difficult. The ease of use of the software tools means complex nonlinear dynamic modeling is now accessible to anyone, regardless of computer skills or mathematical background. Obviously, some training in mathematics and an understanding of decision-making behavior and complex dynamics are important for developing insightful, robust models. The software allows a modeler to spend his or her time thinking about system structure and behavior rather than spending time programming. Researchers interested in evolutionary dynamics will find that such software can be used for "rapid prototyping" and testing of models with considerable complexity.

The model represents the competition among firms in the presence of a learning curve. The simplest version of the model, presented first, is one in which the only feedback loops are those created by the learning curve. This version shows how a learning curve can create path-dependent dynamics. The model is then extended to consider imperfect private appropriability of experience, introducing additional feedback complexity and yielding much richer dynamics.

The model assumes that all firms are identical in structure, parameters, and initial conditions. Two firms are assumed for simplicity, although the model readily generalizes to a population of N firms, which may be heterogeneous. The equations[13] are:

$$\text{Firm\_1\_Demand} = \text{Firm\_1\_Market\_Share}^*\text{Industry\_Demand} \qquad (1)$$

Each firm's demand is the industry demand multiplied by the firm's share of that demand.

$$\text{Firm\_1\_Market\_Share} =$$

$$\text{Firm\_1\_Attractiveness}/\text{Aggregate\_Attractiveness} \qquad (2)$$

Each firm receives a share of the industry demand proportional to the "attractiveness" of that firm's product compared to that of other firms (see eq. 12).

---

13. For brevity of exposition only the equations for firm 1 are shown. The equations for firm 2 are identical.

Firm_1_Attractiveness =

Firm_1_Random_Disturbance*(Firm_1_Price^

($-$ Consumer_Sensitivity_to_Price))   (3)

Firm_1_Random_Disturbance = 1 + STEP(1,1)*NORMAL(0,.1)   (4)

The attractiveness of each firm's product is determined by price and a random disturbance. (The character "^" denotes exponentiation.) The elasticity of attractiveness with respect to price is high but finite: the products are not perfect substitutes but somewhat differentiated. In addition, each firm's attractiveness is influenced by an independent random variable representing the stochastic influence of factors of attractiveness not captured in price and by variations in consumer preferences. The disturbances are specified as normal random variables with standard deviations of 10 percent (the STEP function prevents the random disturbances from having any impact until time 1, so that the model begins in an initial equilibrium where the two firms are identical). Models with more sophisticated determinants of product attractiveness, including product attributes such as delivery delay and reliability, product quality and functionality, service, network externalities, and so on, are described in Paich and Sterman (1993) and Sterman (1988a).

Firm_1_Price = Firm_1_Unit Costs*(1 + Firm_1_Margin)   (5)

Firm_1_Margin = 0   (6)

Price is determined by unit costs and a target margin, assumed to be constant and set to zero for simplicity. In more complex models the margin is a strategic variable that can be used to capture firm strategy, such as an attempt to gain initial market-share advantage to profit from the learning curve (Beinhocker et al. 1993).

Firm_1_Unit_Costs =

(Firm_1_Cumulative_Production)^ (Firm_1_Learning_Rate)   (7)

Firm_1_Learning_Rate = LOGN(.80)/LOGN(2)   (8)

In the spirit of Arrow's (1962) original work, equations 7 and 8 portray the learning curve. Following standard learning-curve theory and empirical research, the unit production costs of each firm fall by a fixed percentage with each doubling of cumulative production experience.[14] An 80 percent learning curve is assumed; that is, unit costs fall 20 percent with each doubling of cumulative experience. The model also assumes, for now, that learning is privately appropriable—each firm can prevent rivals from benefiting from its own experience.

Firm_1_Cumulative_Production(t) =

Firm_1_Cumulative_Production($t - dt$)

+ (Firm_1_Production)* dt

INIT Firm_1_Cumulative_Production = 1   (9)

Firm_1_Production = Firm_1_Demand   (10)

Cumulative production is simply the integral of production. The initial cumulative production levels are set to unity (as specified by the INIT statement). Production is assumed to equal demand. For simplicity, capacity constraints, production lags, inventories, and backlogs that can cause disequilibria in the goods markets are ignored. Models treating disequilibrium dynamics caused by inventories and capacity are plentiful in the system dynamics literature (e.g., Forrester 1961; Mass 1975; Lyneis 1980; Sterman 1989a, 1989b). Models of learning curve environments that treat these sources of disequilibrium include Beinhocker et al. (1993) and Paich and Sterman (1993).

Industry_Demand = STEP(4,1)   (11)

The evolution of the industry commences when industry demand, initially zero, increases suddenly to four units per year in year one. For simplicity, price elasticity and other factors that may affect industry demand (such as word of mouth, marketing, demographic changes, etc.) are ignored. See Paich and Sterman (1993) and Beinhocker et al. (1993) for models with dynamic, endogenous industry demand.

Aggregate_Attractiveness = Firm_1_Attractiveness +

Firm_2_Attractiveness   (12)

---

14. Arrow (1962), however, originally assumed that learning was a function of cumulative *investment*.

The aggregate attractiveness of all firms is the sum of the individual attractiveness levels, ensuring that the sum of the market shares is unity for any number of firms.

$$\text{Consumer\_Sensitivity\_to\_Price} = 10 \tag{13}$$

Each firm is assumed to operate in an imperfectly competitive environment. Each firm's demand curve is highly, but not infinitely, elastic (assuming no reaction by the other firm).

Obviously the model is highly simplified. Yet it contains sufficient feedback complexity to show interesting path-dependent behavior. The feedback structure of the model is shown in figure 2. The learning curve creates a positive or self-reinforcing feedback process within each firm (loops 1 and 2 in the figure). These loops act to differentiate the two firms from one another by progressively reinforcing and amplifying any initial difference in prices and market shares. In addition, the coupling of the two firms through competition creates a third positive loop (the "figure 8" loop denoted as loop 3 in fig. 2) whereby greater market share of, say, firm 1 boosts its cumulative output, lowering its price and reducing firm 2's market share, thus slowing the rate at which firm 2 gains experience and can lower its price, further boosting firm 1's market share. Though both firms are identical at the start of the simulation, the random disturbances in product attractiveness will give one firm a small initial advantage in market share. In the simulation shown in figure 3, the initial edge goes to firm 1. Firm 1 develops a slight lead in the accumulation of production experience, and moves down the learning curve faster than its competitor, thereby gaining a slight price advantage. Lower price then yields additional market share and still faster accumulation of production experience, while the competitor's rate of experience accumulation slows. The process continues until the leading firm captures essentially the entire market, driving the competitor out of business. The competitor's costs stabilize well above those of the dominant firm.

Figure 4 shows the result of fifty simulations, differing only in the particular sequence of random disturbances realized in each case.[15] As expected, each firm dominates about half the time, and the envelope of market-share paths traces out a "lobster claw" shape. Because costs fall most rapidly in the early years, when cumulative production is doubling rapidly, small initial advantages rapidly differentiate the two firms. Later, the cumulative cost advantage of the dominant firm is simply too great to overcome and the system locks in to the particular equilibrium chosen. Indeed, in most cases the

---

15. The simulations were run under the Euler integration method with a time-step $dt = .25$ years.

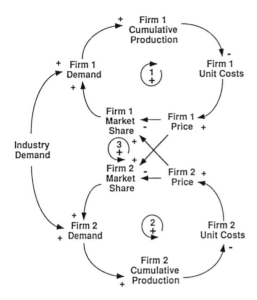

Fig. 2. Causal loop diagram of the learning curve model. The arrows indicate the direction of causality. Signs ("+" or "−") at arrow heads indicate the polarity of relationships: a "+" indicates that an increase in the independent variable causes the dependent variable to increase above what it would have been, *ceteris paribus* (and a decrease causes a decrease). Similarly, a "−" indicates that an increase in the independent variable causes the dependent variable to decrease below what it would have been. That is, $X \overset{+}{\to} Y \Rightarrow (\partial Y/\partial X) > 0$ and $X \overset{-}{\to} Y \Rightarrow (\partial Y/\partial X) < 0$. Positive loop polarity (denoted by + in the loop identifier) indicates a self-reinforcing (positive feedback) process. Negative (−) loop polarity indicates a self-regulating (negative feedback) process. See Richardson and Pugh (1981). The learning curve creates positive feedbacks within each firm (loops 1 and 2) whereby accumulating production experience lowers costs and prices, leading to greater market share and still faster learning. The coupling of firms to one another through market share creates the "figure 8" positive feedback (loop 3) through which one firm's gain also slows the learning rate of its rivals.

loser has been driven out by year 10. Occasionally, however, the random disturbances roughly balance during the period in which the learning curve is strongest, leading to slower differentiation. However, the positive feedback loops through which success begets success always lead eventually to the dominance of one of the firms. That is, the model has only two equilibrium states: Firm 1 market share must tend toward 100 percent or 0 percent. Furthermore, the particular equilibrium realized depends on the particular sequence of events in the early history of the industry. Here these events are

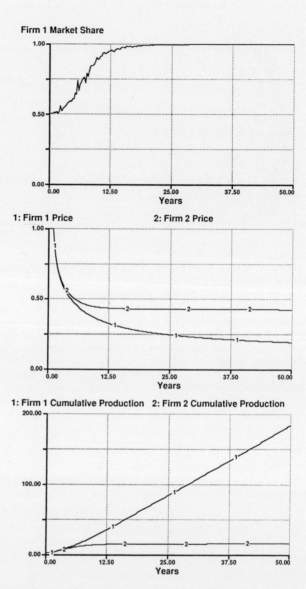

Fig. 3. Simulation run where firm 1 "wins." Small initial differences in cumulative production caused by random disturbances are amplified by the positive feedback loops until firm 1 forces firm 2 completely out of the market, despite equal initial conditions.

Firm 1 Market Share

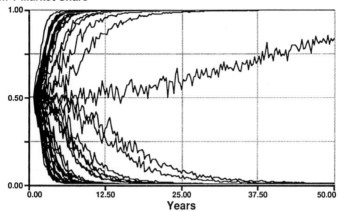

Fig. 4. Fifty simulations of the model. Despite the homogeneous initial conditions where all firms are identical, the positive feedback loops created by the learning curve rapidly drive one firm out of business while the other grows to dominate the market. The winning firm in any given simulation is determined by the particular sequence of random disturbances that perturb the model. In most simulations the winner is determined early, though occasionally the differentiation of the two firms takes many years.

modeled as random, though in reality they also depend on the strategic moves of the contending firms as well as the parameters governing the learning curve and other aspects of the firms' structure and decision-making behavior (which need not be the same).

It is worthwhile to consider more subtle dynamics that can arise when the feedback environment is richer, containing multiple positive and negative feedbacks, some of which are nonlinearly coupled, so that the dominant loops or active structure can shift endogenously as the system evolves. To illustrate, the model is now generalized to include imperfect appropriability of learning. In reality, a firm may often benefit from the production experience of its rivals by imitating their practices and techniques, learning from suppliers or customers they have in common, sending their employees to trade shows and professional conferences, hiring competitor employees, and reverse-engineering rival's products (von Hippel 1988). The equations of the model are modified as follows:

Firm_1_Unit_Costs = (Firm_1_Cumulative_Production +

Firm_1_Cumulative_Learning_from_Competitors)^

(Firm_1_Learning_Rate)   (7')

Unit costs are now determined by the sum of the firm's own cumulative production experience and the stock of cumulative experience the firm has been able to glean from its competitor.

Firm_1_Cumulative_Learning_from_Competitors(t) =

Firm_1_Cumulative_Learning_from_Competitors($t - dt$) +

(Firm_1_Learning_from_Competitors) * dt

INIT Firm_1_Cumulative_Learning_from_Competitors = 0   (14)

The stock "Cumulative Learning from Competitors" reflects the amount of the competitor's relevant production experience the firm has been able to acquire. Thus, to the extent a firm can learn from its competitor, it will move down the learning curve faster than when learning is privately appropriable. Initially, none of the competitor's experience is known to the firm.

Firm_1_Learning_from_Competitors =

(1-Appropriability_of_Firm_2_Experience) *

MAX(0,(Firm_2_Cumulative_Production-

Firm_1_Cumulative_Production) *

NORMAL(1,.1)/Firm_1_Experience_Diffusion_Delay)   (15)

Firm_1_Experience_Diffusion_Delay = 1   (16)

The rate at which each firm accumulates knowledge about the production experience of its competitor depends on several factors. First, each firm may benefit from the competitor's experience only to the extent the competitor's production experience is not privately appropriable. Hence the potential learning rate is reduced according to the fraction given by one minus the appropriability of the competitor's experience. Second, the model assumes that learning is only beneficial to the firm (hence the MAX function to ensure nonnegativity of the learning rate). Third, the model assumes that the firm can only learn what it does not yet know. Thus the rate of learning is proportional to the difference between the competitor's knowledge and the firm's: the greater the lead of the competitor, the more the firm might benefit. The time constant over which the gap in knowledge is closed is determined by the Experience Diffusion Delay. The diffusion delay represents the time required for one firm to learn about and implement the knowledge of its competitor. A one-year average delay is assumed in the simulations below. Finally, it is assumed that a firm's learning from its competitor is stochastic, with multiplicative disturbances in the learning rate of each firm determined by an independent normal random variable, with a standard deviation equal to 10 percent of the expected learning rate.

Appropriability_of_Firm_1_Experience =

GRAPH(Firm_1_Market_Share) (0.00, 0.00), (0.1, 0.00), (0.2,

0.00), (0.3, 0.05), (0.4, 0.15), (0.5, 0.3), (0.6, 0.7), (0.7,

0.95), (0.8, 1.00), (0.9, 1.00), (1.00, 1.00)   (17)

There are many possible hypotheses regarding the appropriability of learning. To illustrate the concept of shifting feedback-loop dominance, the appropriability of each firm's experience is assumed to vary nonlinearly with market share, where market share is used here as a proxy for market power (e.g., control of suppliers from whom competitors might glean knowledge of the firm's practices and techniques). When the competitor's market share is low, their production experience is assumed to be nonappropriable—i.e., the firm cannot protect its knowledge from larger and more powerful rivals. As a firm's market share rises, however, the degree of appropriability rises until, for high market shares, its knowledge is assumed to become fully appropriable (fig. 5). The software program STELLA allows this relationship to be captured through a GRAPH function. The GRAPH function allows the model-builder to specify arbitrary nonlinear relationships as a series of x-y pairs. The software then interpolates linearly between the points. Analytic functions can also be used easily (a logistic or Gompertz function might be used here). Clearly the relationship between market share and appropriability of knowledge in the model, particularly the numerical values, is speculative; they are chosen simply to illustrate the ways in which complex hypotheses about decision-making behavior may be represented easily in models of this type.

The feedback loop structure of the revised model is shown in figure 6. Inspection of the figure reveals that there are now more complex interactions

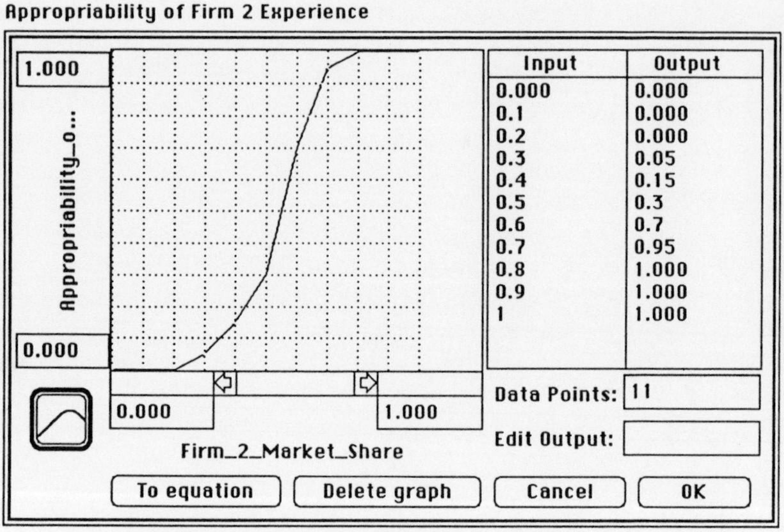

Appropriability of Firm 2 Experience

	Input	Output
	0.000	0.000
	0.1	0.000
	0.2	0.000
	0.3	0.05
	0.4	0.15
	0.5	0.3
	0.6	0.7
	0.7	0.95
	0.8	1.000
	0.9	1.000
	1	1.000

1.000

Appropriability_o...

0.000

0.000   1.000

Firm_2_Market_Share

Data Points: 11

Edit Output:

[To equation] [Delete graph] [Cancel] [OK]

Fig. 5. Graphical function showing assumed dependence of knowledge appropriability on market share, for Firm 2 (eq. 17). The curve reflects the assumption that the larger firm 2's market share, the more it can appropriate its experience and prevent rivals from benefiting. The software interpolates linearly between the specified points. The user can select any domain and interval for the independent variable, thus controlling the smoothness of the relationship. While analytic expressions can be used to capture such nonlinear functions, the ability to specify arbitrary nonlinearities as look-up tables greatly speeds model development, enhances flexibility, and makes complex nonlinear modeling accessible to students, managers, and others who might not have extensive training in mathematics.

between the model's feedback loops. The positive feedback loops created by the learning curve are now potentially offset by negative feedback loops created by the process of learning from competitors (loops 4, 5, and 6). A firm that finds itself falling behind can learn from the practices of its rivals and thus close the gap in unit costs, restoring market share, staying in the game— perhaps ultimately using the learning curve to its advantage. The relative strength of the positive experience-curve loops and the negative cross-firm learning loops determines the nature of the equilibrium achieved. As seen in the simple model, fully appropriable learning means the positive loops dominate and one firm must drive all others to extinction. If learning were not appropriable, and the time constant for knowledge diffusion were short enough, the negative loops that tend to equalize learning would dominate. Thus, whenever a firm began to develop a lead in experience, and hence a cost

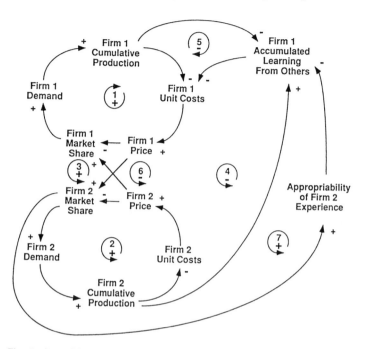

Fig. 6. Causal loop diagram showing the feedback structure of the extended model, in which firms can benefit from the accumulated experience of their rivals. For clarity, the structure for interfirm learning is shown for firm 1 only. The structure of interfirm learning for firm 2 (not shown) is symmetrical and creates many more loops than are shown in the diagram. Interfirm learning introduces negative feedback loops that tend to equalize prices (loops 4, 5, 6), while the assumed dependence of knowledge appropriability on market share creates additional positive feedbacks (loop 7).

advantage, its competitor would rapidly learn from the experience and neutralize the leader's advantage. The industry equilibrium would be an even split of the market among the different competitors. Industry leaders would emerge from time to time as a result of the random component assumed for customer preferences, but such periods of leadership would be short-lived and would not favor any particular firm.

In the full extended model, the relative importance of the positive and negative loops varies endogenously as a function of market share, introducing another set of positive feedbacks. As illustrated by loop 7 in figure 6, the assumption that market dominance allows a firm to prevent rivals from benefiting from its experience creates a positive loop whereby an increase in market share reduces the rate at which other firms can learn, slowing the rate

Firm 1 Market Share

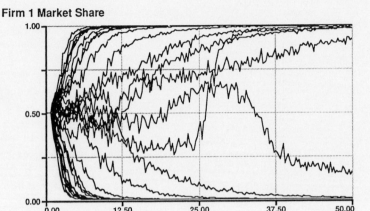

Years

Fig. 7. Thirty simulations of the extended model, showing many more complex paths of industry evolution arising when firms can learn from one another. Note the cases where market leadership reverses through interfirm learning. The ultimate winner is often not selected for decades, and long periods of market share dominance no longer guarantee a firm will ultimately triumph.

at which the negative learning loops 4–6 can equalize costs, giving the firm still greater opportunity to move ahead on its own learning curve. In contrast to the two extreme cases of complete private appropriability or rapid knowledge diffusion, it is not obvious from inspection how the full model, with this complex nonlinear feedback structure, will behave.

Indeed, simulations of the extended model show a variety of complex paths for the evolution of the industry. Figure 7 shows thirty simulations of the extended model. In most cases, one firm establishes dominance quickly and drives the other to extinction before the losing firm can learn enough from the competitor to close the experience gap and equalize unit costs. In these cases the positive learning-curve loops dominate, and the farther behind a firm gets the less it is able to benefit from competitor experience.

In other cases the initial leader finds its rival is able to close the gap, equalize market shares, and essentially begin the game again. Figure 8a shows such a case. Firm 1 gains initial advantage, but is not able to prevent firm 2 from learning from its experience. Despite firm 1's market share advantage of nearly two-to-one in year 5, firm 2 eventually wins. Occasionally, the initial leader suddenly loses, after a long period of high market share, as shown in figure 8b. Here, industry leadership passes between the two firms several times. Around year 18, firm 2 is able to reverse the advantage of firm 1

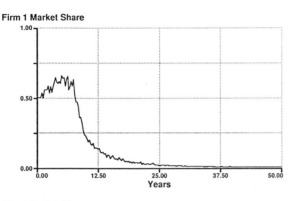

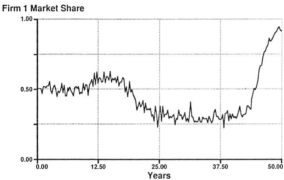

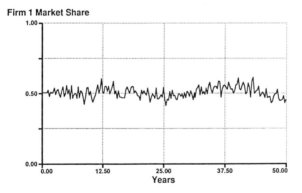

Fig. 8. Three simulations of the extended model, showing the diversity of paths of market evolution

through learning, and dominate the industry with about a 70 percent market share from years 25 through 40. Nevertheless, firm 1 ultimately emerges the winner. The interesting feature of this simulation is the speed of the ultimate triumph for firm 1 after decades of slow change. In still other simulations, the equilibrating negative loops caused by the exchange of knowledge dominate the differentiating effects of the positive experience-curve loops and the two firms remain roughly equal for very long periods of time, as in figure 8c.

Obviously, though only two firms are treated here for simplicity, the model generalizes readily to N firms, so the interaction of large populations of firms can be studied. Further, one can easily extend the model to include explicit entry and exit; heterogeneity of firm attributes, customers, and technology; more sophisticated representations of decision making; and more sophisticated representations of technology and organizations, including changes in fundamental architectures that may destroy firm competencies (Henderson and Clark 1990; Tushman and Romanelli 1985).

Despite the simplicity of the model, the simulations exhibit a number of key features of evolutionary models. First, the dynamics are strongly path-dependent. Second, the behavior is self-organizing: what begins as a market of identical agents rapidly organizes itself into a highly differentiated structure. The particular firm that dominates cannot be predicted in advance, yet the model spontaneously organizes itself into characteristic patterns. Third, the landscape within which the different firms compete against one another is changing as they move through it: as production experience and market share change, so does the strength of the various feedback loops, thereby conditioning the future evolution of the market. In the language of feedback control theory and system dynamics, the evolution of the industry endogenously alters the dominant feedback structure of the system. These changes in active feedback structure then feed back to condition the dynamics of the system.

Software and Other Resources for System Dynamics Modeling

Over the years, a variety of software packages, books, and professional journals have been developed specifically for the field of system dynamics. In terms of software, DYNAMO (Pugh 1983), DYSMAP2 (1992), and NDTRAN (Davisson and Uhran 1979) are available for both mainframe and personal computers; Vensim (Eberlein 1991) is available for PCs and some UNIX-based workstations; and STELLA (Richmond and Peterson 1992), I Think, and MicroWorld Creator (1990) are available for the Apple Macintosh.

Basic textbooks describing the system dynamics method include those by Forrester (1961, 1968), Goodman (1977), Richardson and Pugh (1981), Roberts et al. (1983), and Richmond and Peterson (1992). Since 1985 the international System Dynamics Society has published a scholarly journal, the *System Dynamics Review*, covering the theory and application of system dynamics in a wide range of disciplines.

Conclusions

Recent developments in nonlinear theory, the psychology of decision making, and experimental economics have joined to form the basis for empirically testable, nonlinear, disequilibrium theories of evolutionary economic dynamics. Advances in the mathematics of nonlinear dynamical systems allow modelers to represent the nonaverage behavior of individual agents and to portray systems far from equilibrium. Advances in simulation techniques, software, and computer hardware make such capabilities accessible to anyone with a personal computer and knowledge of basic mathematics.

However, evolutionary economics cannot succeed merely as a technical undertaking. If evolutionary approaches are to generate penetrating insights into the behavior of actual economic systems, the tools of modeling must be complemented by appropriate tools of empirical investigation, so that theories are grounded in experimental tests and field studies of economic decision making. Evolutionary models should portray the decision-making behavior and heuristics of the people in the system as they exist, warts and all, including explicit attention to the many limitations of cognitive capabilities and the role of habits, emotions, culture, and other bounds on human rationality. Though traditional tools of econometric estimation will continue to be useful, the decision rules used in evolutionary models must be investigated firsthand, in the field and laboratory. The findings and methods of economic historians and institutionalists, psychologists, sociologists, anthropologists, and experts from other areas have much to offer in this endeavor.

System dynamics is well suited to the development and testing of evolutionary models. With its historic emphasis on explicit modeling of stocks and flows, nonlinearities, feedback processes, and behavioral decision making, it provides a well-developed body of theory, technique, and examples for modeling disequilibrium dynamics in economic systems. Further, system dynamics practitioners have developed diverse methods for investigating decision making in the field, eliciting the mental models and decision rules people use and testing the resulting formulations. Modern developments in system dynamics software and pedagogy have so simplified the mechanics of the model-building process that precollege students are regularly building evolutionary models. Firms and government agencies are using such models to help design corporate strategy and public policy. Research into new applications of evolutionary dynamics awaits us.

Part 3
Evolution and Social Institutions

The world economy is an intricate, evolving game with nearly four billion players. The players are organized into literally millions of overlapping organizations.

—Richard H. Day (1975)

An Evolutionary Approach to Law and Economics

Warren J. Samuels, A. Allan Schmid, and James D. Shaffer

The question of the relationships between legal and economic (generally meaning *market*) processes has been a central preoccupation of moral philosophy, political theory, economics, and jurisprudence at least since the time of John Locke and Adam Smith, when the idea of an economy at least conceptually separable from the polity came to the forefront. Within these disciplines, there have been understandings—sometimes explicit, but more typically implicit—of the critical importance of government in economic affairs and of the economy for governmental affairs.

Most attempts to analyze legal and economic processes have been unilineal: either the economy is seen to be a function of law or the law a function of the economy. A few writers have attempted more ambitious models of interrelationships between the two spheres, but most work has dealt with parts of the larger subject in such a way that conclusions on particular topics, or solutions to particular problems, have been driven by the treatments of what is endogenous and what is exogenous. For example, analyses of certain putative or potential rights, or of certain governmental processes, have been conducted in such a way that the results depend on the identification and treatment of the particular rights or processes and on whatever factors and forces are begged by their omission.[1]

The authors are indebted to Jeff Biddle and Richard England for helpful comments on an earlier draft of this chapter.

1. This situation is very much parallel to the microeconomic static partial-equilibrium analysis of resource allocation using a demand and supply model in which the identification and distribution of existing rights, technology, preferences, institutions, and natural resources are taken as given, that is, treated as exogenous variables. The price mechanism operative in that model can be modeled in various ways, and in each case analysis would both directly reflect the form of modeling and indirectly acknowledge the operation of the exogenous variables in real-world (that is, nonmodel) circumstances. Even so-called general equilibrium theory is closer in fundamental conceptualization to this static partial-equilibrium theory than to what will be identified below as evolutionary theory.

Furthermore, most writing on the subject of the economic role of government has been either straightforwardly normative or heavily constrained and channeled by normative, ideological, material, or subjective considerations. Perhaps all social science analysis necessarily is so constrained and channeled, but work on the economic role of government has been particularly normative in character. Arguably all theories of the economic role of government, even those that were presented as minimalist and noninterventionist, constitute agendas for government, giving affect to selective, largely implicit, antecedent normative premises. Ideology in particular has influenced the specification and treatment of endogenous and exogenous variables in economics.

The principal technical approach to law and economics found today in the literatures of economics, political science, and law is that of the neoclassical school. Its genesis can be traced to the work of Coase (1960) on transaction costs, albeit with numerous precursors. Parallel movements include public choice, property rights, rent seeking, and similar versions of neoclassical economic reasoning (for example, Buchanan and Tullock 1962; Posner 1973; Williamson 1985; Eggertsson 1990). Much of this work involves the normative application of microeconomic reasoning to reach determinate, optimal, and, where feasible, equilibrium solutions to technical problems of theory and policy.

The objective of this chapter is to identify the nature and content of a positive (nonnormative) evolutionary approach to law and economics. At this point it may be stated that the evolutionary approach presented here focuses on, first, a multiplicity of sources of change and adjustment processes;[2] second, the open-endedness of legal-economic processes; and third, the treatment of economic and political agents and variables as both dependent and independent variables in a type of model that can be designated evolutionary, coevolutionary, cumulative causative, or overdeterminist.[3]

It should be understood from the beginning that the evolutionary approach presented here is fundamentally different from the ostensibly deterministic and predictive method conventionally associated with mainstream economics.[4] An evolutionary approach to law and economics is content with a

---

2. The term *adjustment process* is used instead of *mechanism* because the emphasis is intended to be on the ongoing and choice nature of what is involved, rather than on something transcendental, automatic, and mechanical.

3. The influence of writers such as Max Weber, Karl Marx, Pareto (1963), Schumpeter (1976), Heertje and Perlman (1990), Nelson and Winter (1982), North (1981), Hodgson and Screpanti (1991), and especially the evolutionary institutional economics of Veblen (1919), Commons (1924), and Hodgson (1988, 1993) will be obvious. See also Bromley (1989) and the writings collected in Samuels (1988) and Tool (1988).

4. We say *ostensibly* deterministic and predictive for specific reasons. First, because in order to reach determinate results, the conventional procedure is to exclude all variables that otherwise would interfere with reaching determinate results—so that the determinate results give

different agenda. It is content with an identification and understanding of what is going on; an understanding specifically of the operative processes, mechanisms, patterns, connections, features, and properties of the interrelationship between legal and economic processes, of the economic role of government, or of the legal-economic nexus. The evolutionary approach is additionally different from the neoclassical approach in that it does not seek optimal solutions, or judgments of fitness (in the sense of rightness, as in social Darwinism). It is content with identifying the sources of change (and of countervailing continuity) and the processes of adjustment during the interaction between legal and economic processes.

The evolutionary approach therefore uses models that do not take positions on questions that in the real world still have to be worked out, and it thereby does not foreclose the operation of process and substitute the ideas (including definitions of reality and preferences) of analysts for those of actual economic actors. The open-ended nature of the evolutionary approach follows from this sort of skeptical practice.

Another way of making these same points is to echo Holmes's dictum in *The Common Law* ([1881] 1945, 1) that

> the life of the law has not been logic; it has been experience. The felt necessities of the time, the prevalent moral and political theories, intuitions of public policy, avowed or unconscious, even the prejudices which judges share with their fellows, have a good deal more to do than the syllogism in determining the rules by which men should be governed.

Considered as a positive statement, this means, in part, that an evolutionary approach must examine the larger questions that more static approaches either take for granted or evade by substituting the premises and preferences of analysts for those of actual legal-economic processes.[5]

In the following pages our purpose is to identify, schematically and

---

effect to and are tautological with the narrowing assumptions. And second, because prediction in economics, when it is not merely a ritualistic epistemological invocation, can properly take place only in the context of a model and not in regard to the real world.

5. It should be understood that—because the actual legal-economic world is complex, multifaceted, and kaleidoscopic, filled with plural theories and models—it should be anticipated that there can be multiple evolutionary approaches. It is for this reason that we have used the word *an* rather than the more presumptuous *the* in the title of our chapter. We are confident, however, that the fundamental characteristics of our approach are reasonably sui generis to the class of evolutionary approaches. The approach taken here is generally consistent with the evolutionary treatments of technology and the firm developed by such writers as Nelson and Winter (1982), Dosi (1988), Freeman (1987), Clark and Juma (1987), Elster (1983), and Screpanti (Hodgson and Screpanti 1991). See also Anderson and Sturis 1988; Silverberg 1984, 1987; Lazonick 1991; Hodgson, Samuels, and Tool 1993; and various works by Nathan Rosenberg.

programmatically, the principal characteristics of an evolutionary approach to law and economics and to contrast it with the quite different neoclassical approach. Insofar as the two approaches define their respective scope and central problem differently and are not endeavoring to answer the same questions, they are not in those respects competitive. However, they are competitive in the sense that they present different definitions of the legal-economic world and different assertions of what legal-economic theory should do and the way it should be done. While the authors find the questions addressed by an evolutionary approach to law and economics, and the types of answers that such an approach can properly provide, more interesting and less presumptuous and tendentious than those addressed and provided by the neoclassical approach, they do not denigrate either the questions or the approach taken by neoclassicism. Our position is that "there is, there can be, no economic theory which will do for us everything we want all the time" (Hicks 1981, 233), including the evolutionary approach.

General Characteristics of an Evolutionary Approach

What, then, constitutes an evolutionary approach to law and economics?

1. It is conventional to write of the economic role of government and of the interrelations between legal and economic processes as if the two sectors were both substantively separate and normatively different. The evolutionary approach affirms that the economy and the polity are neither given nor independent nor self-subsistent spheres but are continuously reformed in what may be called the legal-economic nexus (Samuels 1989a). The economy and the law mutually create each other; what goes on is not just a matter of interaction between the two spheres. Rather, each sphere is itself determined through the process of interaction; the two spheres coevolve:

> The legal-economic nexus is the sphere in which government operates to (re)define and (re)create the economy, and in which nominally private interests, perhaps especially economic interests, operate to (re)define and (re)channel government, given the dominant belief system, which is itself reformulated and rechannelled through the uses selectively imposed upon or made of it. (Samuels 1989a, 1571–72)

Selective perception influences what is taken to be mutable and immutable, what is changeable and what is natural and given. Law is a function of experience, which itself is a function of selective perception (for example, what constitutes and what exemplifies "fairness"), which is itself influenced by law.

2. The evolutionary approach rejects single-factor and linear explana-

tions in favor of systemic multiple-factor and curvilinear explanations. Each variable is both dependent and independent relative to the other variables. The economy is a function of law and the law is a function of the economy, but both emerge from a common nexus of activity, activity that is simultaneously both economic and political-legal in character. The spheres that seem so separate emerge from a larger nexus characterized by cumulative causation, coevolution, overdetermination, and evolutionary general interdependence. Neither economy nor polity is self-subsistent; each is reformed through its interactions and, especially, through activities in the common, underlying legal-economic nexus.

Individual agents may be selectively perceived as economic or legal, or as private or public, whereas all units in actuality have both economic and legal aspects to them.

Individual units have variable degrees of autonomy but are also constrained by the system in which they operate and by the aggregation of interactions with other units. But much more than constraint is involved. Institutions constrain, but they also shape what people see and want, as well as liberate and empower individuals to act. Laws help shape preferences, procedures, and habits. Laws help define what is regarded as progress (growth) and productive. Law, in specifying ideals, can sometimes affect behavior toward these ideals and toward other people, even when explicit incentives and sanctions cannot be administered. Experience with collective action can build trust and lessen opportunism, which is useful for future collective action.

3. The key legal-economic questions, the questions that all legal-economic processes operate to resolve, are, first, who is to control government for what purposes; and second, whose interests are to count, how, and how much.

4. The driving forces of legal-economic behavior are: first, ideology and the selective identifications and attributions of ideological patterns and metaphors to policy positions; and second, the continuing contest over the distributions of income and wealth. Each force profoundly influences the other. We cannot stress too much the importance of income and wealth distributions as the key objective of control in capturing and using government.

5. The legal-economic nexus is, in the modern world, the sphere in which resolutions of the problem of order are continually being worked out. The problem of order involves the conflicts between freedom and control, continuity and change, and hierarchy and equality.

6. The legal-economic nexus is not given. Its substance is a matter of the social reconstruction of reality, driven by activity that is, in the present context, simultaneously both legal and economic. The general process through which this social reconstruction of reality takes place is coevolution or over-

determination (see the contributions of Norgaard and of Resnick and Wolff to this volume). Central to the social construction of reality is the manufacture of and power play over cultural symbolism and meaning, ultimately governing whose interests are to count.

7. Power, ideology, and institutions are important dependent and independent variables endogenous to the legal-economic nexus.

8. The key adjustment processes[6] are: public opinion, learning and selective perception, expectations and discounting, legitimation, control of government (that is, of the uses to which government is to be put), administrative agencies, the legislature, and the courts. These are illustrative of the many and varied processes and transactions through which issues are worked out and conflicts resolved. On the one hand, these processes generate the implicit assumptions underlying operative premises as to rights (entitlements), risk identification and assumption/avoidance, and social goals. On the other hand, these processes are the objects of efforts to capture, channel, or otherwise manipulate them. At the constitutional level the processes are those by which the rules for making rules are generated, these rules being both dependent and independent variables in different circumstances.

9. The principal characteristic of the operation of the legal-economic nexus is *process*. Although it may be useful to use equilibrium models to produce deductively correct and determinate results, in the real legal-economic world all variables and interrelationships are in a continuous process of flux, without either given or actually achieved end points. The legal-economic nexus is a process of working things out, not a matter of the application of technical formulas.

10. In an evolutionary approach to law and economics, the substantive results generated by legal-economic behavior and the operation of the aforementioned adjustment processes are treated objectively and nonnormatively. They are neither affirmed in an optimizing/productivity paradigm nor denigrated in an exploitation paradigm, but are treated simply as results, albeit results that can be evaluated differently by economic actors with different perspectives and interests.

11. The substantive results generated by legal-economic behavior and the operation of the adjustment processes manifest the principle of unintended or unforeseen results. That is to say, the results are due, in part, to the interaction between and/or aggregation of behaviors and adjustment processes. This is not to say, however, that various economic agents do not attempt to control or channel behavior or the adjustment processes; nor is it to treat the principle of unintended or unforeseen results as anything but a positive proposition, that is, not as itself a principle of policy.

---

6. Processes in the sense of having to be worked out, thereby including relevant structures.

12. In society—for present purposes, especially regarding the legal-economic nexus—parts are a function of wholes and wholes are a function of parts. Individual units have degrees of autonomy but also are constrained by the system in which they operate and the aggregation of interactions with other units. The evolution of parts is thereby influenced by the evolution of wholes, and vice versa. Evolutionary paths are influenced by enterprise organization, technology, economies of scale, and, inter alia, the extent of the market. Private choice in each of these matters (for example, corporate form) is both influenced by and influences corporate and other (for example, antitrust) law.

The same is true of different aspects of economic life: for example, production and distribution are in fact intimately interconnected. Their separation for analytical purposes does not negate the situation that production is a function of distribution (for example, the distributions of income and wealth) and distribution is a function of production (for example, technology and the relative scarcity of factors of production).

Causal chains in the evolutionary approach to law and economics are long and complex. For example, resource allocation is a function of market demand and supply, but market demand and supply is in part a function of power structure (including wealth effects) and therefore of legal rights; and legal rights are a function of government, whose actions are a function of who is in a position to control the choices that are made through government determining whose interests are to count.

Conceptual designations in the evolutionary approach to law and economics are problematic, rendering reductionist analysis highly suspect. For example, the distinction between private and public is fundamentally ambiguous, because "public" is ultimately influenced by "private," and "private" is what it is in part because of legal action (see the treatment of the corporation as a legal "person" in Samuels and Miller 1987).

For the foregoing and other reasons it is extraordinarily important in evolutionary analysis to avoid reductionism. This does not mean that the analyst cannot make analysis manageable. It does mean that the analyst must make ample room for multiple, two-way, cumulative, and curvilinear causation.

The Neoclassical Approach in Contrast

The neoclassical approach to law and economics is very different. Preferences are stable and law is modeled as either a constraint or the fulfillment of those preferences. The neoclassical approach seeks determinate optimal equilibrium results to problems of explanation and of policy. It seeks determinate results because it embodies a particular conception of science; equilibrium results because it embodies a unilineal mechanistic conception of the economy; and optimality results because neoclassicism has both a maximizing and a harmonistic conception of the economy and because it embodies a desire to be relevant to questions of policy.

The neoclassical approach is manifestly normative. It is used to purportedly address such questions as who should have what rights; what is the best design of institutions; and why, or by what criteria, the status quo is the best of all possible worlds. The neoclassical approach tends to legitimize, selectively, either some specification of the status quo or some alternative to it. For example, it condemns some legal change as rent-seeking and applauds other legal change as wealth-creating. It tends to promote the conclusion that market or marketlike processes select individual units or performance results that are globally efficient or in some sense superior or comprise a compelling orderliness. It thereby tends to promote the conclusion that surviving arrangements are to be explained in terms of their utility or function, or by their having been selected for their efficiency in serving some purpose. The conclusion is promoted that surviving arrangements represent greater efficiency of, or greater benefits for, the whole, or that there is a single, universal, conclusive indicator or definition of fitness, etc.; that is, that survival connotes something transcendent to survival per se.

Yet such conclusions are highly presumptive and give effect to an assumption that "what is, ought to be" (Samuels 1992). Survival may have no transcendent meaning. Survival, or an optimality result, may only reflect the initial starting point. A local optimality result may conflict with a more inclusive, global one. A particular optimality result may be inconsistent with the maintenance or improvement of the environment. A particular inferior technology may be locked into because of temporary circumstances. And so on.

The microeconomic orientation of the neoclassical approach tends to a focus on simple natural selection and evolution of a unit within an environment, without consideration that the environment itself is subject to selection and evolution. The neoclassical approach, except insofar as it affirms the operation of market process qua market process, is disinterested in the environment-specific character of fitness or optimality; in how changes affect the environment itself; in how the environment of the individual unit is the system of social relations itself, which is subject to change; and in how individual behavior is both the consequence and the cause of environmental change.

Users of the neoclassical approach tend to affirm the existence of a single, universal, conclusive mechanism guaranteeing determinate and optimal results. Yet individual users, while generally affirming the market or price system as the overriding mechanism, tend to further specify quite variably other adjustment processes such as entrepreneurship.

In contrast, therefore, with the evolutionary approach to law and economics, the neoclassical approach has a very different conceptualization of legal-economic reality and a very different agenda as to what its scope and central problem, or analytical and policy objectives, are to be. The neoclassical approach is more apt to seek conclusions as to the optimality or nonoptimality of allocative and other performance results. It also has a narrower range of variables and it tends to treat those variables as given and self-subsistent in a unilinear way. Both the neoclassical and the evolutionary approaches to law and economics are interested in the operation of legal-governmental processes, in the jockeying for position to control government, and, inter alia, in the generation of impacts. Each, however, comprehends these subjects quite differently. Both approaches are powerful, but the respects in which they are powerful are quite different.

The Principal Elements of Developmental Analysis

A distinction must be made between theories of development and theories of impact, although the line of demarcation ought not to be too strictly held. For our purposes, theories of development focus on the operation and evolution of institutions or systems that produce policy; theories of impact focus on the consequences of policy. The following discussion centers on developmental considerations. But it must be recognized that impacts and consequences are steps or facets of development: from one perspective, development includes both the ex-ante changes and the adjustment processes that they set in motion; and impact includes the ex-post situation after the adjustment process has run its course, the results.[7] From another perspective, the impact of the developments of one period constitute the foundation or initial condition of the next period. Impacts are part of the developmental process. Among the relevant impact-oriented themes are: performance as a function of structure, behavior as a function of structure and performance, and the importance of unintended and/or unforeseen consequences.

How do these precepts shed light on the legal-economic nexus? What is important when one examines that sphere in the context of the evolutionary paradigm? It would be contrary to the evolutionary approach to say, in answer to those or comparable questions, that a certain outcome inexorably must happen or does happen. The evolutionary process contemplated here is open-ended and contingent, or problematic; it is a matter of working things out. The answers to these questions must be put in terms of processes, patterns, connections, features, properties, and adjustment processes.

---

7. With due regard to the fact that such periodization is an arbitrary model, and that initial changes and adjustments and results comprise ongoing processes.

Although legal-economic theory qua theory cannot properly say whether one rights-claimant will or should win out over another, this does not mean that nothing important can be said about the evolutionary legal-economic nexus and its adjustment processes:

1. Economies require fundamental institutions that are basically legal in character, though informal cultural institutions are also relevant. Markets are formed by the institutions that operate through them. In order for the Western market economy to have evolved, there simultaneously evolved, and had to evolve, a network of laws—legislative, judicial, and, to a lesser extent, executive—to permit orderly economic activity. These were the laws of property, contract, business organization, negotiable instruments, money and banking, sales, agency, torts, and so on—the very laws that the populations of the former Soviet Union and states of Eastern Europe must somehow have if their hitherto centrally planned economies are to become what are known as "market economies."

These legal institutions did not emerge on their own. They were the result, in part, of governmental agencies, such as courts, deciding conflicts between litigating parties and thereby establishing the rules of the game or the working rules of the market. They were also in part the result of interested parties who wanted, with legal security, to be able to do things in certain ways that they hitherto had been unable to do. In each of these situations, manifest or latent conflicts of interest were resolved and new law and new market arrangements were created, typically incrementally. Yet the Emancipation Proclamation radically changed property law in the United States in one day. Some actors within government saw in the economy an object of legal control, some seeing perhaps that such control was simply necessary, others that control could be exercised to their material or ideological, perhaps political, advantage; other actors, nominally within the economy, saw in government the means to economic gain and/or other advantage.

Much of this activity was, in the United States, at the state and local level (see, for example, Heath 1954; Nelson 1975; and Primm 1954). In the late nineteenth and twentieth centuries, as national markets emerged and as the advantage of national solutions appeared, such activity was increasingly undertaken at the national level.

The transformation of the U.S. economy from a rural, agrarian, and largely precapitalist one to an urban, commercial, industrial, and fully capitalist economy took some two hundred years. It involved the creation of the legal foundations of capitalism and the transformation of law. (We have in mind the work of such writers as Commons [1924], Friedman [1985], Nelson [1975], Horwitz [1977], and various works by James Willard Hurst and Carter Goodwich.) The economic and legal-political changes were two sides of the same coin, both taking place in the legal-economic nexus. The additional critical point is that the transformation of law, the creation of the legal foundations of capitalism, and the rise of a business civilization and culture itself took place gradually, incrementally, evolutionarily, with changes in one area leading to changes in another and then back again ad infinitum, such that each area, the economy and the law, was itself changed in the process: coevolution or overdetermination has been the rule.

The foregoing amounts to a recognition that, with regard to the necessary legal framework within which economic activity can be undertaken, the "planning" inherent in court decisions and statutes in a very fundamental, system sense is inevitable: different configurations of law, including different definitions and assignments of rights, lead to different economic outcomes. Moreover, the specific details ensconced within this legal-framework planning have particular consequences with regard to economic performance. Different systems and structures of rights yield different performance results.

2. According to the dominant ideology of the United States, which is very much a projection of a vibrant individualism, government is exogenous to the system, something that creates rather than solves problems, and therefore should be kept to a minimum. The economy is projected as a natural phenomenon, government as an artifact, something artificial. Contrary to this ideology, the manifestly evident "natural" tendency is for people to resort to government to accomplish their goals, including the therapeutic use of government in the face of perceived problems and untoward developments.

On the plane of ideology, a fundamental breech between economy and polity is posited; whereas on the plane of practical affairs, government is envisioned to be a pragmatic, instrumental, utilitarian tool or vehicle. The resulting cognitive dissonance is overcome by the formula that we resort to government only in emergencies, a model of intervention that can be called "laissez faire with exceptions." But ideology and psychology aside, resort to government has been continual, and the system transformations indicated above took effect, without design in the large, by incremental changes in law and in economic practice related to law. To repeat, judging by experience, the natural, or historical, tendency is to use government to accomplish economic purposes.

3. At every point in history there generally has been a body of law relevant to the interdependencies at hand. Not always, however; for example, new laws had to be made as technology opened up new ways of doing things, new social relationships, new ways of benefiting and of injuring others, and it was in the variably intensive interest of the relevant parties to have the law made in their interest. The body of law that is relevant to a new situation is often itself subject to dispute, but there are almost always people who believe that at least some body of law is relevant. (A contemporary example is the technology that permits surrogate motherhood. Many believe that ordinary

contract law is relevant, but others believe that law prohibits anything that amounts to the purchase and sale of a human being.) Conflict proceeds in part by arguing that the new interdependence is similar to a prior one, and thus it is implicitly ordered by existing law A rather than law B, or it is argued that no precedential sequence is relevant; in both cases, some choice (of analogy and of law, or of interest to be promoted) is made. The critical point is that given the existing network of rights and duties, the legal-economic process continuously involved legal selection and change, direct change in the existing network of rights and duties and indirect change in them through the adoption of complementary new rights and new duties. Most legal and jurisprudential analysis, including court decisions, tends to focus backwards on precedent and origins. But the fundamental significance of law and of legal change is in the future. Law may be made with a view to the past (for guidance as well as for legitimation) but its functioning is in the future; it is future organization and life that is governed by law.

4. As the U.S. economy became increasingly a capitalist, urban, commercial, and industrial economy; as the territory of the nation expanded across the continent; as its population increased; and, inter alia, as its technology became ever more sophisticated and roundabout, the economy became increasingly complex and its organizational forms and modes of doing business became increasingly diverse. These changes placed great and increasing pressures on the legal system to accommodate new conditions and various interests. These economic changes also brought about changes in government and law. Historical stages, using the term loosely, have involved both changes in economic and in governmental-legal relations. Each market, each political jurisdiction, became a site in which legal-economic experimentation took place (for example, state public utility regulation, commencing in the late nineteenth century). And, as we might expect, evolution has meant increasing complexity and diversity.

5. Every society necessarily confronts the problem of order, meaning thereby the continuing need to reconcile conflicts between freedom and control, continuity and change, and hierarchy and equality, with each of the terms of each conflict being subjected to selective perception. If legal change is the most critical, even dramatic, feature of the legal-economic nexus, legal changes, as both dependent and independent variables, are functional with regard to the three subsidiary components of the problem of order. For example, conflicts over the distributions of income and wealth involve all three conflicts and are such that the initial distribution of any period is the basis for the pursuit of those conflicts during the period. The temporary resolutions of those conflicts constitute the resulting distribution for that period, which becomes the initial or ex-ante distribution for the next period. There is not one single solution to the problem of distribution (or to the three conflicts compris-

ing the problem of order) that can be reached once and for all time, and what transpires in one sphere is both cause and consequence of what happens in other spheres.

The foregoing analytic period analysis is useful in describing other processes and properties of the evolutionary legal-economic process. Agents adapt to the system and agents adapt the system. Agents adapt to their environment but also adapt their environment to their needs, interests, and desires. One mode of adaptation is the law and one source of change necessitating, but not strictly dictating the substance of, adaptation is economic, including technological, change. Both actors and markets change, in part through the process of economic market change and in part through the process of political market change. "Initial" conditions change from analytic period to analytic period, as behavior both changes and is changed by boundary conditions, often those stipulated in law. The initial conditions of any one period are those produced by the adjustment-selection processes of the preceding period(s). Central to the process of changing initial conditions from period to period is the typical, but not necessarily gradual, transformation of rights and other entitlements.

6. Legitimation of the existing status quo is a principal social process. Legitimation tends to be absolutist; even in a pluralistic society, the justification of an institution or other arrangements tends to its affirmation in exclusivist, absolutist terms. Law in particular tends to be treated as an absolute, whereas social evolution indicates the relativity of law to changes in social power—continual change in the status quo, law in general, the interpretation of constitutional and common law doctrines, and judicial choice of precedential alternatives.[8] The practices of absolutist legitimation obscure the artifact and, therefore, the choice character of social control through law. Absolutist legitimation is a technique of both selective social control and social change. On the one hand, it influences the development of social arrangements; on the other, it serves to legitimize whatever arrangements emerge through the social processes.

The ceremonial legitimation of legal-economic arrangements (existing arrangements or some revision thereof) and the formulation of definitions of reality functional with regard to policy, together with the quest for certitude (the former constituting a social control and the latter a psychic balm function), lead to reductionist, unilineal, teleological, and deterministic arguments. The evolutionary process, however, manifests complex, curvilineal, open-ended, and random features. Operating as both cause and consequence of the legitimation cum certitude functions is the law-taker mentality, which

---

8. To affirm the "original intent" of the Founding Fathers, the writers of the Constitution, is to assume a particular reading of the document.

induces individuals to accept either existing law or proposed law as either given or transcendent to them; conversely, the evolutionary process manifests law-making as the actual state of society.

7. The social (re)construction of reality, in modern times especially operating through the legal-economic nexus, exhibits dual tendencies. On the one hand, there is considerable openness of evolutionary direction, considerable social discretion as to both the broad outlines and particular details of legal-economic and other arrangements. On the other hand, social evolution, including legal-economic, is path-dependent, heavily constrained by the dominant socioeconomic philosophy of life, that is: (1) economic ideology and/or religious value system—and the particular arrangements selectively rationalized by that value system through identification with its elements; (2) the existing power structure—social, political, and economic, insofar as these may be differentiated; and (3) the social psychology of peoples, with its selective susceptibility to political mobilization and manipulation. There is frequently a tension between one set of values and another—for example, the emerging legal crisis in the Islamic world (Iran, Algeria, Pakistan) between modern commercial values and traditional values. Modern economics supports some, and conflicts with other, traditional religious values.

Path-dependency and openness are simultaneous properties. Path-dependency constrains current choices and decisions, but current decisions govern path-dependency and the potential traverse (in the sense of Hicks 1969) from one path to another; in both respects future actions and performance results are affected. What is possible is influenced by what institutions came before and the environment of other institutions, as well as by the particular change-oriented decisions that are made (with due regard to the principle of unintended and unforeseen consequences).

This last point underscores the dual aspect of the tension between openendedness and path-dependency: the importance of both choice as to when path-dependency is to be challenged and the personnel who are to exercise authoritative discretion and make those choices. *Authoritative* here does not necessarily mean *official*, for business positions are loci of entrepreneurially generated acts of creative destruction—legal and cultural as well as narrowly technological. The same is true of political entrepreneurs, even in a society in which businesspeople enjoy a privileged position (Lindblom 1977).

Insofar as the social reconstruction of reality is a function of power, knowledge, and psychology, knowledge (or what is accepted as knowledge) is an instrument of power for the manipulation of individual cognition and psychology, ultimately for control of the state and the processes governing legal change. Contests over economic theory, like those over public opinion, contribute to the definition of reality and thereby to the mobilization of political psychology as the basis of policy.

Writers who have analyzed technology have identified such properties as technological innovation, diffusion, and interdependence; technological regimes and trajectories; development paths, path-dependency, and lock-in; and the cumulative nature of technological change (see the works of Dosi, Freeman, Silverberg). Similar points have been made with regard to entrepreneurship. Throughout such studies one finds but openness and constraint, change and continuity. Such dynamic features also appertain to the economic role of government and law. Just as technological change takes place within technological regimes, legal-economic change, including technological change itself, takes place within particular legal-economic-nexus regimes. Neither type of regime is treated in evolutionary analyses as a black box (or as necessarily producing the "right" results). Both types of regime, technological and legal, have both stable and unstable trajectories of development and each can be evaluated differently by different criteria. In both regimes are the processes that govern the direction or substance of economic growth, the distributions of opportunity and sacrifice as well as of income and wealth, and the selective release of entrepreneurial and other energy.

The legal-economic nexus, comprehended in terms of the evolutionary approach, is a system of self-organization, somewhat in the sense of Ilya Prigogine (Prigogine and Stengers 1984). There is no design external to human beings and society imposed on legal-economic affairs. Human beings organize their own systems, including the legal-economic. All of it is a matter of individual action, some that of individuals acting alone and some, actually very much, that of individuals acting as members of social groups and organizations, including government. One of the reasons why consequences are typically unintended and unforeseen is that such actions are matters of interaction and aggregation, the processes of interaction and aggregation constituting principal elements of self-organization, some of which are deliberative and some nondeliberative.

8. One of the critical features of the legal-economic nexus is the hierarchical nature of the relevant processes. Several points relate to this: First, participation in market choice and public choice in liberal democratic governments tends to be more pluralistic (that is, to have a wider diffusion of power) than the alternatives, though that is not to say that neither markets nor governments do not have hegemonic powers. Second, the evolution of the modern democratic state has specifically involved governments becoming increasingly responsive to a wider range of interests. Access to government remains heavily asymmetric, but over the last two centuries government in the West has become less the vehicle of rule and opportunity of permanent upper classes, and income has become more equal. Third, both belief in and descriptive accuracy of individualism and democracy should not obfuscate the centrality of the problem: *which* individuals, or *which* individual units, are to have their preferences and interests count.

9. The sources of legal change are numerous and operate on what may be called the demand and supply side. Some interests constitute the demanders of change and other interests constitute the suppliers of change; often the former are self-interested economic actors, sometimes public-spirited reformers of various types; and the latter are those who occupy positions of formal and informal governmental decision-making authority, often with their own ideological and material-interest agendas. Use of the metaphor of a demand and supply model, while it can help identify the operative forces of an evolutionary situation, should not, however, lead to a nonevolutionary equilibrium model of social change.

More broadly, economic forces, during the last several centuries, have generally, but by no means completely, replaced or supplemented political forces as the prime mover of historical change. Industrialization, commercialization, and political and economic liberalism (Enlightenment values) have introduced and sustained diversity of mutations or variations and sources of variation, and the consequent necessity to choose. Technology; changing values; power play; war; externalities; selective perception of "problems"; secularization; improved knowledge of the physical and biological world; heightened sense of policy consciousness (that social arrangements are not given but a matter of human construction); mobility; ease of communications; the widened availability of liberal democratic governments; experience and learning; changes in population level, density, and interaction; changing relative prices, power relations, and perceptions of opportunity; and so on—these have fueled the dynamics of legal-economic evolution, largely through their interactions.

The evolutionary approach to law and economics identifies both the multiplicity of sources of change and the multiplicity of adjustment and selection processes. It therefore underscores the importance not only of conflict and of the legal resolution, as well as prevention, of conflict but also of legal conflict resolution as an object of control and use by interested parties—in a truly coevolutionary, overdetermined, and/or fundamentally general-equilibrium way.

10. Lending elements of subjectivism, spontaneity, and surprise to legal-economic evolution is selective perception. Selective perceptions of government, rights, legal change, I-thou, freedom, control, continuity, change, hierarchy, equality, progress, growth, decay, and so on, provide inputs to the legal-economic process. In this respect, selective perceptions are independent variables. But selective perceptions, because they are subject to deliberative and nondeliberative political (and religious, etc.) psychological manipulation, are also dependent variables. Institutions selectively provide cognitive frameworks for learning and interpreting sense data and for transforming such data into putatively useful knowledge, such as: what constitutes individualism and what interventionism; what constitutes democracy, the nature and significance of chance, personal character, social relationships, and individual respon-

sibility; and, inter alia, the source of selectively perceived policy problems and solutions. Therefore both institutions and the processes of selective perception are the objects of control and use.

11. Several open-ended interactive processes operate in the legal-economic nexus. These may be identified as follows: (A) The dual processes through which (I) efficient-optimal solutions are worked out, given the identification and assignment of rights, and (II) the identification and assignment of rights, including the creation of new rights and duties, that is, the power structure, is changed such that it is through both processes together and interactively that it is determined whose interests and values are to count. (B) The value-clarification process through which values are identified, contrasted, evaluated, and chosen. (C) The interaction between power, knowledge, and psychology, each understood as comprised of multiple variables (for example, in the Paretian model of power, knowledge, and psychology, and their interactions, going far beyond the limited domain of Pareto optimality; see Samuels 1974). (D) The combination of politics, elections, court appointments, class, material interests, and ideology.

A wide-ranging and suggestive evolutionary model of legal-economic policy can be illustrated using the familiar concepts of a production possibility curve and a social welfare function, with values or goals on the respective axes. This model indicates four fundamental interactive (coevolutionary, overdetermined) processes: the process by which the values on the axes are chosen, which is to say the values on the agenda of public choice; the process determining the slope of the production-possibility curve applicable to the values, that is, the necessary trade-offs between the values; and the processes governing both the relative preferences for the values that people have and the power structure governing the weighting of the preferences. Another such evolutionary model posits different economic agents, each with its own respective opportunity sets. Each realizeable opportunity set, over time, is a function of (1) power and the bases of power, for example, legal rights; (2) the choices made at various points in time by individuals (according to their capabilities) from within their respective opportunity sets influencing their opportunity sets in the future; and (3) the impact decisions made by others have on each agent's opportunity set. Putatively included in the opportunity set is the opportunity to seek legal change of the rights of the respective parties and therefore change of their respective opportunity sets (see Samuels 1989b).

Conclusion

The foregoing has outlined the principal characteristics and important developmental elements of a nonnormative evolutionary approach to law and economics. Once one both escapes from the narrow and misleading thinking that posits determinate optimal equilibrium solutions to problems of law and economics and considers just what a meaningful evolutionary analysis requires, the approach outlined here enables the analyst to identify fundamental processes and problems that are worked out in the legal-economic nexus, processes and problems that the conventional mode of analysis forecloses.

But the important matter is not the critique of the neoclassical approach to law and economics. It tells a story, or set of stories, and these stories are valuable, however limited. Inasmuch as no theory can answer all questions, there must be room for multiple theories in law and economics. The questions raised by and dealt with by an evolutionary approach to law and economics are fundamental and important, and techniques of analysis must be adopted that are suited to deal with them in their enormity and complexity. The important point is that the results of a partial, single-factor, unilinear, and static approach should not be taken for those of a comprehensive, multifactor, curvilinear, and evolutionary approach.[9]

---

9. In addition to authors already cited we want to call attention to the work of such writers as Bromley (1989), Hirschman (1970), and Vanberg (1986).

Communication in Economic Evolution: The Case of Money

Michael Hutter

Among numismatic scholars, there is widespread agreement that the first coins were stamped in Asia Minor during the seventh century B.C., and that the use of the new money form had spread to most Ionian and Greek cities by about 580 B.C. There is also agreement that the first coins were pieces of electrum, conforming to the weight standards in force along the Ionian coast. The most primitive variety had a striated surface and a punchmark on the reverse side; a slightly earlier variety substituted a lion's head for the crude striations.

However, there is a remarkable difference with respect to dating the exact decade of emergence. There are, it seems, two schools of opinion. Both opinions are based on the evidence of a single hoard located underneath the temple of Artemis in Ephesus, which was excavated in 1908. So the issue boils down to differences in interpreting the same evidence. The dominant opinion today argues that the oldest coins could not have been in use for more than a generation, which sets their issue around 630 B.C. (Robinson 1956; Kraay 1976). A divergent opinion, based on literary sources and on an analysis of the stylistic properties of the lion-head coins of the Artemis hoard, argues that these coins were already in use around 700 B.C. (Ure 1922; Weidauer 1975).

Why does a squabble about events that happened almost three thousand years ago matter? The emergence of coin money was one of the major transformations in the history of our economy's transaction medium. Therefore, the episode contains a good part of the empirical evidence available to test competing theories. If the first coins emerged around 630 B.C., then the new "invention" of stamping molten lumps of silver, gold, or its alloy on both sides must have spread quickly among those engaged in the trade of goods, particularly the trade of those goods that were precious enough to be traded externally. Quite clearly, this interpretation supports the theory of money emergence first formulated by Menger and adhered to ever since: according to

111

that theory, money forms emerge as the result of unintended agreements between partners in commodity exchange. Once a new form has been found, it is observed and imitated by others. Therefore, new monetary inventions spread quickly.

If, however, the use of coins began around 700 B.C., then the new money form must have taken more than a century to really catch on. This interpretation calls either for a theory of slow continuous change, or for a theory predicting bursts of rapid change, interrupted by periods without change. In the latter view, new forms are not readily accepted, and variations of the stamps in use are a highly improbable event. In principle, evolutionary theories are able to account for such complex processes.

It is the object of this chapter to formulate an evolutionary theory of money that explains and, thus, supports the 700 B.C. interpretation. The impetus for such an effort does not stem from an interest in archaeological issues. It stems from basic logical problems in contemporary monetary theory. To put it into a nutshell: money is, in most modern models, conceived either as a rule or as a special asset. Both approaches neglect the communication property of money.

The "rule approach" has been expressed most poignantly by Hahn:

> Tobin . . . has splendidly remarked that money is like language. My speaking English is useful in so far as you do also: just so, money is acceptable to me provided it is acceptable to you. One can think of this argument as a Nash equilibrium. Once there is a rule that transactions should proceed via money, it is not advantageous to deviate from this rule. (1982, 21)

It is, first, interesting to note that Hahn invokes a notion that is based on reciprocal expectations of the actors. We will return to this point later on. Even more surprising is the reference to language, and the implicit premise that such a complex arrangement of sounds comes about by adjusting to a myriad of little rules. How these rules come about is, according to Hahn and to most of the contemporary game theorists, beyond the economist's reach.

The "special asset approach" focuses on the effects of the asset that has been chosen or produced to be used as money. In general, reference is made to "search and information costs" (Brunner and Meltzer 1971) or to "reduction of uncertainty" (Niehans 1971). Information, then, is considered a key quality of the money asset. However, in a general equilibrium model, it is difficult to assign a status to information. Either it is a commodity, or it is a property of an observer. In the first case, information is indistinguishable from material features—monetary assets are just another kind of commodity. In the second case, information becomes part of unobservable subjective minds, linked to properties like trust, reputation, and confidence. There is an obvious link to he language metaphor used by Hahn. But that "special" feature of money cannot be expressed in the categories available to the theory.

Apparently, our theoretical grasp of money depends strongly on our ability to integrate the process of communication into economic models, be they verbal or formal. In order to gain that ability, we will take advantage of the results of a number of modern research programs in other scientific fields. These results affect our way of communicating about economic action and about social evolution. To illustrate the explanatory power of that theory, I have investigated the historical pattern of events surrounding the emergence of coin signs. In conclusion, a few implications and applications of the proposed integration of communication into economic theory are discussed.

Changing the Primary Distinction: From Observer to Observation

The basic claim can be stated in a few words: communication is a process that has the same logical status as consciousness. The argument begins with us, the observers. We divide the world into conscious minds and the world outside the minds, and each observer is one of these conscious minds. This distinction seems quite natural today, but, in fact, it is one of the accomplishments of the philosophical discourse called "enlightenment." Descartes was the first to use the distinction between *res cogitans* and *res extensa*, and it took a few centuries before the difference between objective (external) and subjective (internal) truth began to appear self-evident. The method has helped to describe the world external to conscious minds in a "rational" manner, and it has been particularly successful in leading us to understand our natural environment.

The object/subject distinction has not been quite as successful in those fields that involve communication processes, i.e., the humanities and the social sciences. The reason for this difficulty is a logical implication of this primary distinction: if communication happens in the outside world, then it must have objectlike properties. In consequence, "information" is perceived as something that is, like a parcel, transmitted from one subject to the next.[1] If communication happens within the inside world, then it is part of the internal cognitive world of the mind. It is described as learning, as knowledge, or as creativity.[2] In both cases, communication must appear as a secondary prop-

---

1. Such a view is at the base of technical treatments of information in the Shannon-Weaver tradition.

2. On the borderline between subjective and objective worlds, there are interesting skirmishes for territory. Expectations were originally a subjective category. The Vienna school treated them that way, and so did Keynes, Shackle, and the post-Keynesians. A subset of expectations, however, is now assumed to be determined by rational, i.e., outside, communication. The "rational expectations" approach is based on that assumption.

erty. In the external world, the signs and symbols are "really" special objects; in the internal worlds, signs and symbols are "really" the idea, the creation of single individuals. If we are right in suspecting that communication is a process of the same logical order as consciousness, then the traditional distinction won't do. We need a distinction that will preserve the continuity of communication, instead of splitting it into objective information and subjective creation.

The new primary distinction runs between the continuity of communication and the world outside of communication. Communication is a process observable in signs, symbols, and gestures. How do the signs turn into a process? The continuous nature of signs is only observable in *events*. The events, however, are a construction within another, observing text. The written letters of a Shakespeare sonnet, for instance, are interpreted against the background of their use in other texts, and they are open to contemporary interpretation because the verses have remained in use since then (P. Smith 1988).

The basic operation is one of *observing repetitions* —repetitions within the text, or between the text and its interpretations. The same operation takes place in observing less well-structured sequences of signs. A phenomenon— rising smoke, or resounding vocal chords, or a human motion—is interpreted as a sign by an observation registering the repetition of the sign. The observed first appearance of the sign is considered part of an event involving a preceding sign, and the observed second appearance will be followed by a succeeding sign. Such events cannot be reduced to single, individual actors, either in their operation or in their observation. Every sign needs another sign to validate its existence: only the next sign proves that the prior sign had meaning, i.e., *was* a sign.

One is tempted to state the point simply in one sentence: The observer picks a short sequence of events out of an infinite chain consisting of nothing but signs. However, the word *observer* is actually without meaning under the new distinction. There are only chains of signs, like texts or conversations, and something outside these chains. The self-restriction of the theory holds for the notion of the observer as well. He or she has now become a secondary distinction. If I am an *external* observer, then I register the communication nature of an event without being able or willing to participate in it. I observe that others are understanding each other, that they continue to use the same language. I have no knowledge of that understanding, but I infer that it works just the way my own messages work. This is actually the perspective chosen in the above paragraph. Or, alternatively, I am an *internal* observer. I understand what is being said to me and know how to interpret meaning. That is a purely experiential process, surrounding us since our cradle days. We always believe that "everything" is within the reach of what can be said and understood, because "everything" is what can be articulated on the inside. The observer operates in the sequence of communication events around him, without access to the world outside of his communication. These two positions are so important for the theory to be formulated that their logical structure will be examined more carefully.

The basic characteristic of the internal continuity of communication events is their *self-reference*. By this, we mean that the signs emitted refer to nothing else but other signs. To sketch the process: Site A emits signs containing many differences; A observes that B reacts to the message by repeating some of the differences; A then continues the conversation by repeating some of the differences in B's message. The point is: neither of the two will ever know how its counterpart has processed or "understood" the message. All it can refer to are previous and expected signs. The two sites are able to continue their dialogue under the supposition that they understand each other.[3] The self-referential nature of the process implies its logical closure. Understanding appears always complete, because it contains its own foundation. Understanding operates blindly, and it has to. The sense of completeness is an eminently helpful property; without it, we would probably die of fear and insecurity. However, it is a powerful hindrance to change. In what instances, then, can we observe an opening in the closure of our own communication? Two examples are offered.

The first case is the learning of language: a baby makes noises from which parents select those sounds that they interpret as "messages"; they answer with their own noises and gestures. A year later, the baby begins to select from the surrounding noises those that he or she can use for its own messages. The baby tries out sounds and words and watches the effects of such actions. After many infantile failures, the grown-ups answer with a repetition of the sound or sign. Thus, the field of meaning of the signs becomes more and more determined, until the point is reached when the field of meaning cannot be altered at will anymore. The child has learned to use a word, or a phrase. But the word and the phrase were there before the child and before the grown-up. The two preserve the meaning of the word by reproducing it in their messages. The continuity of the already-existing communication process has been extended in time.

The second case is the acceptance of a new theory. New theories tend not to fit into the communication mold of their predecessors. But the continuity of a specific scientific tradition has to be assured. One of the ways of making new contributions understandable is to couch them in old terms. Our own science is a good example: new theoretical features, like the variability of

---

3. The phenomenon has already been observed by Parsons (1968, 436), who emphasizes the "double contingency" of the communication process.

property-right structures, were generated in order to correct inconsistencies in the old theory. The "Coase theorem" is a prominent example: out of a formulation that was, and still is, considered by many as an extension of the existing paradigm, new conclusions about the nature of organizations and institutions have been drawn—conclusions that are severely at odds with the premise of full information. A further example is the present text: if the basic object/subject distinction of current scientific thought creates a closed universe of discourse, then the distinction between communication and its environment is bound to introduce terms that seem familiar but are, in a rigorous logical sense, inconsistent with the old premise.

The conditions of external observation of communication events are clear by now: the external observation mirrors a communication event in another closed system of reference. The observation cannot enter the discourse.[4] It can only assume that a process of "understanding" takes place. If the observation were able to continue a chain of communication events, it would become a *message*, a part of the process. If it is a message in a different discourse, then it regards the observed process as *information*. The observation links itself to a communication event in the (internal) form of a message, or in the (external) form of observing information.[5] In both cases it is clear that the observation is made of the same "stuff" as the events observed.

If we, as outside observers, cannot see what we cannot see, then how can we determine that we have some closed discourse of communication before us? We can determine it because we know the logical structure of closure: in the world of signs, only signs can be used to distinguish a specific discourse from its communication environment. Such a distinction cannot be part of the discourse in question. It is the borderline of the discourse, part of it and yet not part of it: therefore, it has the logical structure of *paradox*.

The phenomenon of paradox is well known in the history of logic. From Epimenides to Russell, it has been treated as an anomaly to be avoided. Recent contributions, from Hofstadter to von Foerster, have established the fundamental importance of paradox in structuring our universe of communication. A particularly precise argument has been developed by Krippendorf (1984). He shows that the information content of paradox is infinite in statistical terms, and he draws the following conclusion:

Infinite quantities of information simply indicate a state of paralysis. In such a situation, observers are unable to process information about their world and will remain so incapacitated unless they "think twice," exam-

---

4. The term *discourse* describes the condition of closure quite well, even though most authors continue to connect it with traditional observers. An interesting attempt is McCloskey's application to the discourse of economists (McCloskey 1985).

5. The term *information* is now used in the sense suggested by Bateson: "Information is a difference which makes a difference in some later event" (1972, 381).

ine some of their own axioms, and resolve the descriptive problem giving rise to the paradox. . . . Unless one is able to escape a paradoxical situation, which is what Whitehead and Russell achieved with their theory of logical types, paradoxes paralyse an observer and may lead either to a collapse of the construction of his or her world, or to a growth in complexity of his or her representation of this world. It is the latter which should be characterized as morphogenesis. (51–52)

The implication of these arguments is quite straightforward: if an observation encounters paradox, then it is unable to articulate fully what is being communicated in that specific communication event. The communication event is distinguished by the premise of an "origin," which, to the outside, looks like paradox. This is, for example, why religions tend to look so incredible to "heathens." There is another, more general phenomenon that helps to understand the situation: when we speak of a play, we mean by that a phenomenon of communication without any serious ground. The play seems arbitrary, yet the events belonging to it are delineated clearly against other events that are not part of the play. This means: all events have something that characterizes them as parts of the play. A gesture that says openly, "This is a play," is not part of the play, whereas a gesture that says playfully, "This is not a play," is part of the play.

The kind of play to which the metaphor relates is not the kind of entertainment game that is determined by a finite set of rules, like board games. It is the kind of improvised play typical for music and theater. Here, we can experience most vividly how our own observation is drawn into worlds that have their own deeply convincing inner logic, yet it is decidedly not the logic of daily communication. Every play move, every note or every gesture, is coded for recognition by other, possible play moves. In the code of the play, there can be no observation of the play's own boundary,[6] of the difference between the play and its environment. The play, we might say, observes its environment and possibly itself only in the terms of its own code. In understanding such plays, it is not enough to learn the rules. As Wittgenstein has observed, one can find out about understanding language plays (and *Sprachspiele* is what we are talking about) only by playing them.[7]

We will see below that the logical structure of plays can be found in discourses that seem to have little in common with children's play or operas.

---

6. Which is not to overlook attempts by authors like Pirandello, who have contributed to understanding the nature of the border. Just a line from "Six Persons in Search of an Author": "What do you mean, truth! I beg your pardon, here we are in the theater. Truth has its limits, too."

7. The notion of play has been in the epistemological debate at least since Kant. Huizinga (1940) gave a thorough empirical account of the importance of plays in cultural history. Bateson came to similar conclusions using his ethnological evidence (1972) and then translated his findings into more general theoretical terms.

And yet, the notion helps us to recapitulate the entire story told in this section: as we introduce the distinction between communication events and their environment, we place our observations in a world consisting of such events. The totality of these events is called "society."[8] The boundary of understanding is marked by the condition of double contingency: it works only if someone plays that it works.

The total stream of communication called society happens in highly conditioned environments of humans and specialized machines.[9] Within society, we can observe smaller, more elaborately coded subsystems or organizations. They all are self-referentially closed: their internal operations reproduce only other internal operations. In some of these plays, we are able to "connect"—our own signs are interpreted as messages. In other plays, we can only register the event of communication without being able to influence the internal course of the play's development. In any case, however, "we" are talking as a text among texts. The complexity of the communication play takes precedence over the complexity of the mental structures of consciousness that contribute to it. That's just the way the new distinction is played.

Economy and Money

In this section, we want to follow one basic rule: to stick to the self-imposed constraints of the theory outlined in the previous section. If we are able to do that, we gain the opportunity to perceive the economy and its environment in

8. "Society consists of communication, it consists only of communication, it consists of all communications. It reproduces communication through communication. Whatever happens as communication is thus operation and, at the same time, reproduction of society. Neither in the environment nor with the environment of society can there be communication. In consequence, the communication system society is a closed system. It is, however, only possible in an environment, thanks to psychic consciousness, thanks to organic life, thanks to physical materialization, thanks to the evolution of suns and atoms. Society registers this situation by establishing itself as an open system. It communicates about something—about topics which concern its environment or itself or the actually occurring communication. Thus, society is a closed and an open system at the same time, and communication is the form of the elementary operation which performs and reproduces this combination" (Luhmann 1984, 311; all translations are by the author).

9. Individuals do not disappear in communication systems theory, as it is often claimed. Rather, they are split into two kinds of appearances: first, they appear in social systems inasmuch as they contribute to the ongoing communication. But only the communication acts are observed. Second, they appear as separate consciousnesses, which are, in themselves, self-reproducing systems. But the reproduction of consciousness takes place outside of communication, and communication takes place outside of consciousness. The neglect of that basic distinction has led the idealist movement following Hegel into mistaking consciousness for communication. The distinction is logically necessary because systems are distinguished from their environment through the environment's higher degree of complexity. For communication events, consciousness and life forms constitute their environment, and they are inaccessibly complex. Communication can only respond to events that have been brought down to its level and form of complexity.

a way that is new and therefore revealing. The observation of the economy begins, again, with itself. The observing messages are part of the scientific discourse: they are intended as messages to be reproduced in future scientific discourse. The messages follow, though not in a rigorous way, the conventions set for the particular play of economic science. They take as their outside reference another communication play: the economy. If the economy is a communication play, it must be possible to determine its paradox, its medium of communication, and the specific form of the operations in which the play reproduces itself. All three of these issues are traditional to economic science.

The basic paradox that closes off the economic discourse is the distinction between scarcity and abundance. There is no such distinction in nature. The distinction is entirely man-made or, to be more precise, communication-made. Scarcity may be "explained" through rarity or production costs, but it is not identical with such notions.[10] Scarcity is a state that is produced through the act of avoiding it. In securing the use of resources and commodities, the condition that motivated the move to secure the "good"[11] in the first place is created: a perfect example of self-referential closure.[12]

All the talk about scarcity in the environment of the economy is meaningless to the continuity of the play. The economy has its own medium of articulating the attribution of that self-invented property called "scarcity" to specific parts of the environment or even itself. This medium is called "money." At this point, only the basics are noted: Money is a construction that articulates the "value" of parts of the environment with respect to the notion of scarcity.[13] The signs and symbols of that specialized language are therefore selected[14] in a way that expresses or codes that property. The term *value* has, in consequence, no meaning outside of the communication play driven by the scarcity paradox. Every communication play has such an inner sense of its baseless base, and in every case the observations speak of *value*. Here, we clearly speak of economic value, and economic value is created and reproduced *exclusively* in communication events involving money (Mirowski 1990).

Describing a complex system in a linear fashion is an awkward task. Of course, the economic play consists of nothing but communication events, and

---

10. Note also how earlier societies looked at economic communication from the outside: they focused on abundance—the switch to scarcity is not more than two hundred years old.

11. The property of being a good emerges, self-referentially, in the same act.

12. "The taking (Zugriff) creates what it wants to remove. It wants to secure a sufficient quantity, and thus it creates the scarcity which makes it meaningful to secure a sufficient quantity" (Luhmann 1988, 179).

13. Scarcity is used as an anchor in an otherwise open world of meaning.

14. The term is to be understood in an evolutionary sense.

they haven't even been mentioned yet. But the preceding paragraphs should help in analyzing their highly specific structure. Economic communication events have already become the object of scientific investigation. The most frequently used term is *transaction*. Transaction analysis has taken two major forms: one branch is concerned with the cloud of negotiation and control communication that surrounds real, material exchange; that approach has been extended to intrafirm events where the material concreteness of exchange becomes tenuous (Williamson 1985).[15] The second branch is concerned with the "uncertainty-reducing" properties of media of payment in facilitating real exchanges (Hahn 1982).

All we have to do in order to adapt these efforts to the new perspective is to combine the two branches. According to the suggested theory, transactions must be communication events. This implies that the central process of a transaction is the pure communication of value transfer that takes place in an act of payment. The act of giving a coin, of underwriting a credit, of changing positions in a book of accounts is entirely meaningless outside the self-referential logic of the scarcity play. We also infer that the act of payment is basically endless, that there must always be the premise of a prior and a subsequent payment. We will return to this property below, after considering the "real" side of the transaction.

If payment is central, exchange must be peripheral. Exchange is something that goes on in the environment of the continuous, closed process of payment communication. The payments use the reference to aspects of their environment, which are, in this context, regarded as goods and services. The payments comment on changes in the environment, and thus the chain of payments reproduces itself. The outside events are undoubtedly of an existential importance for the continuity of the play. If there is nothing to comment on, the play vanishes. Yet, in a strictly logical sense, the real events take place outside of the economy as it is interpreted here. We have turned around the priorities: the payment events are regarded as the central, continuous process, while the changes and exchanges in the environment are peripheral and discontinuous. It seems that the fascination of the moving stream of payments is enough to drive the process of production. To put it into one phrase: the economy is fiction driving matter.

This concludes a first rough observation of the economy based on the communication distinction. Quite expectedly, the result differs widely from the mainstream interpretation. There, the term *economic* has become synonymous with a specific kind of human action, namely, the rational choice of complex actors called individuals. It is a kind of behavior that can be applied

---

15. The notion of contract has interesting implications from a communication perspective. After all, the intention is to set two wills into one with respect to the content of the contract.

to all kinds of human action; commodity production and exchange just happen to be particularly convincing examples. Not surprisingly, that approach works quite well for explaining short-term choices between given alternatives. In such cases, the theory just stylizes everyday impressions. But if we want to understand long-term change, the way the choices and the actors came to be, then we cannot start our observations at a point where the constitution of self-conscious actors has already been achieved. The object/subject distinction, however, leaves no other possibility: the moving forces must be subjects, and the subjects must act according to a logic that is transparent to the observing scientist. In contrast, the new distinction adds motion to the communication events, and it transforms the universe of logic into a "multi-verse" of different logics.

We can now move on to a closer examination of money and the conditions of its emergence and development. Payment, the monetary aspect of transactions, is a communication event. Payment communication utilizes materials and symbols to code economic value in money units.[16] It is quite common to call such money signs "a medium." But what, exactly, is meant by that? Here, we suggest a precise definition. Every communication act has to be shaped by combining simpler events into a complex shape that can be recognized as a message. Vocal sounds are shaped into words, letters are shaped into texts, cello sounds are shaped into a suite. Whenever we observe a rigid coupling of those basic events, we call it a *form*. Whenever we observe a loose coupling of the same events, we call it a *medium* (Luhmann 1990a, 53f.).

We can rephrase the relationship between payment and money signs in this fashion: the actual payment events are the rigid communication forms shaped out of the loose medium of various money signs. When this distinction was originally suggested by the psychologist Heider in 1926, it was intended for the performance of language in the natural medium of air. Now, we use it in a communication-made context. The medium does not exist naturally but rather has to be created and reproduced by society. If the quantity of the medium or its consistency are insufficient for reproducing economic value, then that should affect the immediate environment of the economy, i.e., the production processes.

Money articulates a message of scarcity and transfer under widely differing circumstances. Both of these properties must be reflected in the forms[17] of money. In archaic societies, the basic quality of scarcity was articulated

---

16. Barter becomes observable after payment. Before, it is restricted to the territorial or social border of a community.

17. The term is used in the same sense, but in a different context: money signs are, in turn, rigid combinations of loose elements, partly taken out of religious and political imagery. There are no "final" elements in self-referential processes.

through material substances whose high production costs were known. But that is only part of the story. Invariably, the money material was associated with the communicative value of another discourse, either that of the community or that of a religion. Tool money always grew out of local religious or decorative practice, and precious metals always had magical properties. As economic discourse separated itself from the rest of a society's discussions, the coding of scarce money was taken over by organizations that were trusted to regulate an economy's money supply. But until today, it has been necessary to use a variety of symbols, like gold reserves and interest-rate declarations, in order to assure a sense of scarcity. The second quality is the indication of transfer. Scarcity has its meaning in an environment of goods and services. The taking or nontaking of the most varied components of that environment is thus given a particular meaning.

The code of money, therefore, presupposes a coding of the environment in terms of property. Payment only makes sense after the distinction between having and not having has become part of a culture.[18] Once that has been established, then the acts of payment can symbolize the transfer of property rights. They do so by letting money change hands. The transfer of money must therefore be understood as part of a symbolic language rather than as an action of material consequence.

Payment communication extends into the past and into the future between a large variety of persons and between a wide variety of items. Every one of these dimensions demands its own form to ensure value reproduction. In fact, there are specific kinds of credit money for preserving value through time, there is book money to transfer value between the accounts of various persons, and there is exchange money to establish value relationships between commodities. These money forms tended to evolve separately, and the recognition of the fact that they are part of the same discourse came rather late in historical time. The claim to the earliest form probably goes to credit money, which emerged almost imperceptibly in agricultural societies. Yet, we will focus our further observations on exchange money. The reason is not, as in traditional monetary theory, the quasi-material nature of "bullion and specie." In fact, that association has contributed to the difficulties in perceiving the language property of money. The advantage of exchange money lies, however, in its visibility. Whereas many of the connotations around credit money and book money are coded into the banking institutions and are thus totally immaterial, exchange-money signs are preserved in the shapes and symbols of tools, coins, and notes. I will use these signs as evidence when I apply my theory to concrete episodes in monetary history.

---

18. Luhmann (1988) compares the relationship between property and money with the relationship between spoken and written language.

Conditions of Evolutionary Economic Change

Up to now, we have primarily considered static structural features of money, as they are observed when we start from the premise that an economy is a communication play. Surely, even the structural observations imply the passage of time since communication events have replaced material elements. Yet, we have not given any attention to questions of long-term, historical change. Observations of long-term change pose no particular problem in a theory of self-referential communication systems. In fact, the theory gains a major competitive advantage when it is applied to such questions. In doing so, we will draw from a field of science that has had dramatic success in explaining historical change of forms in the world of organic forms: the theory of biological evolution.

When economists speak of evolution, they have very different notions in mind. Radzicki and Sterman (in this volume), for instance, draw up a list of authors, ranging from Marx to Prigogine, that indicates their understanding of the basic characteristics of an evolutionary approach. The key conditions are irreversibility of time and change *within* a structure.[19] Irreversibility of time is consistent with the event structure of self-reproducing communication plays. "Changes within" can be interpreted in various ways. Quite common is a distinction between biological structures and engineering structures. The former evolve autonomously within natural environments, whereas the latter experience change within the constraints set by a power in their environment, for instance, by the engineer. The majority of evolutionary approaches to economic change seem to favor the engineering approach: multiple equilibria, path-dependence, feedback loops, and nonlinear couplings are studied. But an engineered evolution is a contradiction in terms, and even within a self-structuring process, as it is studied in limit-cycle and chaos models, we cannot observe the emergence of new economic forms. Biological structures are a far better orientation for economic evolution.

Economists can choose to regard the economy either as a constructed entity or as a process of autonomously emerging "spontaneous order" (to borrow Hayek's term). If we choose the second alternative, then we commit ourselves to an explanation based entirely on internal change. There is no deus ex machina who can twist the knobs and fine-tune the parameters. The study of organic evolution has given us an immense amount of insight into such processes of internal change. Two issues stand out in contemporary biological discussion: (1) What are the advantages to an increase in internal complexity as opposed to an adaptation to external change?; and (2) What are the empirical and logical prerequisites for successful internal change?

---

19. For some other examples of evolutionary approaches see Witt (1991).

The dominant "neo-Darwinist" position in evolutionary biology claims that evolutionary success is determined by the degree to which a system is able to adapt to its external environment (Mayr 1982). That position coincides nicely with the optimization hypothesis in economic theory: systems compete under external constraints, and those systems that adapt most efficiently will survive. Recent authors, however, favor another interpretation: external pressure establishes a minimal standard for survival. Above that standard, a variety of evolutionary alternatives are able to survive.[20] The only condition of that survival is maintenance of the organism's internal self-reproduction or "autopoiesis."[21] That result has an important implication for our observation of evolutionary processes: We do not observe forms that adapt to a given, unchangeable environment, but forms that establish an increased independence from their environment.

The argument goes as follows: Variations in reproduction lead to increases in the organism's internal complexity. That complexity increases the organism's degrees of freedom with respect to its environment. The organism detaches itself from the environment and its constraints: it is able to flee, to attack, or to migrate.[22] To be sure, the "autopoietic" interpretation of evolutionary change does not replace the exclusive emphasis on the phenotype with an equally exclusive emphasis on the genotype. The entire process of "gene-organism-interaction" (Roth 1986, 166) is considered, but always with a view to the autonomy of the entire system. It should be clear that such a growth of internal complexity is a highly improbable development.

We now turn to the process of internal change. Its major components are fairly well established in evolutionary biology, although there remains a surprisingly vivid debate (Oyama 1985; Ingold 1986). For the purposes of economic theory, the task consists in identifying those aspects that are of general

20. "The scenario of Ernst Mayr and the neodarwinists is a special case of evolution. If the environment of a population changes, there are two normal cases: either none of the carriers of alternative traits survive, or several of them survive. . . . All that matters is to find a state of equilibrium with respect to the organism's autopoiesis, and these states of equilibrium can be quite different" (Roth 1986, 163).

21. The notion of "autopoiesis" is of particular relevance for the biological context. Research in the reproduction of cells has shown how simple organisms are able to produce their own elements out of structures that consist of the same elements. Autopoiesis has been introduced into the discussion of communication systems as well. Any direct analogy between organic and social processes is unwarranted and misleading. The self-reproduction of cells is a closed system, following its own laws. But the focus on molecular reproduction has brought into focus the "informational" aspects of biological change. See Varela (1979) and Roth and Schwegler (1981).

22. "Not the ability to adapt, but the ability to detach itself explains the immense stability and tenacity of life and all systems based on that principle. . . . The question is: How can a system which regulates its operations through its internal structures change these structures with the very same operations even if the system, bound by the given structures, is not able to replace them with new ones in a planned fashion" (Luhmann 1990a, 556–57).

relevance for evolutionary social processes. At this point, it is quite helpful that biological research has given such close attention to the "informational" properties of organic reproduction. We know that the reproduction of elementary units within organisms takes place through the ability of certain chemical material to exactly reproduce itself (genome) within a specific enzymatic structure (Roth 1986, 166). Such operations consist of material molecular changes, but the pattern of self-reproduction can be interpreted in logical terms: continuity is assured by a process of self-reference.

To express and articulate such continuous chains of duplication in scientific discourse, three aspects of evolutionary change are customarily distinguished: variation, selection, and stabilization. All three are hierarchically ordered: "variation" relates to differences in the reproduction of genetic material; "selection" relates to the adoption of a specific variation by a gene-organism-system; "stabilization" relates to steady states of such systems within their environments. Furthermore, events on the various hierarchical levels are brought into a circular temporal sequence: variation precedes selection, selection precedes stabilization, stabilization precedes new variation (Luhmann 1990a, 557f.). The relationship appears circular, or, more precisely, endless, because of the "strange loop" (Hofstadter 1979) that connects stabilization and variation—events on differing logical levels. This seems to be the basic reason for using the double distinction variation/selection and selection/stabilization: One is able to "model" the endlessness of biological reproduction in language. It is a notational structure enabling biological observers to communicate about the evolution of organisms.[23]

It remains to be shown that the basic distinction that characterizes organic reproduction, namely the distinction between genotype and phenotype, has its correspondence in social reproduction. The task can be solved on a general level, and on the specific level of single operations. On the general level, we note that biological science has taken its terminology for processes of genetic reproduction straight from the social world: genetic "information" is said to be reproduced through a genetic "code." At first, the terms may have been intended as simple analogies. But by now, biologists have discovered that they are dealing with a process that is quite distinct from the nature of material change. Genetic information, it seems, does not inform "about" an already-existing identity; instead, it shapes the new form through its own form—through the improbability of its sharply reduced contingency.[24] This means that the process of genetic reproduction is observed as a process of communication reproduction. Otherwise, our observations would not be able

---

23. A single distinction, like between variation and selection, is not enough. Single-distinction approaches invariably use environmental change as a driving force.

24. Particularly convincing arguments are found in Polanyi (1968), Oyama (1985), and Ingold (1986).

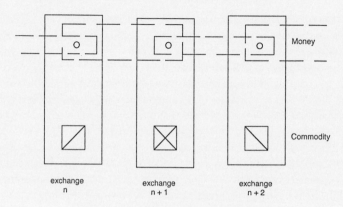

exchange n   exchange n + 1   exchange n + 2   Money   Commodity

Fig. 1. The reproduction of payments

to register it. Genetic reproduction is, in logical terms, a communication process.

We will now pursue the same distinction on the level of single operations by examining the single transaction. It has already been shown that transactions consist of a continuity of payment events that relate to changes in the economy's environment. We will now take a closer look at the reproduction of payment events. Figure 1 visualizes the process: the upper row shows the sequence of payments, symbolized by a single coin. The lower row shows the goods to which the coins relate. Traditionally, that situation had been represented by economists as a sequence of exchange acts in which two kinds of matter are compared. The sequence was, as it were, divided vertically into single pieces. The division did not matter because continuity was assumed to reside in the consciousness of the actor. Now, continuity is placed into the duplication process of the upper row.

Within the sequence of payment events (dotted rectangles), every sign appears twice. A coin is accepted, and the same coin is offered in a different context: at a different time, to a different person, for a different item. The same sign, thus, appears in two different contexts: the sign has duplicated itself. This duplication has the same effect as the duplication of genetic material in organic reproduction. As in organic reproduction, the normal case is an exact duplication. In almost all instances, errors in duplication lead to a rupture in the continuity of the system. However, a few aberrations prove to be viable. They are selected, in the sense of being adopted by the system. Out of them develop new phenotypic variations and mutations that will be, in an open future, registered as new forms. The implication of the above argument for a theory of monetary change should be quite clear: money signs provide the medium for payment sequences. Payment reproduction relates to changes in goods production and exchange in a way that corresponds logically to the relationship between gene reproduction and changes in an organism's shape and behavior.[25]

How can something change while it continues to be the same? We are now ready to formulate two necessary conditions for evolutionary change in systems that reproduce social values, like the economic value reproduced in payments. The first condition is observed on the level of single communication events. As a sign is reproduced, it may, despite the identity, be used differently in the next event. The sign has changed meaning. Usually, the difference is noted and corrected, or it does not matter. The different usage can continue, however, if the meaning of the sign can be kept ambiguous for a sufficient period of time: two meanings are reproduced simultaneously. In that case, the traditional use of a medium runs parallel to the new, aberrant use until the new interpretation has been selected by the system.

The variation may start either as a promise or as a mistake.[26] In the case of promise, some address connects a present event with a future event and then tries to find others to accept its understanding. In the case of mistake, some address connects its understanding of a present message with a previous operation that never took place. In both cases, *ambiguity* bridges the gap. Thus, new variations seep into the code. The variations are reproduced many times before they are selected internally. After that, they can be noticed "consciously," i.e., outside of the economy. Only then, a new alternative of action has become observable.

The code of a communication system does not change instantly throughout a play. The starting point must be, in order to be consistent, another communication play. Such a play can be introduced as a secondary distinction. As noted above, such an internal *circle of communication* may be a group, a clan, an organization, etc.[27] Within the circle, the code variation

---

25. This implies, admittedly, a surprisingly close homology between the observations of biologists and those of economists. But the argument of the comparison rests on entirely different grounds than the metaphor of the "social organism." There, individual humans were taken to be the "elements" of the organism, thus confusing material, organic, psychic, and social reproduction. In the view suggested here, these different kinds of self-referential systems are strictly kept apart. Because of the distinction, structural and functional similarities can be observed. If the metaphor is not transferred adequately, if individuals are identified with their biological characteristics, then the result is a race-oriented theory that dresses up as social theory. The disastrous consequences of using such a theory as a basis of political action are well known. Hegelian philosophy seemed to offer a solution: the social entity continues itself through dialectical movement, one idea leads antithetically to the next one. The social continuity is transferred to a continuity of thoughts in individual minds. But the continuity is only observable in explicit messages—which brings us back to communication (Hutter 1992).

26. The German word *Versprechen* contains the ambiguity of speaking of something that is not yet (promise) and something that is not (mistake).

27. The closure of such circles has been noted by Coleman (1988).

through ambiguity finds a protected environment. It is, through repetition, brought into a standard form. From such starting plays, the change in the code spreads through imitation to other plays. Most changes never diffuse throughout the entire economy. Sophisticated coding skills need culture-rich environments, which are rare even in modern societies. There will always be a periphery where the older, less independent code variations are still current procedure.

The two conditions merge into one: ambiguity of messages in closed circles is the basic condition for evolutionary change in a communication code.[28] With this result, we have a theory of evolutionary monetary change. Is that theory consistent with the slow and halting change in the coin signs that were first used during the seventh century B.C.? The next step is to investigate in detail whether the course of historical events, as it can be reconstructed today, coincides with the pattern predicted by evolutionary theory.

The Evolution of Money during the Seventh Century B.C.

There is, as previously noted, general agreement that some time during the seventh century B.C., coins began to be used for transactions. Using the available numismatic and literary evidence, the change of coin forms during that period, up to the point when the form stabilized in the shape of the Athenian "owl," will be observed. The process has been divided into five steps.

Bean-shaped lumps of precious metal had been in use in various places throughout the eastern Mediterranean at least since the twelfth century B.C. The lumps, molten and flattened, conformed to the units of the weight standards of the local culture (Balmuth 1973). Such "precoins" were made of gold, silver, or electrum, which is a naturally occurring alloy of the two metals. Precoins have been found in sizes down to .13g. Even such small pieces had considerable purchasing power. Slaves, livestock, and long-term services could be bought with them (Kraay 1976). Like other forms of precious metal, the lumps were used in far trade, usually in order to equalize values in commodity exchanges (Heichelheim 1938).

This custom remained stable until about 700 B.C. At that point in time, punchmarks began to appear on the metal lumps (see coin 1 of fig. 2). However, they are documented only in electrum precoins, as they were in use in Lydia. Electrum, being an alloy, posed the problem of a fluctuation in the ratio of the two metals. By punching the metal, the content of the lump could

---

28. To clarify the terminology: language, observed from the outside, appears as a medium; from the inside, it appears as code.

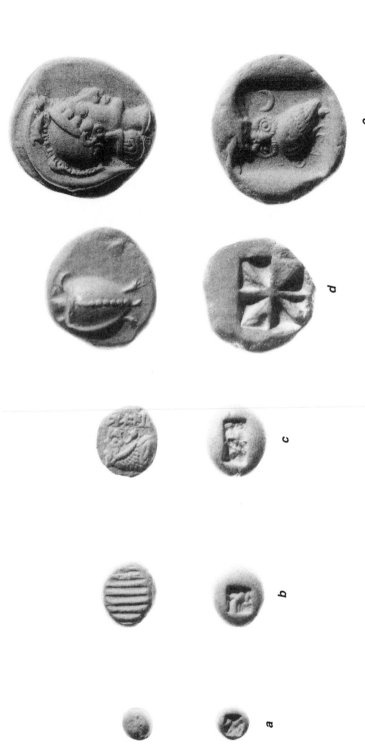

Fig. 2. The evolution of ancient coins. *a*, Coin 1: Ionia, electron, 1/48 stater, ca. 650 B.C. *b*, Coin 2: Ionia, electron, 1/4 stater, ca. 650 B.C. *c*, Coin 3: Lydia, electron, 1/3 stater, ca. 600 B.C. *d*, Coin 4: Aegina, silver, 2 drachmas, ca. 550 B.C. *e*, Coin 5: Athens, silver, 4 drachmas, ca. 520 B.C. (Permission by Ashmolean Museum, Oxford.)

be tested. But in addition, the person stamping had a means of *recognizing* pieces that carried its own mark:

> The merchant's mark was often no more than the end of a particular broken iron nail hammered into the metal, but it could be readily identified by the man whose mark it was. This eliminated the necessity for the weighing and testing for purity of each piece of the precious metal every time it passed through the merchant's hands; he knew his mark. (Davis 1967, 21)

The point to be noted is the relevance of *recognition*. The mark communicated a quality of the material, just as we know it from the marks on livestock or other moveable property. The continuity of the evaluation was restricted to the absolute minimum of one dimension: the dimension of time. The place and the person remain unchanged since the act took place in the memory of the merchant. When a message is entirely new, there is no one who understands it except the person who tries it out in itself. This is the way every sign appears to begin: as a perception in memory, as a sign to oneself. The sign to oneself could be recognized by others as well. The person who had marked the pellet guaranteed its weight. Material testing was substituted by trust in the marker.

The effect of the new sign was considerable, particularly within the household or *oikos* of merchants. The archaic *oikos* was a considerable enterprise, which often included more than a hundred individuals. An important payment purpose seems to have been workers' or mercenaries' long-term services. For such purposes, coins could now circulate more rapidly in and around the *oikos* than other money forms. The stamped pieces of electrum were easy to control and could be passed back to the center of the *oikos* in order to pay for services and commodities received by workers.

Eventually, the marks lost their testing function. They only signified the marker and were applied in order to fill the space of one coin side: small pieces carry one punchmark, medium-sized pieces and large pieces two and three punchmarks, respectively. The punchmarks were hammered independently, yet in one manufacturing process.[29] The typeless side usually showed irregular patterns. Around 670 B.C., coins appeared whose obverse side had been arranged into regular striations (coin 2 of fig. 2). The minting of that type can be located quite clearly at Sardes, the major city in Lydia. Again, there is a plausible *material* explanation: the striations facilitated the grip of the anvil onto which the metal lump was placed in order to be marked. But there is,

---

29. Evidence of this is the lack of any signs that a double impact would leave on the obverse, typeless side of the coin.

again, a *communicative* aspect to it: the punchmarks fill the "upper" side,[30] the striations fill the lower side of the coin. The entire piece has now been shaped into a form. Thus, a double ambiguity is introduced.

In order to appreciate the improbability of the new coin form, a little historical information is necessary. Sardes was the town where the trade route from Assyria branched off to the various Ionian settlements along the coast (Heichelheim 1938). Thus, Sardes was positioned at the periphery of two vastly different cultures. Toward the east, the Mesopotamian empires had found their continuation through the Assyrian rise to power in 745 B.C. Toward the west, the Ionian migration had led to a string of coastal settlements that still operated according to the rules of their rural ancestors. In Assyria, various commodities were used as media of exchange.[31] Gold and silver bars were also used as stores of value. The fineness of material was held constant, while weight changes were measured with sophisticated accuracy. As long as the value ratios of the exchange media remained constant, this code had the advantage of continuous measurement up to very high value accumulations. But the complicated verification procedures limited the use to a small set of public officials and traders. The system did not have one generally understood and accepted monetary medium. The basic social codes of Assyria were still religion and power.

The Ionians, like other peasant societies, used livestock and tools as media of payment and exchange. These tools must be viewed with a predominantly religious connotation. Sticks, tripods, knives, and rings invariably had been part of religious sacrifices. What worked in the "exchange" with supernatural powers was considered trustworthy in the exchange with humans (Laum 1924). Such esteem, however, was limited to the narrow boundaries of a particular community. For purposes of tribute or far trade, the tools were of little use. The code had the advantage of discreteness, since the single pieces could be added up easily without testing for material content. But the validity of the medium was restricted to small areas. For purposes of far trade, the Ionian towns also used precious metal, particularly silver, which was more easily found in the region settled by the Greeks.

The striated electrum coins of Sardes were understood as money in both of these vastly different cultures. The pieces were, simultaneously and ambiguously, perceived as Eastern signed metal (with the shine of gold) and Western metal signs (with the shine of silver). The effect was, literally, unconscious: the new form made a new medium of value communication available. Transactions that had never been possible could now be articulated. The coins were

---

30. On the earliest pieces, this must be considered the front side. Once the side facing the anvil begins to be filled with types, the upper side is considered the reverse side.

31. Heichelheim (1956) lists more than a dozen, from precious metals to foodstuffs, weapons, and shells.

understood in a wide area outside the merchant's internal play. The scarcity coding of the precious metals was combined with the property coding of tokens. That highly improbable change in the monetary code of archaic societies found the conditions for its selection in the transactions of early seventh-century Lydian traders.

If the impact of that particular ambiguity was as tremendous as claimed here, then there should be some trace of it in the history books. Indeed there is such a trace: the rapid circulation increased the money supply available to the merchants. As a result, the financial power of the traders who stamped money grew so great that it not only eclipsed political power, but created a new form of it—tyranny. "It was the monopoly in stamped pieces of electrum that brought the first tyrant to the king's palace and placed him on the throne" (Ure 1922, 152). Literary sources suggest that there was a considerable time period between the "tradesman king" Ardys (766–730 B.C.), who ousted the then-ruling king with the money of an "inn-keeper and waggon-builder," and Gyges (687–652 B.C.), "who completed the evolution of metal coinage by making it the prerogative of the state after he had first used it to obtain the supreme power" (Ure 1922, 143). During that period, the rather innocuous innovation of striated coins must have created an impact that changed the entire society—an effect that was far beyond the expectations of the traders involved.

The early trader-tyrants seem to have ruled under precarious circumstances. Gyges, however, was able to found a dynasty that remained in place until King Croisos was ousted by the Persians in 546 B.C. This fact, and the phenomenal wealth that has been associated with his name, seem to be connected with the third step in the development of the coin: instead of the older striations, a lion's head appeared on the side facing the anvil, while the punchmarked "back" of the coin remained unchanged (coin 3 of fig. 2).[32] The lion was the sacred animal of Astarte, the supreme Lydian deity. Its image contained a powerful message: "Whoever bears the totem sign is in magic communion with the totem community, the sign is a legitimation of tribal participation" (Laum 1924, 140). In other words, a communication form that had been developed in *religious* discourse was first adapted to *political* discourse and was then used to secure *economic* value communication. Once the coin issuer had become the holder of public power, he was in a position to use public images. Thereafter, totem animal images could be used and the advantages of coinage to public finance could be exploited. In addition, the internal circulation of services and commodities could be extended to the entire circle in which the political power was accepted.

---

32. There are, however, other images found on coins of the same period. It seems probable that private circles continued to experiment with coin signs. But the religious-political connotation led to the selection of that particular coin form.

It was this form of the electrum coin—totem animal type on the front, ornamental punchmarks on the reverse side—that spread first to Milet, Ephesus, Samos, Phokaia, and, a little later, to Smyrna, Chios, Kyzikos, and Lampsakos (Heichelheim 1931, 42–43). The coins show, in variations, the sacred animal of the power that minted the coin. Thus, after the innovation had been monopolized in its original territory, it was now adopted by other, competing powers in the region. Again, the sources report remarkable economic growth in the Ionian towns during that time period. Far trade with standardized products, intensive regional trade, and investments in agriculture and crafts became possible (Heichelheim 1931).

At this point, we can return to the introductory question about the time span necessary for the evolution of the coin. The conventional archaeological interpretation holds that not more than thirty years passed between the use of the first striated pellets (coin 2) and the minting of animal-type coins (coin 3) throughout Ionia. The alternative interpretation allows about one hundred years for the process.[33] The traditional theory of monetary development is consistent with rapid diffusion: once the innovation had been made, it spread quickly due to individual rational choices. But slow diffusion can also be explained in the context of a consistent theory: through improbable perturbations of ambiguity, new variations seeped into the established code, without being noticed by the operations of the code. The variations changed the code or, in other terms, the "institutional" environment without any willful decision on the part of those who participated in the ongoing sequences of transactions.

The fourth step in the development of the new payment form entailed a change of only one dimension, namely the material of the coin. The Ionian electrum coins increased in silver content to almost 100 percent, but they still were considered nominally as electrum coins. The first explicit silver currency was minted on the island of Aegina, probably somewhere around 600 B.C.[34]

---

33. As mentioned at the beginning of this chapter, most of our knowledge about the first coins comes from a "construction sacrifice" hoard of nineteen electrum coins, nine precoins, and several precious objects found in the base of an Artemis temple. One of the coins bears an inscription that was, for a long time, interpreted as part of the name of the Lydian king Alyattes, whose reign began in 610 B.C. Assuming, furthermore, that coins were not in use for more than a generation, the first coins were dated no later than 630 B.C. (Robinson 1956; Kraay 1976). In the light of more recent research, the attribution to Alyattes is improbable. On the contrary, the following points speak in favor of an earlier emergence: (1) there is solid evidence for a Kimmerian attack that destroyed the temple and that cannot have occurred after 626 B.C., since the Assyrian sources can be dated by the death of Assurbanipal; (2) coins were in use for a much longer period than just one human generation; and (3) there are strong stylistic similarities between coin types, particularly lion heads, and other artistic objects that were made during the first half of the seventh century (Weidauer 1975).

34. There is a literary tradition going back to Herodot that attributes the introduction of silver currency to King Pheidon of Argos (Ure 1922). That would set the date around 650 B.C., a date that is not supported by the coins that have been found. Since the Aeginetans were an active clan of far traders, a more circle-oriented theory of emergence seems plausible. Herodot's story

The form had not changed: sacred animal (sea turtle) on the front, ornamental "Quadratum" on the reverse side (coin 4 of fig. 2). But the material had changed to pure silver, and the denominations of the coins were extended to much smaller fractionals. This way, local trade could now be "driven" by the new monetary code. In addition, the weight system was adapted to the peculiarities of the code.[35] The communication quality of the new device had become more important than its material quality.

A final step brings us to the coin form that remained stable for the following centuries.[36] Around 520 B.C., animal heads appeared inside the incuse square of Athenian coins for the first time.[37] The punchmark, which had become more and more ornamental yet had remained a part of the money sign for more than a century, disappeared. Shortly thereafter, the tyrant Hippias "reformed" Athenian currency by replacing the existing coin varieties with one standard form. The reverse side now showed, still inside the incuse square, a standing owl with an olive branch. The obverse side showed the helmeted head of Athena (coin 5 of fig. 2). The sign of the owl would have been sufficient to indicate the origin of a coin. Athena's image is a reference to the gods that were common to the entire Greek culture. With respect to this image, even observers outside Athens were inside the relevant circle of communication.

The power of the religious interpretation of the image remained, but the religion had changed from an archaic local reference to the much wider reference of a unifying culture. This coin was to remain virtually unchanged until the third century B.C. It was minted in thousands of tons of silver, mainly in tetradrachms.[38] Some of the coins left the circuit of Athenian trade and became the dominant medium of exchange in far trade from Asia Minor to Afghanistan. The popularity of the coins was reaffirmed by numerous local adaptations and imitations.

It seems that Hippias's reform had effects far beyond the original intentions. There is reason to believe that the rise of Athens as a center of finance and commerce was partly due to the performance of the payment medium at its disposal. The complexity of public tasks grew, and the new money forms

---

also indicates that Pheidon called in the archaic spits that had been used as money before. Again, the willful act is probably a literary interpretation. But it is still remarkable that tool money was still in active use even among "advanced" economic powers.

35. The Aeginetan drachma was designed to "make ten silver pieces worth one gold when gold was 15 times as precious as silver" (Ure 1922, 172).

36. The account follows Kraay (1976, 55f.).

37. Athens was not the first town to have coins with images on both sides—the priority goes to Corinth.

38. In 454 B.C., Athens appropriated the treasure of the Delian League and minted it in order to pay for the building program of the Acropolis. The size of the treasure amounted to 125 tons of silver, or 7.5 million tetradrachms.

could deal with harbor fees, fines, taxes, payment for soldiers, and expenditures for public works. The sources also report that the money economy virtually exploded in Greece at the end of the sixth century. The country began to be covered with mints, and banking emerged as a separate occupation. The new medium was being produced on an industrial scale. From now on, the developing economies contained a "pure money complex" (Crump 1981), i.e., a network of institutions and organizations whose function it was to produce and process the monetary code. A new era in the evolution of the European economy was about to begin.

To summarize the historical account: the evolution of coin forms became observable whenever particular variations or "steps" were selected in a money-production system. Other variations are known from the historical evidence, but they remained without influence on the long-range development. The decisive mutation of the code occurred when the Lydian electrum coins were interpreted ambiguously as signed metal and as metal signs. After that, selection of the new form spread. But the form did not stabilize until double-image silver coins with a more sophisticated cultural interpretation became part of economic transactions. At that point, a wavelike expansion of coinage began, affecting the total social and natural environment of the payment code. Similar dramatic social changes occurred when, during the third century B.C., Rome began to mint coins and, more than a thousand years later, when the Carolingian currency reform provided the base for the reestablishment of a pure money complex, driving the emergent medieval economy. In all cases, the result was not an economy that was better adapted to a given environment, but an economy that had gained increased independence from that environment.

Final Remarks

The episode just reported was part of a concrete period in the history of money. It allows us to compare alternative explanations for changes in the value medium. The episode showed how "genetic changes" in the continuing sequence of payments succeeded only rarely but, when they did, led to dramatic changes in the "phenotype" of economic production. It is striking to observe how all changes of the form safeguarded the continuity of the "value message." The value medium changed imperceptibly around the players, in a process literally outside of rational choice, while the players continued their own self-reproduction by participating in the play.

This example was restricted to exchange money, but it could be extended to credit and book money, even to contemporary monetary processes. Modern economies are, of course, far more complex in structure and much faster in their rhythm of transaction. Trade is not limited anymore to a few staples or luxury goods. It has expanded into a global activity, fueled by the transformation of entire landscapes. The money media available are not limited to metal coins, harvest credits, and temple treasures anymore. Today, transactions are surrounded by a host of financial institutions and markets that constantly produce and process the forms needed for value reproduction. Still, the transactions are the language in which value reproduction takes place, and the money forms are, to stay with the metaphor, the air in which that language can formulate itself.

At the very horizon of that monetary environment, we observe lenders of last resort: the central banks. They are indeed the borderline between the fictional world of economic value and all other kinds of communication. They are, however, observed as borderline only from the inside—the observing position of transactions. We are familiar with that position from our everyday experience as participants in an economy. From the observing position of scientific discourse, we have a much more detached view. Now, central banks appear to be at the center of a pure money complex of institutions, which, in turn, is at the center of the communication play we call "economy."

There is reason to believe that the self-organization of economies through autonomous central banks or a network of central banks will eclipse political systems, just as religious systems were eclipsed by political systems a few hundred years ago.[39] When that will happen, or if it will happen at all, remains uncertain. It depends on the emergence of ambiguities inside the money complex that make it possible that the ongoing operations continue, while, at the same time, a new form of influencing currencies is already in operation. Thus, the process of economic evolution continues.

---

39. This is a final feature of a communication theory of economic evolution: Although the future remains open in principle, the theory generates projections that reach far into that future. It does so because the projections are built on observations that reach into the past in similarly large time horizons.

Part 4
Innovation and the Firm

The chief fault, then, . . . [of] Ricardo and his followers . . . was that they did not see how liable to change are the habits and institutions of industry.
—Alfred Marshall (1879), quoted in Pigou 1956, 154–55

The Coevolution of Technologies and Institutions

Richard R. Nelson

In our 1982 book, *An Evolutionary Theory of Economic Change*, Sidney Winter and I presented a quite complex analysis of how technologies develop. One central theme was that technological development must be understood as an evolutionary process, in which new technological alternatives compete with each other and with prevailing practice, with ex-post selection determining the winners and losers, usually with considerable ex-ante uncertainty regarding which ones the winners will be.

However, while we highlighted the elements of uncertainty in technological evolution, we stressed as well the strong systematic selection that many market environments provide. We also argued that the generation of alternatives often was highly focused. In most modern fields of technology there is a considerable body of technological understanding that provides guidance as to what kinds of projects are likely to be technologically successful and what ones not, as well as an understanding of user needs, which provides strong guidance as to what advances would have value. Thus the technological "mutations" offered to the market-selection environment are far from strictly random. This, as well as selection, provides direction to technical advance.

We argued that detailed studies of technological advance had shown that the development of technologies often followed what we called "a natural trajectory," where the generation of innovations is constrained by both kinds of understanding—what technologists understood would likely work, and what entrepreneurs judged would likely be profitable—with ex-post selection further winnowing the innovative ideas that survive. We also proposed that in many fields technological advance was what we called "cumulative," in that today's technological advances tended to proceed from yesterday's, with today's in turn becoming the basis for tomorrow's. We discussed the cognitive aspects of such dynamics, introducing the term "technological regimes" to

The author is indebted to the Sloan Foundation for financial support, through its funding of the Consortium on Competition and Cooperation.

describe them. Later, Dosi (1988) called this cognitive structure a "technological paradigm."

In our work we paid some attention to how firm size and industry structure change over the course of development of a new technology. We also referred to the coevolution of institutional structure with technology more generally. However, our discussion of these matters was much more limited than our discussion of the evolution of technologies, because at the time we wrote there was much less research on those issues from which we could draw.

Since that time a considerable amount of research has been done that leads to a fleshing out of the character of the coevolution of institutions and technology. Some of that work has been largely empirical, or has taken the form of what Winter and I have called "appreciative theorizing." (More on what we mean by this later.) But another part of the work has been quite formal in nature, and oriented toward examination of the mathematics of evolutionary processes involving dynamic increasing returns.

The purpose of this essay is to pull together a portion of this recent work and to point to some promising analytic implications. I begin by discussing several different strands of the recent literature, which together suggest some very interesting patterns of coevolution of technologies and institutions as an industry develops. Recognition of these patterns and what lies behind them has significance in analysis of a wide variety of economic questions.

I then turn to some of these areas. I briefly discuss the implications of these ideas for analysis of productivity growth and the dynamics of industrial organization. Then I consider at somewhat greater length issues relating to the building of comparative advantage, the topic central to the "new trade theory." Finally, I provide a reprise on appreciative and formal theorizing and their complementary roles in economic analysis.

Recent Research Bearing on the Coevolution of Technology and Institutions

Almost all of the research I report here has as its unit of observation a particular broad technology or industry, or a connected group of these, as contrasted with being focused at the level of the overall economy. A good portion of this research effort is concerned with developing generalizations that hold across technologies or industries, and that will be the orientation of this review, although an important open question is how widely these generalizations hold. For the most part, the bodies of research I report here have been developed separately, and there is little cross-referencing from one to another. My intended contribution is to show that when these pieces are fitted together, a very interesting picture emerges.

It is analytically convenient to begin with a body of research that purports to identify a "life cycle" through which many technologies seem to go. At the present time a number of scholars, including both economists and organization theorists, are doing work that I would put in this category. However, much of the contemporary formulation was offered over a decade ago by Abernathy and Utterback (1978), who had been studying automobile technology. The basic starting argument is that when a new technology comes into existence there is considerable uncertainty regarding which of a variety of possible variants will succeed. Different ones are tried out by different parties. However, after a period of time and competition, one or a few of these variants come to dominate the others, and attention and resources become concentrated on these at the expense of the others. In the parlance of several of the workers in this field, a "dominant design" emerges.

There are several different stories about how a dominant design comes into existence. In the most straightforward of these, one variant simply is better than the others and, with time and experimentation, the best basic design comes to be identified and widely recognized. However, according to another story, while an initial concentration of attention and resources on a particular design may have been the result of chance, once those resources are so concentrated, improvements of this variant will, relatively quickly, make it and its further development the only economic way to proceed. Winter and I suggested this as a possibility some time ago, and some of Arthur's recent modeling (1988) can be interpreted this way. In such a context there is no reason to believe that the dominant design society fixed upon is the best one. It could well be that other broad configurations would have turned out better had resources been allocated to advancing these in the technological race.

While these two stories are analytically very different and point normative assessment in different directions, I suspect it is very hard to distinguish between them empirically. The question of what would have happened had a particular alternative not been abandoned—whether it would actually have won out or been confirmed as a bust—is not an easy one to answer.

Still a third story, or rather a family of stories, has some commonalities with the second, but stresses systems aspects. In particular, the focus is on interaction economies that may occur when the number who own and use a particular variant grows, as skills develop that are particular to a certain variant, or through investments in complementary products designed to fit with a particular variant.[1] While sometimes used more generally, the special term *standard* tends to be used to denote the key mechanism or configuration that defines and delineates the dominant *system* when it emerges. As the authors writing in this field argue convincingly, there is no reason why the standard that emerges and, in effect, "locks" in the system need be optimal.

Standards in the above sense can come about through a variety of pro-

---

1. See, e.g., David (1992), Arthur (1988), and Katz and Shapiro (1985).

cesses. In many cases a standard emerges through market competition without any explicit agreement. In others, members of the industry and other interested participants (for example, users or financiers) may get together to agree upon standards. Particularly where there is a major governmental involvement, as through a regulatory mandate, the government may declare standards. In the latter case, there is a rapidly developing literature about when and how the standard should be chosen.

In the original Abernathy and Utterback story, once a dominant design comes into existence, radical product innovation slows, and product design improvements become incremental. There may, however, be a considerable period of time when there is substantial improvement of process technology. If the advancing process technology is specific to a particular product design, cumulative process innovation further locks in that design and makes it even more difficult for different designs to compete. This story line is quite consistent with that being spun by economists interested in systems technologies and standards.

When Abernathy and Utterback first spun out the dominant design story, they based it on detailed observation of only one industry, automobile manufacturing. Since that time the basic story line has been tried, and found to be fitting, in a wide range of industries. (See in particular the work of Tushman and colleagues.) Some writers clearly believe it is a universal. I confess some skepticism about that. The story seems to fit best industries where the product is a "system," and where customers have similar demands. It is not at all clear that the notion of a dominant design fits the experience of the chemical products industry, where often a variety of quite different products are produced for similar uses, or where customer needs are divergent and specialized. Nonetheless, the dominant design theory certainly has proved illuminating in a wide range of industries.

And where it does seem applicable, that theory raises very interesting, and troubling, questions about the nature of economic explanation, about whether one can presume that market forces generate efficient outcomes, and even about what one means by market forces. In the first "story" economic logic prevails. But in both the second and third story of how a dominant design emerges, there are stochastic forces at work that can be decisive. Particularly in the third, there also may be processes of coalition building that can nudge the outcome one way or another, which may have little to do with projections of long-run economic efficiency.[2] Some writers have gone so far as to argue that it is power, or social consensus, rather than economic efficiency, that determines which broad path ultimately is followed. This raises the question of how far economic selection arguments can take one in an evolutionary analysis of economic change, and the extent to which political

---

2. See, e.g., David (1985, 1992) and Tushman and Rosenkopf (1992).

and social forces need to be taken explicitly into account, not simply in influencing transient or short-term developments but in determining the broad paths along which technology proceeds. More on this later.

There is another body of research that uses concepts similar to those in the technology life-cycle literature, but with a different focus—in particular, it looks at what happens to firm and industry structure as a technology matures. Until recently, the bulk of the research in this area has been done by economists, who made little reference to the technology life-cycle literature.[3] The basic propositions are the following: During the early period of experimentation and flux, before a dominant design emerges, there are no particular advantages to incumbency. Market demand is fragmented across a number of variants. Firms producing particular designs tend to be small. Model changes may be frequent. Exits from and entries into the industry are common.

However, after a dominant design becomes established, firms that do not produce a variant of it tend to drop out of the industry or into small niche markets. With product design less unstable, learning by incumbent firms becomes more cumulative, and potential entrants increasingly are at a disadvantage. With the market less fragmented and more predictable, firms try to exploit latent economies of scale, and advances in process technology both reflect and enforce this. Generally, scale-intensive technology is capital intensive as well, and so the cost of entry rises for this reason too. There is "shake out" in the industry and structure becomes more concentrated, with the surviving firms tending to be relatively large.

As with the theory about dominant designs, there is a question about how universal is the pattern of industry birth and evolution proposed by Mueller and Tilton (1969). The empirical work by Gort and Klepper (1982) shows that the basic story does seem to fit a wide range of industries in the United States. Utterback and Suarez (1993) similarly claim wide applicability. However, there may be an issue of industry definition. Consider radically new products, like television sets, that are produced by established companies that had been producing related products, like radios. In such cases one is inclined not to see or define a new "industry," but rather simply to say that there is a new product produced in an established industry. And there also is the issue that almost all the empirical research on the topic has been on patterns in the United States. At least in the post–World War II era, there is reason to believe that new products that were pioneered by new firms in the United States were pioneered (somewhat later) by established firms in Europe and Japan. If so, these international differences seem interesting to explain.

The story about industrial maturation and changing firm and industry

---

3. A number of economists have contributed to this line of research and "storytelling." Mueller and Tilton (1969) wrote a pioneer piece along these lines. Recently Gort and Klepper (1982) and Klepper and Grady (1990) have developed the empirical and theoretical argument further.

structure is tied to the notion of organizational learning. That part of the story can be enriched considerably, I believe, by tapping into another body of research associated with the proposition that successful firms develop a complex of "core capabilities" that enable them to be effective in the context in which they operate.[4] The basic argument is that firms have (at best) a limited number of things they can do well, which include operating and advancing the particular technologies they know well, their particular approaches to marketing and purchasing, their ways of identifying and responding to environmental changes, etc. Further, ability to do even a limited number of things will usually take a considerable amount of learning by experience, and other investments in those "core capabilities." Chandler (1990) has stressed the investments in production, marketing, and management that are needed for a firm to become and remain competitive in an area.

The research on "dominant designs" suggests that these capabilities and investments cannot be developed when a technology still is in flux, but only after broad orientations have become clear. On the other hand, the proposition that a firm's core capabilities have a limited domain of applicability suggests a tailoring of firms to the requirements of prevailing dominant designs. In turn, this suggests that established firms may have considerable difficulty in adjusting, in gaining control of needed different capabilities, when important new technologies that have the potential to replace prevailing ones come into being. I will pick up this issue later.

Firms do not stand by themselves, of course, but rather in a context in which they compete with rivals, are served by suppliers, sell to customers, and draw on particular talents and skills. Granovetter (1985) has argued that a new industry takes on a sociological and communal aspect when the people and the firms in it begin to see themselves as an industry. Industry or trade associations then tend to form. These may be active in standard setting and in organizing collectively funded research on common problems. For better or worse, these also give the industry a recognized organization that can lobby on its behalf for regulation more to its liking, public programs that support it, protection from outside competition, etc. This is another feature of an industry's development that can lock in the status quo.

For an industry with special input and skill needs, growth and effectiveness is strongly conditioned by how rapidly and effectively a support structure grows up. Recently several scholars—Piore and Sabel (1984), Lazonick (1990), and Krugman (1992) quickly come to mind—have resurrected Marshall's notion of an "industrial district," which includes most of the firms

---

4. Among the new articles on this topic are those by Winter, Teece, Dosi, and myself, separately and in various combinations; by Prahalad and Hamel (1990), Kogut (1991), Henderson (1991), Cantwell (1991), Langlois (1992), and Pavitt (1988); and (in somewhat different spirit) by Chandler (1990) and Lazonick (1990).

in the industry itself, specialized suppliers, and concentrations of workers with the particular needed skills. The latter may be associated with the presence of training institutions and programs. If the technology on which the industry is based has novel characteristics, new technical societies and new technical journals tend to spring up. In some cases, whole new fields of "science" may come into being.

Research by Rosenberg and myself (Nelson and Rosenberg 1993) has called into question certain popular notions about the relationships between science and technology. Conventional wisdom has it that the sciences, in general, do not aim to solve practical problems but rather to advance basic understanding of nature, but that enhanced basic understanding makes technological advances possible even if the work is not aimed to do that. Thus the work of Maxwell on electromagnetism, which was an exercise in pure science, ultimately led to radio. The case of Carnot, who launched the field of thermodynamics largely because he wanted to understand what was going on in steam engines, is recognized but generally considered something of an exception.

Our research suggests that these kinds of "exceptions" well may be the rule. Quite often when a new technology comes into existence, there is very little scientific understanding relevant to it. However, the appearance of that new technology then induces scientific research to understand it, and lays the basis for its subsequent development. The result may be the creation of a new scientific field related to that technology. Thus, the field of metallurgy came into existence because of a demand for better understanding of the factors that determined the properties of steel. Computer science is the field that was brought into existence by the advent of the modern computer. Chemical engineering and electrical engineering rose up as fields of teaching and research because of industry demand for them that occurred after the key technological advances had launched the industries.

The appearance and development of these technology-oriented sciences tend to tie industries to universities, which provide both people trained in the relevant fields and research findings that enable the technology to advance further. The development of these sciences naturally tends to lend extra strength to prevailing technologies. On the other hand, the presence of university research tends to dilute the extent to which existing firms have knowledge advantages over potential entrants. Also, research at universities may become the source of radically different technological alternatives.

Recognition of the role of technical societies and universities in the development of modern technologies opens the door to seeing the wide range of institutions that may coevolve with technology. Often, legal structures need to change. Thus there may be intellectual property-rights issues that need to be sorted out—biotechnology is a striking contemporary case in point. There almost always are issues of regulation, as was prominently the case in radio and, in a different manner, biotechnology again. Hughes (1987) has described in great detail the wide range of legal and regulatory matters that had to be decided before electric power could go forward strongly and how the particular decisions affected the evolution of the technology and the industry.

In many cases new public-sector activities and programs are required. Thus, mass use of automobiles required that societies organize themselves to build and maintain a system of public roads. Airplanes required airports. The development of radio required mechanisms to allocate the radio spectrum. Development of commercial television required frequency assignments and also depended on governmental decisions about design standards.

These examples indicate that the evolution of institutions relevant to a technology or industry may be a very complex process, involving not only the actions of private firms, but also organizations like industry associations, technical societies, universities, courts, government agencies, legislatures, etc. The "new institutional economics" started with a broad theoretical stance that, somehow, institutions changed optimally (if perhaps with a lag) in response to changes in economic circumstances that called for those changes. Recently, however, scholars in that field are beginning to highlight the interest group conflict often involved in public responses and the strong sensitivity of outcomes to political structures and processes.[5] Not only is there an abandonment of the assumption of "optimality" of institutional response, there now is strong recognition that one needs a process model to predict and understand what the institutional accommodations will be.

This leads me to the last set of strands I want to gather here: those concerned with what happens in a mature industry when radical new developments come about that call for significant change. An example would be the effect of the advent of transistor and, later, integrated circuit technology on the mature electronics industry, which had been dedicated to vacuum tubes. Another would be the effect of emerging biotechnology on the mature pharmaceuticals industry.

Perhaps the largest body of writing addressing this issue has been concerned with who adopts and brings to practice such a new technology. In particular, do incumbent firms adopt it, or does its adoption depend on new entrants? The proposition advanced by this literature is that the answer depends on whether the new technology employs roughly the same kinds of understandings and skills as does the old. If so, firms in the industry tend to be able to switch over to it. If not, new firms will tend to enter the industry, and the failure rate among incumbents may be very high.[6] However, as with the

---

5. North (1990), Shepsle and Weingast (1981), Cohen and Noll (1991).

6. Work along these lines has been done by Tushman and Anderson (1986), Tushman and Romanelli (1985), Hannan and Freeman (1989), and Henderson and Clark (1990), among others.

empirical literature on the evolution of firm and industry structure, virtually all of this work has been on industries in the United States. As I noted earlier, there is reason to believe that in Europe and Japan new firms do not seem to enter the picture so readily, and incumbent firms thus have more time to adjust.

A broader question, of course, is whether the larger set of institutions supporting the established technology and industry are able to adapt, or whether they make it very difficult to shift away from old practices or for new firms to enter and take over. Lazonick (1990) has elaborated the theme that the broad organization of work and institutions for training labor that worked so well for British industry in the late nineteenth century became a handicap in the twentieth. Veblen's famous essay (1915) on the rise of Germany as an economic power stressed more generally that British industry was in effect sorely handicapped in adopting the new technologies that were emerging around the turn of the century, due to an interlocking set of constraints associated with her institutions and past investments, whereas Germany could work with a relatively clean slate.

One thing Germany had going for her that Britain did not was a set of universities dedicated to the ideal of research and science. This system was in place before the rise of modern science-based industry but surely was a powerful asset in supporting that development. In contrast, the United States had to build a system of research universities in order to get into the new game, but it did this much more rapidly than did England.

By the 1920s the U.S. university system still was lagging relative to the Germans, but, because it was built up with economic applications in mind, it was arguably more responsive. Landau and Rosenberg (1992) have argued that the speed with which the American university system adopted the field of chemical engineering was a major help to American companies in the new chemical products industries that opened up in the 1920s. In contrast, the German universities lagged in adopting chemical engineering, and German industry paid the price.

The most sweeping of the propositions along these lines has been made by Perez (1985) and Freeman (1991), who have developed the concept of a "techno-economic paradigm." Their argument starts along lines developed by Schumpeter many years ago: different eras are dominated by different fundamental technologies. Perez and Freeman then propose that to be effective with those technologies a nation requires a set of institutions compatible with and supportive of them. The institutions suitable for an earlier set of fundamental technologies may be quite inappropriate for the new. Their arguments clearly are similar to those of Veblen, in the particular case he addressed. Thus while Britain lagged, Germany and the United States had, or quickly adopted, institutions that could support the rising chemical and electrical industries that were the basic ones from 1910 to 1960 or so. The authors propose that the period since 1970 or so has seen the rise of "information technologies" as the new basis of economic effectiveness and argue that effective accommodation requires a very different set of institutions from those required in the earlier era. They see Japan as coming closest to having them.

One can be skeptical about these propositions simply because they are so grandly stated. However the basic point—that new technologies often are not well accommodated by prevailing institutional structures and require institutional reform if they are to develop effectively—squares, I think, with the historical record.

Implications for Economic Analysis

I believe that these new understandings about the dynamics of technical change at a sectoral level, and about the various ways in which technology and institutions coevolve, are important. They illuminate several areas of economic inquiry.

First, they suggest interesting things about the interactions among technical advance, capital intensity, and scale economies as factors contributing to productivity growth at the level of an industry, or cluster of connected ones. In particular, the argument outlined above leads one to expect that rising capital intensity and the development of large-scale units are phenomena that go together and occur after a dominant design has been established. One might suspect that these developments also would be associated with an acceleration of growth of labor productivity. However, particularly if effective use of the potential latent in a new technology requires significant institutional accommodations, it might take a long time before there is much effect on productivity. David's study (1991) of electric power is consistent with this story.

Second, the arguments suggest strongly that one must see the "industrial organization" of a field as something that evolves with the technology and with the broader pattern of institutional change. Firm size and market concentration can be expected to increase as a technology matures, and the pattern of entry and exit also will change. However, one might expect that the extent of latent economics of scale would differ from technology to technology, and undoubtedly also vary with the extent to which learning by incumbents is of major significance compared with more generally accessible sources of technological know-how. Both of these variables should affect the size of firms and barriers to entry in a field. The latter might have something to do with whether a field of science develops around the technology and whether university researchers are active in that field.

More generally, the arguments would seem to call for a significant broadening of what economists include under the rubric of "industrial organization." Economists have looked a little at industry and trade associations, but mostly as vehicles for collusion. They may be that, but they also serve other functions, from standard setting, to establishment of cooperative R&D funding of university research, to lobbying for protection. Where there are technologies that are especially important to an industry, there are likely to be important university connections, and other industry-linked research or training organizations. A number of industries have government agencies linked closely to them as providers of needed complementary services, major customers, clients, and protectors.

These new understandings also provide a broad point of entry into analysis of how countries or regions come to establish comparative advantage in an industry. The "new trade theory" recognizes, in stylized form, that comparative advantage in certain fields is created rather than being innate in broad country-level variables and that both private and public actions may be needed for comparative advantage to be built. However, the stories sketched above provide a much richer and variegated account of how comparative advantage is built. While I have only sketched applications to understanding of economic growth and industrial organization, I think it useful to flesh out in somewhat more detail how these ideas apply to at least one area of economic inquiry, and here I have chosen trade theory.

One can identify three basically different bodies of writing on the sources of competitive advantage (as business school scholars would put it) or comparative advantage (as economists would call it). Recently much of the writing has been concerned with trying to explain why the Japanese are now beating out the Americans in automobiles and RAMs and to divine what the future holds.

One important body of writing locates advantage in the strategies, structures, and core capabilities of particular firms. The book by Womack, Jones, and Roos (1991) comparing automobile firms of different nationalities is an excellent example. The authors identify the sources of Japanese advantage in the policies and characteristics of Japanese firms and argue that firms of other nationalities could, if they chose, learn to look like the Japanese firms. The authors expressly play down general features of the Japanese economy that differentiate it from the American economy. In this theory, competitive advantage is something that individual firms create.

This perspective could not be more at odds with the theory of comparative advantage put forth in traditional economics. In that paradigm, comparative advantage in an industry depends on broad national conditions, for example, climate, or the cost of capital, or the broad education of the work force, which determine what products domestic firms can produce more economically than can firms abroad. What the firms themselves do is viewed as being largely determined by the national economic environment. Thus while scholars like Womack and his associates consider the short-time horizons of American managers as something they should and can correct, traditional economic analysis would propose that these short-time horizons are a rational response to the high cost of capital and a justified fear of takeovers. According to this theory, comparative advantage is made through investments that affect the economywide climate, as contrasted with efforts focused on particular sectors.

Recent writings on competitiveness have opened this theory to include broad national institutions as variables influencing where national firms will be strong and weak. Thus, several writers have argued that, far from representing choices that firms in different environments could have made, the way Japanese firms are structured, and their broad strategies, are largely the result of their attempts to accommodate particular aspects of the broader Japanese political economy. Bank finance and the tradition of close and long-run firm-bank relations enable and encourage firms to take a long-time perspective. Lifetime employment is, to a considerable extent, the consequence of the breaking of militant unions that occurred many years ago and their replacement by company unions. In turn, major investments by firms and workers in firm-specific training are supported and encouraged by long-term employment relationships.

The other side of this analytic coin is that American financial institutions have been assigned blame for the decline of the American automobile and semiconductor industries. Traditional loose attachment of workers to particular firms is recognized as a possible factor explaining why American firms do less training than Japanese or German enterprises. But in any case, the emphasis here, in contrast with that in Womack, Jones, and Roos (1991), is on national level variables, rather than policies at the discretion of firms, as the factors that make for comparative advantage.

Still a third body of writing identifies the sources of competitive advantage as residing in institutions and investments tied specifically to a broad industry or sector, as contrasted with being economywide, or being associated with individual firms. Porter's recent book (1990) has this orientation, and so, to a considerable degree, does that of Chandler (1990). (I noted earlier that Piore and Sabel [1984] and Krugman [1992] recently have resurrected Marshall's concept of an "industrial district," which connotes a complex of complementary activities supporting a particular industry or industry complex.)

Much of the writings about "industrial policy," both by economists and noneconomists, identify industry-specific institutions, investments, and government policies that lend a competitive advantage to an industry or industry complex. Thus, the rise of the Japanese semiconductor and computer industries is seen by some as having been spurred by the VLSI project. Much of the current dispute between the United States and Europe regarding trade in commercial aircraft involves the United States claiming the Europeans are blatantly subsidizing Airbus, and the Europeans rejoining that the United States aircraft industry is specially advantaged by military procurement and R&D contracts.

The body of writing surveyed in the second section bears on all of these themes about the sources of competitive (or comparative) advantage and is especially illuminating, I believe, about how they fit together. Thus the concept of a technology life cycle suggests that the relevant firm capabilities may differ depending on the stage of that cycle. And the argument that core capabilities are specific to particular contexts would cast doubt on the notion that there is a general purpose best way of organizing firms that is independent of the industry, as seems to be suggested by Womack, Jones, and Roos.

The technology life-cycle schema, and appreciation of the ways in which technologies and institutions coevolve, can lend insights into how broad country-level variables influence development of comparative advantage. Countries clearly differ in the ease with which new firms can form and get funding and in the degree to which markets are open to new sources of supply. They also differ in the speed with which universities are able to adopt new sciences, in how adaptable legal structures are to changing demands put on them by new technologies, in how supportive public sector programs are of the new as contrasted with protective of the old, etc.

Consider the questions of why the United States gained strong comparative advantage in the semiconductor business when it was relatively new, but may be losing that advantage in recent years, and why the United States seized comparative advantage in the new biotechnologies and continues to hold that advantage. Both of these new broad technologies involved very different sets of skills from those possessed by the established companies that were producing products for which the *new* technologies promised potentially superior substitutes. The old electrical equipment suppliers who produced vacuum tubes had no expertise relevant to transistor design and production. The old pharmaceutical and agricultural chemicals companies had virtually no in-house expertise in biotechnology. Thus the incumbent firms had no advantages over potential new entrants, except money and extant organization, and arguably they were disadvantaged relative to them in some respects.

There were several *general* characteristics of U.S. institutions that enabled new firms to implement these new technologies more quickly than firms in other countries. One was the presence of a venture-capital market. A second was the flexibility and responsiveness of the university research system, which led to very rapid incorporation of the new technologies into the U.S. academy, and also the tradition of entrepreneurship by academics. Put another way, one can argue that the United States has a general comparative advantage in new science-connected technologies and industries.

However, in both of these cases, one can identify a number of industry-

or sector-specific sources of comparative advantage. The Department of Defense and the National Institutes of Health were, and are, the two largest governmental supporters of research in general and of academic research in particular. The DOD was strongly interested in advancing semiconductor technology, and the NIH had very strong interests in biotechnology. Thus public funding of research supporting these two new technologies was quick and large.

In the case of evolving semiconductor technology, for the first decade or so the U.S. military was overwhelmingly the largest purchaser of products and gave strong preference to domestic suppliers. Also, and of major importance, the DOD and the military services stood ready to do business with new American firms. In the case of biotechnology, while no one would characterize the general regulatory environment in the United States as unusually adaptable, regulations proved far less constraining on biotechnology than did regulations in the country one might have expected to become a strong competitor in the field—Germany.

In both of these arenas, the argument that a dominant design ultimately emerged requires at best considerable delicacy and several grains of salt. However, with the advent of the broad design for very large-scale integrated circuits, one certainly did see the subsequent rapid growth of scale and capital-intensive production, cumulative learning advantages gained by incumbents, and increasing barriers to entry.

Interestingly, as these developments occurred, the United States began to lose its comparative advantage to Japan. Several arguments attempt to explain why. Specific Japanese industrial policies have been put forth by some. Recently the argument has been made that the Japanese financial system is superior to that in the United States (at least as of the 1980s) in providing secure low-cost, large-scale funding to established firms.

Something similar, although not as pronounced, appears to be going on in biotechnology. As the first products of biotechnology research and development have entered the market, the advantages of production expertise and marketing loom more and more important and, in general, these were not included in the core capabilities of the biotech start-up firms. We thus are witnessing a rash of mergers between the now older start-ups and the older companies in pharmaceuticals and agricultural chemicals who do have production and marketing competence. We also are seeing these older companies growing their own R&D competencies. It is noteworthy that many of the companies engaging in the buyouts are foreign owned.

A few years ago, Ergas (1989) put forth the proposition that "technology policy" in the United States was splendid in achieving breakthroughs but rather bad at supporting follow-throughs. I would suggest that it is not so much "technology policy" as the broader set of American institutions that has that characteristic and that leads to the United States gaining comparative advantage early, but then losing it later in the history of the technology. Florida and Kenney (1989) make a similar argument. I should note that the old "product cycle" theory in international trade also posited this outcome. However, in the two innovative fields considered here it certainly is not the case that technological advance has basically stopped, which was the point of shifting advantage posited in that theory. I also should remark that if the statement by Ergas is true about U.S. institutions today, this is likely to be a recent development. Chandler and Lazonick, among others, have commented on the ability of American companies to make large, long-time horizon investments before the 1940s.

These remarks should not be understood as a careful examination of the building and losing of comparative advantage in two technical fields, but rather simply as a trial exploration of how the broad theory sketched in section 2 might be applied to examine how comparative advantage is built. I think there is considerable promise here.

Reprise

It has now been a decade since Sidney Winter and I published *An Evolutionary Theory of Economic Change*. The views we expressed there on the determinants of firm behavior and performance, on the nature of competition, and on the primary processes driving short- and long-run economic change diverged strikingly from the views articulated by most economist theorists then, and they have yet to be seriously entertained by most economists.

However, since 1982 a number of economists have come around to an evolutionary perspective on economic change. We like to think that this is partly because we have persuaded some people. But a good part of the movement clearly has been due to the fact that, since we wrote and independently of what we wrote, a number of economists have come to recognize that even relatively simple dynamic processes may display "increasing returns," that there might be multiple alternative equilibria for those processes, and that these facts may call for major reinterpretation of certain observed economic phenomena. I would like to suggest that there is considerable promise in merging the general theoretical framework that Winter and I proposed with the new insights about dynamic increasing returns, and that this marriage might be able to shed powerful light on economic phenomena and issues of the sort considered in the preceding section.

Evolutionary theory, at least as Winter and I have tried to develop it, is a broad and roomy thing.[7] Its central premises are these: The cognitive capacities of humans and organizations are very limited compared with the actual

---

7. See also Silverberg, Dosi, and Orsenigo (1988); Metcalfe and Gibbons (1986); and Metcalfe and Saviotti (1991).

complexity of the contexts in which they operate. Hence, one cannot presume that they actually see or think their way through to an "optimal" behavior and then adopt it. Further, neither learning processes nor selection pressures can simply be presumed effective enough so that behaviors actually observed at any time can safely be presumed optimal. On the other hand, humans and organizations do learn, if the environment permits them to do so and the incentives and pressures are there. In some contexts there are selection forces that induce expansion of organizations that do relatively well and contraction of those that do poorly. A consequence of these central premises is that in order to understand and predict behaviors, one needs a dynamic process model, which treats both individual and organizational learning and also selection.

Winter and I came to these judgments largely from our studies of how individuals, organizations, industries, and economies seemed actually to work, strongly influenced of course by theories about individual and organizational behavior we found persuasive. It seems fair to say that many of our recent fellow travelers reached the same conclusions through another route. That was to notice certain features of simple dynamic processes and to recognize that, to the extent they were governing, it simply is impossible to predict where the system will go and hence impossible for an individual or organization to "think through" to an optimal strategy. The same understanding is becoming widespread among game theorists who now are taking more seriously the fact that many games have multiple possible "equilibria" and that "out of equilibrium" play may persist for some time (Kreps 1990b). Again, there is no substitute for a dynamic process model.

Thus there now are strong unifying elements binding together the different camps of evolutionary theorists. But there are differences as well. For the most part it seems that the contemporary evolutionary theorists who focus on multiple equilibria also emphasize formal models. The models are motivated by stories, based on certain stylized empirical observations, and are interpreted in terms of those stories. But the emphasis is on the formal models. In contrast, the center of interest for Winter and myself is in empirical phenomena and the stories about these phenomena, which we have called "appreciative theorizing." In our view of economic theorizing, formal models certainly do play an important role but generally not the central role. In particular, we have proposed that for economic understanding to advance effectively, both appreciative and formal theorizing are needed, and they need to interact strongly.

Appreciative theorizing tends to be close to empirical work and provides both guidance and interpretation. Empirical findings seldom influence formal theorizing directly. Rather, in the first instance, they influence appreciative theory and, in turn, appreciative theory challenges formal theory to encompass these understandings in stylized form. The attempt to do so may identify gaps or inconsistencies in the verbal stories, or modeling may suggest new theoretical storylines to explore. In turn, the empirical research enterprise is reoriented.

Since Winter and I take seriously quite complex appreciative stories bearing on the phenomena in which we are interested, formal modeling in our work has taken on the role of serving as a vehicle for building a unified framework for exploring how different processes interact. In general our models have not aimed at explaining or exploring a single phenomenon but often a relatively large set. Thus in our formal model of economic growth we were, first of all, interested in finding out whether an evolutionary model was capable of generating and explaining the kind of macroeconomic time series that was the focus of neoclassical growth theory. But we also were interested in knowing whether that model could generate something like the quite dispersed distribution of productivity levels across firms that industry-level analysis had revealed and that was repressed in neoclassical models. We wondered if it would create S-shaped diffusion curves. We were curious whether the model could generate the distribution of firm sizes that had been explored and analyzed by several industrial organization economists. There were a considerable number of parameters in our model, and we found that by setting these in the appropriate ways our model could generate all of these phenomena. This we regarded as its most important virtue and the strongest evidence that it was capturing important elements of actual dynamic processes.

In contrast, the "evolutionary" models that have been constructed by economists interested in dynamic increasing returns have been rather narrowly pointed at one or a very small number of phenomena. The question has been whether a simple model could explain a small number of things. This certainly is an important role of modeling. However, I think there is great value in treating clusters of economic phenomena that seem to be connected within a single broad model. Where several processes seem to be operative at once, I think it is important to treat these together and to explore how they interact.

This approach would seem fruitful for exploration of a number of interesting questions. One is what it takes for a new, potentially superior, substitute technology to take root given the presence of an entrenched industry backed by a strong support system. Another is how comparative advantage shifts when the old leaders possess considerable advantages in the competition, at least at the early stages. In a way these are both "infant industry" or "infant firm" questions. What keeps the new infants alive and growing until they can stand on their own?

More generally, when there is competition among broadly different technologies and their associated organizations and institutions, what determines which one wins? Economists have been inclined to argue that relative economic efficiency, in a broad sense, almost always is determining. However, when there are dynamic increasing returns, this argument becomes at best complex and at worst empty.

Exploring issues like these requires both modeling and detailed empirical investigation. Linking the two and, in my view, the principal way economists structure their understanding, are our stories. Good stories in these areas are going to have to be both evolutionary stories, in the broad sense that Winter and I have used the term, and increasing-return stories, in the sense of that new work. The combination could be very powerful.

Some Elements of an Evolutionary Theory of Organizational Competences

Giovanni Dosi and Luigi Marengo

Only recently has the economic theory of the firm begun to address the issue of the role of different organizational structures. Traditionally, the neoclassical theory explained all economic phenomena in terms of individual agents (households or firms) and markets, which through the price mechanism convey all the information necessary to individual decision making and therefore coordinate all interactions among individuals.

The basic tenets of neoclassical theory are summarized with remarkable clarity by Arrow (1974a, 1–3):

> The neoclassical model is founded on two concepts, which are considerably different in nature. One is the notion of the individual economic agent, whose behavior is governed by a criterion of optimization under constraints which are partly peculiar to the agent, such as production functions, and partly terms of trade with the economic system as a whole. The other is the market; here the aggregate of individual decisions is acknowledged, and the terms of trade adjusted until the decisions of the individuals are mutually consistent in the aggregate, i.e., supply equals demand.

Indeed, the reduction of rationality to maximization makes it possible for the neoclassical economist to ignore the psychological and cognitive aspects of decision making (Simon 1976): the rationality of a decision resides solely in the optimality of the decision itself, regardless of the procedure that led to it. Symmetrically, the reduction of all coordination modes to the market—exemplified by the general equilibrium theory but also, in strategic contexts, by most game-theoretical models—brings the issue of organization outside the domain of economic theory: organizations such as firms might indeed exist, but their internal structure is immaterial for the allocation of resources at the level of the entire economic system.

Recent streams of research, e.g., Williamson (1975, 1985), Sah and Stiglitz (1986), Crémer (1980), and Aoki (1986, 1988), have progressively challenged the latter assumption and analyzed coordination modes different from that of the market. Aoki, in particular, has extensively studied the potential for learning within and resource generation of different organizational setups. However, the primary emphasis of most of these studies is upon learning in activities involving information processing, which can be fundamentally reduced to Bayesian estimation of random variables with stationary means and finite variance. Certainly, along these lines of research, major progress has been made in highlighting the different efficiency properties of alternative combinations of market mechanisms and hierarchies in the organization of economic activities.

In essence, whenever one abandons the most restrictive assumptions on information perfectness and symmetry among agents, organizational forms do matter because incentives, information flows, and behaviors differ according to the particular "institutional architecture" of each system. In particular, if each system's performance rests on specific learning dynamics by individuals or groups of them (such as "firms"), the institutional architecture affects the scope and rate at which such learning can occur. Even more so, all of this applies whenever one considers environments characterized by permanent opportunities for technological and organizational innovation.

As argued elsewhere, for example, Dosi (1988) and Dosi and Egidi (1991), innovative activities involve also a kind of learning quite different from Bayesian probability updating and regression estimation: it requires agents to build new representations of the environment they operate in (and that remains largely unknown) and develop new skills enabling them both to explore and to exploit this world of ever-expanding opportunities (Nelson and Winter 1982).

The Notion of Competence

To introduce the notion of competence, one may begin with the puzzle posed by the quite robust piece of empirical evidence that suggests that firms do *persistently* differ in their characteristics, behaviors, and performances. It is a piece of evidence that has been intuitively obvious for a long time to managers, business analysts, and consultants alike. However, these phenomena are also increasingly "tested" according to criteria that satisfy the requirements of the economic profession, and efforts are being made to explain them with a variety of theoretical tools.

Mentions of the evidence here need only be very telegraphic. For example, firms—*even within the same industry*—differ in terms of their propensities to commit resources to innovation and imitation. They differ in their revealed successes in developing and adopting new products, new production processes, and new organizational setups (Freeman 1982; Dosi 1988). They also differ—*also within the same line of business*—in terms of unit costs of production and their profitabilities (Rumelt 1988 and, for a somewhat different interpretation, Schmalensee 1985). Moreover, among firms (often operating in different lines of business) profit differentials are quite persistent over time (Geroski and Jacquemin 1984; Mueller 1986). Finally, differences in innovativeness and production efficiency, although not necessarily in profitability, are even more pronounced and persistent in international comparisons (Patel and Pavitt 1988).

What has economic theory to say about these observations? As is well known, many theoretical accounts with some bearing on this evidence have been proposed over the last decade or so. In a rather sketchy way, we could group them into two different streams. A first class of theoretical interpretations suggests that either asymmetries among firms are wrongly inferred from the data or that they are indeed epiphenomena. For example, interfirm differences in innovation and timing of adoption are explained primarily as the outcome of *equilibrium* strategic interactions. If this were the case, one could account for residual diversity as temporary disequilibrium phenomena. However, persistence of technological or economic asymmetries is strikingly at odds with this kind of interpretation. A second stream of analysis, often in combination with the former, acknowledges various forms of interfirm diversity and explains them in terms of: (1) different utility functions—mainly intertemporal preferences and risk-aversions; (2) different endowments in some production and innovating skills; and (3) asymmetric information.

Let us focus primarily on points (2) and (3) of the latter interpretation. Suppose that the comparison between the performance of two firms (or groups of them) shows a systematic difference. For example, one of them could show systematically higher rates of innovation. But this would not be sufficient to suggest an asymmetry between the two: the other firm could follow an equilibrium strategy of imitation, given some appropriate difference between average costs of innovation and imitation. However, the first one could also be systematically more profitable, while the second subsisted permanently on the verge of bankruptcy. What do we make of all that? Most likely there is an underlying asymmetry between them. Ruling out differences in utility functions and expectations—easy to claim but also ad hoc unobservable—most economists would base their explanation on differences in endowments and/or asymmetric information.

The main points of the "endowments" explanation could be summarized as follows. Individuals and organizations are highly bounded in their performances by their inner features (something analogous to their "genes") but they do not exhibit, ex ante, what they are. The actual process of interaction among agents is in fact a sort of tournament that allows the "inherently best" to emerge as winners (Jovanovic 1982; Lucas 1978). Alternatively, the "asymmetric information" explanation would roughly claim that individuals and organizations, though having virtually similar performance potentials, happen to face asymmetric access to information and therefore reveal, ex post, systematically different performances.

We do not intend to deny the importance of asymmetries in endowments and in access to information. However, we believe that a large class of features exists that characterizes and distinguishes firms that cannot be reduced to either category. Indeed, we propose that competences cannot be reduced to either endowments or information partitions, but represent the *problem-solving features of particular sets of organizational interactions, norms, and*—to some extent—*explicit strategies*. Competences present a significant degree of inertia and firm-specificity. Thus, as a first approximation, they could be considered as firm-specific assets but unlike "endowments" are subject to learning and change through their very application to actual problem solving. Similarly, they share with information partitions the fact that being more competent also implies, loosely speaking, a greater control upon the environment wherein the firm operates. However, competences do not necessarily increase as information becomes more perfect. There are fundamental elements of learning and innovation that concern much more the *representation* of the environment in which individuals and organizations operate and *problem solving* rather than simple information gathering and processing.

Let us illustrate these points by means of a metaphor. What does being a good soccer player mean? Certainly there is a strong "endowment" component. However, the number of those who succeed is most likely much lower than the set of those endowed with an adequate potential. Ultimately, success depends on training, the sequence of teams the individual has played for, his or her coaches, and, last but not least, on chance. In this example one can easily identify some basic features: (1) the existence of some learning process, (2) a puzzling difficulty in stating the exact procedures of this learning, and (3) different performance outcomes that can hardly be attributed to ex-ante recognizable differences in the features of the agents or differences in the environmental stimuli to which they have been exposed.

Competence and Decision Making

In order to clarify what a "competence" is, it might be useful to start from a relatively standard decision-theoretic representation of an agent or a firm. The existing theory of decision making, on which most of the economic theories of the firm are based, characterizes each decision maker by his or her own information partition, which constitutes the decision maker's information processing capabilities. In other words, this information partition embodies the agent's knowledge about the environment in which he or she is operating, his or her "model of the world." Such an information partition is the frame through which the agent can classify the information received from the environment and compute the probabilities according to which conceivable events are expected to take place. Bayes's rule is the rational way of coherently incorporating new information within such a frame, and maximization of expected utility is the rational criterion for taking a decision that is coherent with the probability distribution.

Two key, but often implicit, hypotheses are made about this information partition. First, it is assumed, by definition, to be a partition, which involves postulating consistency and even isomorphism between the real world and the agent's model of it. Agents may differ only because they have "finer" or "coarser" partitions, meaning that they can be more or less precise in responding to events. However, mistakes, surprises, and inconsistencies are all ruled out. Second, the partition is assumed as given, and the study of the decision process is limited to the study of the rules that optimize the use of information within such a frame. It can be contended instead that a crucial part of the decision process is the construction, evaluation, and modification of the frame of reference itself. This very process can be defined as *learning*. Bayesian learning is instead the use of new information in order to update the present probability distribution, within a given and constant frame of reference.[1]

As far as decision making is concerned, this perspective clearly implies a shift of attention away from the objective validity of the rules that determine the optimum use of information and the optimum action toward the *procedures* used by the agents to improve their understanding of reality (Simon 1976). Moreover, whereas with information partitions, more information always means better decisions (or at least not worse ones), without partitions, more information can also lead to worse decisions (Geanakoplos 1990).

This applies to individuals and, a fortiori, to organizations such as firms. Basically, the firm is seen in most of present-day economic theory as an information-processing unit, although the presence of a multiplicity of agents with information asymmetries raises complex questions about the design of coordination and incentive schemes that can efficiently allocate information

---

1. Bayesian decision making reduces all uncertainty to mere risk. It cannot account therefore for another fundamental source of uncertainty: ignorance. On one side there is the uncertainty deriving from the intrinsic randomness of the phenomena the decision maker faces: this kind of uncertainty cannot be entirely eliminated by the decision maker and is adequately handled within the framework of probability theory. But, on the other hand, there exists also the uncertainty that derives from the agent's ignorance of the characteristics of the world he or she is facing. This kind of uncertainty instead can be reduced by the agent through the improvement of his or her own state of knowledge, that is, by what we properly call "learning" in this work.

among them. Thus, differences in efficiency among firms are reduced to differences in their "endowments," i.e., in the information partitions of their members and in the ability of their executives to efficiently allocate information by designing and running appropriate coordination and incentive schemes.

Our perspective characterizes instead firms mainly as *learning organizations*, where the set of "opportunities" open to the organization is not assumed as being known to the decision makers and, therefore, where the members' and the organization's information-processing capabilities and the very decision rules cannot be postulated but are generated and coevolve in a process of learning and adaptation. In other words, organizational knowledge is neither presupposed nor derived from the available information but rather emerges as a property of the learning system and is shaped by the interaction among the various learning processes that constitute the organization.

This interpretation implies a radical shift in the object of analysis. Rather than analyzing the signals that the environment delivers to the unit of decision, it focuses on the inner features of the response mechanisms of the unit itself. It is a perspective that clearly goes back to Simon, Cyert, March, Nelson, and Winter—i.e., to what is often referred to as "bounded rationality" and the "behavioral theory of the firm." As these and other authors have repeatedly emphasized, the very definition of what information is relevant (before its collection, classification, and interpretation) might turn out to be highly problematic and "framed." Individuals and organizations most likely have only a modest control over the world and there may often be an essential ambiguity in the relationship between events, actions, and outcomes (March 1988a). Given all this, it is hard to postulate some invariant optimizing algorithm and to define it.

However, even when the existence of such an optimizing algorithm can be established, its derivation from the available (even perfect) information might still prove problematic. In Dosi and Egidi (1991) the solution of a Rubik cube is considered as a simple and archetypical example. Given the initial configuration, the solution concept and the admissible rules ("information" in the sense of the foregoing decision-theoretic setup) are perfect: there is no environmental uncertainty and indeed there notionally exists a function that maps information into actions that maximize utility (say, by minimizing the number of moves leading to the solution). However, *finding* that optimal procedure or, for that matter, any procedure is precisely the crucial task.

The following should be noted: (1) This is a pure problem-solving task quite independent of any further interaction with the external environment. (2) Despite the known existence of an algorithm, it is no trivial task and in fact many people do give up. (3) It can be shown that human subjects develop *higher-level rules* in order to solve it—rules that are underivable from the original information about the problem itself, that apply to a whole set of initial configurations (i.e., they are *robust* to changes in the initial information), and that can be automatized as *routines*. We believe that this is a highly simplified metaphor of individual problem solving and, even more so, of firms as problem solvers.

"Competences" here are viewed as the properties of the solution procedures. Each set of rules or algorithm may well be different, with different revealed efficiencies, without, however, the possibility of defining ex ante the optimal one and without even the possibility of determining *in general* whether any such algorithm exists before having found it. Both, in fact, are well-known results of computation theory on problem solving. In the foregoing representation of the decision problem, the partition on the set of states of the world and the solution concept are formally equivalent to finite strings of information.

Finding maps from states of the world into action means finding a Turing machine that rewrites the information string into the solution string with a finite set of transformations (Dosi and Egidi 1991). A powerful impossibility theorem from computation theory states that there is no general algorithm that can always decide whether two strings are derivable one from another after a finite sequence of admissible transformations. In other words, there cannot be any general problem-solving algorithm (Cutland 1980). Or, putting it in yet another way, information about states of the world, solution concepts, and admitted rules—no matter how "perfect"—are by themselves insufficient to automatically derive *in general terms* any solution algorithm and hence, a fortiori, the optimal one. In order to do so, one requires also some form of preexisting *knowledge* and some imperfectly definable procedures, which are usually the product of inferential induction, analogy, and problem framing but also of socially constructed norms and bodies of knowledge.

What do we make of all this from the point of view of positive theories of behavior and decision making of individuals and organizations? One epistemology consists in postulating that individuals and organizations do prepossess all the knowledge appropriate to most relevant economic decisions and also that they have already worked out the problem-solving algorithm. Hence, no issue of "competence" arises. The heavy assumption here is that proving an existence theorem requires some innate cognitive and computational endowment of the agents to work out the appropriate algorithm in order to get to the place where the theorem states it is optimal for the agents to be, given the available information.[2]

A second possible approach is to explicitly acknowledge "bounded rationality": memory and the other computational resources are finite, and recur-

---

2. Incidentally, an increasing stream of theoretical results shows that many familiar equilibrium concepts are recursively noncomputable (Lewis 1985, 1986).

sive computability represents the "upper bound" to the perfection of the decision procedures that agents are allowed to possess. Indeed, suggestive results have been recently achieved on the grounds of this methodology, especially in game theory. For example, by assuming that agents are bound to choose sets of algorithmic rules in their interactions,[3] it can be shown that the set of possible equilibria significantly changes as compared to unrestricted rationality setups (e.g., Rubinstein 1986; Abreu and Rubinstein 1988).

This notwithstanding, a lingering issue concerns the procedure by which agents "choose" their appropriate algorithm (i.e., their automaton). In a sense, the question of whether or not agents possess the "competence" appropriate to the solution of the problem they face is only pushed to some meta-level. By assuming that agents possess different and well-constructed (albeit computationally finite) procedures and can choose among them, one attributes to them all the appropriate "competence" to work them out and select them. From a computational point of view, this implies that agents are assumed to possess some unspecified "correct" heuristics of choice among different automata. In turn, this implies—at the very least—a very strong interpretation of Simonian "procedural rationality." Comparisons among alternative algorithms plausibly ought to imply that "problem solving is viewed as *nearly decomposable*, meaning that for the most part each subgoal can be solved without knowledge of the other subgoals of the system" (Forrest 1990, 7).

We want to argue here for a third perspective implying an even more radical departure from the standard representation of rationality. It develops recent modeling on "emergent computation" (Holland et al. 1986; Forrest 1990) and in its spirit directly connects with the analyses of corporate decisions and behaviors by March, Nelson and Winter, and many organizational theorists.

To put it briefly, suppose that—no matter how perfect information is— agents do not prepossess the appropriate "problem solver." Suppose also that the space of "opportunities" is incompletely known by the agents and is possibly modified by their own actions. Finally, suppose that agents start from very simple and rudimentary rules, by themselves inadequate to the solution tasks. Our conjecture is that the problem-solving procedures are emergent properties of interactions, involving also mutation and recombination of these distributed basic rudimentary rules, often drawing on related but hardly codifiable knowledge, experience, and interpretation frames.

The crucial point of this perspective is that learning involves adaptation and discovery of problem-solving procedures that cannot be automatically derived either from the information about the states of the world or from the

---

3. This assumption is usually formalized by such finite automata as "Moore machines."

solution concept. The empirical counterpart of these problem-solving procedures comprises organizational tasks ranging from how to design a product and manufacture it efficiently to how to penetrate new markets—that is, most of the activities of business firms. A few important implications follow from this view of the firm.

First, the difference between the *process* and the *content* of learning is a blurred one, a point repeatedly emphasized by Nelson and Winter (1982) and also in Dosi, Teece, and Winter (1991) and Pavitt (1990a). What a firm "knows" is mainly stored in its behavioral rules and is reproduced, augmented, changed via the actual implementation of such problem-solving routines.

Second, "competences" summarize the effectiveness of firm-specific problem-solving procedures. The "dynamic competences" discussed by Teece et al. (1990) concern higher-level procedures, namely those related to the search for *new problems* and *new problem-solving procedures* (after all, this is an essential part of technological and organizational innovation). Hence, loosely speaking, competences relate to both "being good at doing certain things" and "being good at learning certain things."

Third, this focus on firms as problem solvers may be taken as somewhat complementary to the view of Williamson (1990) that firms are economizers on the costs of transactions. The fundamental divide is between a representation of firms primarily in terms of strategizing versus a representation in terms of learning and economizing. The first view in its essence proposes that firms, *by assumption*, have got their problem-solving procedures and their hierarchical structure right and, therefore, that their primary activity involves playing complicated and devious games with each other. On the contrary, we would argue the latter view to the extreme and claim that most of firms' activities concern *games against nature*, in which strategic interactions induce only relatively minor fluctuations.[4]

The strategic view concentrates on equilibrium interactions among firms,

---

4. Similar remarks were made by Sidney Winter during the conference on "Fundamental Issues in Strategy: A Research Agenda for the 1990's," Napa Valley, California, 1990. To illustrate, in the latter perspective a car manufacturer tries primarily to develop a new type of car with a quality as high as possible and costs as low as possible: the primary activities involve understanding changing consumers' preferences, developing new electronic gadgets, building and learning how to use new machinery, organizing production, etc. Looking at competitors is important mainly to learn from their own problem-solving procedures, but in a first approximation everyone is playing games against nature wherein subtle strategizing has only second-order effects. Conversely, the "strategizing view" would suggest that every competitor notionally knows how to make a new car or a new microprocessor equally well (or at least knows equally well how to draw from a stochastic process such as the "patent race"). Differences are mainly the outcome of complicated strategizing (e.g., preemptive investment) or chance.

on the assumption that each of them is *internally* optimally adjusted, while in the learning perspective the primary explanation of what firms do relates to what goes on *within* them.

Some of these analytically conflicting views could be settled, in principle, on empirical grounds: e.g., what is the variance of interfirm, intraindustry performance that is left unexplained after allowing for the effect of different governance structures? How far can one go in explaining different competences by assimilating them to identifiable assets, however defined? But, of course, even if one subscribes, in a first approximation, to a "learning" or "dynamic competence" view of the firm, a more satisfactory picture would be a model that embodies other corporate functions that have traditionally been the major focus of other theories.

The model of the firm described here suggests that it is a *behavioral entity* (Kreps 1990a) embodying highly *idiosyncratic, specific, and inertial compromises* between different functions, namely: (1) resource allocation; (2) information processing; (3) incentives to individual performance; (4) control and power exercise; and (5) learning.

Remarkably, most breeds of economic theory focus primarily upon one single function, often trying to explain it on the grounds of the usual maximization cum equilibrium assumptions. The perspective proposed here, on the contrary, embodies fundamental trade-offs between the functions mentioned above (e.g., Aoki and Dosi 1991). To illustrate them in a somewhat caricatural way, think of the possible trade-offs between performance control and learning. While the former is likely to imply rigid task specification, the latter generally involves a lot of experimentation, trial and error, and "deviant" behavior.

Competence, Learning, and Organization

We would like to suggest that the notion of competence does not involve only problem-solving skills, concerning the relationship between the firm and the outside environment, but also skills and rules governing internal relationships. The two are strictly interconnected: the rates and direction of learning are shaped by the internal norms of behavior of individual organizations.

Holland et al. (1986) examine the key characteristics of a learning process. As already pointed out, learning takes place in the space of *representations* and cannot be reduced to mere information gathering. In a complex and ever-changing world, agents must define sets of states that they consider as equivalent for the purpose of action. In other words, they have to build representations of the world in order to discover regularities that can be exploited by their actions. These representations have a pragmatic nature and are contingent upon the particular purpose the routine is serving. Second, learning is essentially driven by the search for a better performance. The learning agent must therefore use some system of *performance assessment*. Finally, if rules of behavior have to be selected, added, modified, and deleted, there must exist a procedure for the *evaluation of the usefulness* of the rules. This problem might not have a clear solution when the performance of the system may be assessed only as a result of a long and complex sequence of interdependent rules (such as in the game of chess).

These questions arise in every learning system, individual or organizational. But when learning takes place within a multiagent setting, it requires the coordination of the learning processes of many individuals. This poses some additional questions about representations, performance assessment, and rule evaluation within an organizational context.

Members of an organization will in general have different representations of the environment they are facing. This multiplicity of representations requires the implementation of some mechanisms whose task is to reconcile actual or potential conflicts.

Mechanisms of this kind can be considered from at least two perspectives. The first is a "cognitive" one. From this perspective, conflict resolution requires the definition of a common knowledge basis, a "shared representation" of some parts of the environment that takes the form of a collection of organizational facts, codes, and languages whose meaning is clear to all members of the organization and that enables communication and coordination among them. As with individual representations, organizational common knowledge and languages will also be contingent upon the particular purposes they serve.

The second perspective is a "political" one and encompasses all the procedures that define and govern hierarchical relations inside the organization.[5] It is important to stress that the cognitive and the political aspects of coordination mechanisms are strictly interconnected and cannot be distinguished: the relations that shape the organizational knowledge basis are the same as those that define the hierarchical structure of the organization.

If the multiplicity of representations, on the one hand, raises the problem of coordination in organizational learning, it might also be a source of learning if the resulting variety of organizational knowledge can be exploited. In general there will be a trade-off between the two aspects of multiplicity: on the one side, coordination benefits from a large and consistent "shared representation"; on the other side, commonality of knowledge reduces the scope for learning from diversity.

In addition to a multiplicity of representations, collective decision mak-

---

5. This perspective lies behind the conception of organizational routines as a "truce" among conflicting intraorganizational interests (Nelson and Winter 1982, 107–12).

ing is usually characterized by a multiplicity of systems of preferences. Members of an organization have different goals, which must be harmonized in some way.

It is worth mentioning that assuming multiplicity of representations complicates even more the problem of the multiplicity of preferences. Not only do preferences among states vary across members, but the same state might be differently perceived by different members, making performance assessment highly complicated. Cohen (1987) provides an example: the present state of the firm may be perceived by a functional unit as "we are in our third successive quarter of increasing market share" and by another as "we are in our third successive quarter of decreasing return on capital." Even if the two functional units shared the same system of preferences, their assessments of the present performance of the firm would turn out to be divergent.

Similar problems arise when one tries to evaluate the contribution of single decisions to a complex and interconnected set of actions leading to a certain organizational outcome. Divergent representations and divergent systems of preferences make this evaluation even more complex than in the case of individual decision makers, where already no unique solution seems possible.

As Cohen (1984) pointed out, looking at the incentive problem from a static optimizing or a learning point of view may lead to very different conclusions. From the former perspective, diversity of representations and goals leads to inefficiency and suboptimality ("loss of control"), whereas from the latter perspective diversity of representations and preferences enhances organizational adaptability and learning. All in all, there is no reason why, in general, efficient design of hierarchical structures for allocation and control should coincide with effective design for learning.

Organizations achieve coordination through the definition of a common set of rules, codes, and languages that are well understood and shared by all the members of the organization involved in a given interaction. Such a set is termed by Crémer (1990, 54) "corporate culture" and defined as "the stock of knowledge which is common to a substantial portion of the employees of the firm, but not to the general population from which they are drawn." Organizations are social institutions that shape, preserve, and modify this common knowledge basis.

Let us consider an organizational decision problem where the outcome for the organization depends on the actions of several agents in a nonadditive way. The information-processing capabilities of the members of the organization do not necessarily represent a partition of the set of states of the world but are, more generally, a subset of the power set of the states of the world.[6] A

---

6. Recent critiques of and extensions to the theory of probability, such as fuzzy probabilities and the theory of evidence (e.g., Dubois and Prade 1987), which provide a formal

fortiori, the information-processing capabilities of different members of the organization generally will neither coincide nor be compatible (meaning that given two information partitions, either they are equal or one can be obtained from the other by simply refining or coarsening some information cells).

If agents shared the same model of the world or knew each other's model, the only obstacle to effective coordination would derive from some form of lack, bias, or strategic use of information. In a world instead where decision makers do not entirely share a given model and do not know a priori each other's models, a common knowledge basis must be developed that enables agents to communicate effectively and eventually achieve coordination. If, for instance, one part of the organization communicates to another that, to the best of its knowledge, the present state of the world is X and such communication is truthful (and known as such to the other), the meaning of such a piece of information can still be misunderstood because the receiver has a different information-processing capability than the sender.[7] For example, the proposition "the state of the world is X" can have for the receiver a different meaning (when the considered subset of the states of the world's power set is not the same for the two agents) or even no meaning at all (when X does not exist in the receiver's information-processing capabilities).

As far as organizational decision making is concerned, the problem is therefore first of all to build a common knowledge basis, a common language that enables communication and coordination. At the same time members of the organization, who are involved in learning, do modify their own knowledge basis. Individual knowledge and organizational knowledge *coevolve* through a process of *mutual adaptation*.

In game theory, common knowledge expresses the concept that a group of people know some facts, each of them knows that the others know, each of them knows that the others know that they know, and so on ad infinitum. It is well known that such a chain of conditions leads either to an infinite regress or to a logical contradiction (Gilboa 1988) and that therefore this kind of common knowledge can ultimately only be postulated and not deduced from the agents' information-processing capabilities.

These considerations cast strong doubts on the validity of the neoclassical reduction of the firm to an optimum bundle of contracts that can be entirely deduced from the members' rational interaction. The firm appears on the contrary as a social institution, formed indeed by individuals, but not entirely "transparent" to their rational introspection. People do coordinate their actions and base such coordination on a common knowledge basis that allows them to form correct expectations about each other's behavior and to

---

framework for the treatment of subjective uncertain knowledge, are based on this very representation of the subjective state of knowledge.

7. Similar concepts are expressed in Arrow's (1974b) discussion of the issue of "coding."

"close" the chain of speculations on each other's actions that would be unsolvable on the grounds of mere rationality. Such a common knowledge basis is formed by and *evolves* through the interaction of individual knowledge bases but cannot be reduced entirely to them. It takes the form of social institutions, such as conventions, rules, languages, culture, etc., which embed, preserve, and modify the amount of social knowledge that makes coordination possible.

Marengo (1992) has developed a simulation model of organizational decision making and learning in which the members of the organization do not possess any prior knowledge of the environment they are facing, let alone a given common partition of the states of the world. At every moment in time, each member's state of knowledge is represented by a subset of the power set of states of the world. This very state of knowledge is modified through a process of learning and adaptation, which is driven exclusively by the search for a higher organizational payoff, according to a methodology derived from the classifier systems (Holland 1986; Holland et al. 1986).

Suppose that the members of the organization observe independently the state of the world and do not communicate among themselves. Simulations show that coordination cannot emerge, even in the simplest case where the state of the world is held constant throughout the entire simulation. Such a negative result is obvious when we consider that agents cannot, in these conditions, make any connection between states of the world, action, and payoff, since the latter depends on the other agents' actions as well.

But consider now another agent, whose task is to observe and forecast the state of the world and send a unique message to the other agents, who will now receive only this message and will not directly observe the state of the world. Let us again suppose that this higher-level agent (let us call it "management"[8]) is, like the other ones, completely ignorant at the outset and refines its knowledge according exclusively to the organizational payoff.

Simulations show that in this case coordination can indeed emerge. It may appear as surprising that such a different behavior can emerge since in both cases the members of the organization still observe a unique external message and do not communicate with each other. (Actually in both cases they are not even aware of each other's existence.) The difference is that now the message that is received is not fixed but adapts to the receivers' capabilities of interpreting and using the message itself. In other words, the system builds an internal *language*, a *common knowledge* basis that adapts to and coevolves with the information-processing capabilities of both the management and the other decision units.

A few observations are due on the nature of this language. First, the language has a pragmatic nature. It is developed to help solve a particular

---

8. It could be called, more generally, "institution."

problem and to serve a particular state of cognitive capabilities of both the broadcaster and the receiver. Therefore, the language cannot be directly transferred to another problem or another organization. Second, the very semantic content of the language and the level of understanding of reality that the common knowledge basis embeds are themselves strictly adapted to the problem that is being faced and to the characteristics of the agent's cognitive capabilities. For example, if the state of the world remains constant and the agents are not pursuing a refinement of their information-processing capabilities, they develop a "minimal" language—a single message for all the possible situations—that embeds no understanding at all of the environment but is perfectly apt to promote coordination in the case.

Marengo (1992) considers the role of the structure of the organization in shaping and modifying such an organizational knowledge basis. Organizational structures are characterized by their degrees of centralization/decentralization in the formation and use of knowledge. Suppose again that the organization must adapt its decisions to an environment whose characteristics are not known a priori and that the organizational outcome depends on the actions of all the members in some nonadditive way. At the same time, suppose also that comprehensive detailed planning is not feasible, so that the members of the organization always have some degree of discretion in their decisions.

One way of achieving coordination is by centralizing the formation of an organizational model of the world coadapted with the members' capabilities to interpret it. On the other hand, the formation of such a model can be entirely decentralized, by allowing all the members to observe independently the environment and exchange messages in order to negotiate a common interpretation. Between these two cases—complete centralization and complete decentralization—there exists a range of intermediate ones. For instance, it is possible to centralize the formation of the model of the world but allow subordinate units to communicate and coordinate actions via horizontal communication. Or it is possible both to allow subordinate units to form their own autonomous model of the world and to have at the same time a competing centralized model that preserves the coherence of the organization.

Simulations allow us to test the learning performance of these different organizational structures in different environmental conditions, characterized by varying degrees of being stationary and regular. If the state of the world remains stationary, "simpler" structures such as the completely centralized and the completely decentralized ones are faster in achieving coordination, while changing environmental conditions and the need for reorganizing routines that have already been accumulated through past experience favor structures where forms of centralization and decentralization coexist.

In particular, when environmental changes follow some regular and detectable pattern, the discovery and exploitation of such regularities seem to require organizational structures that allow subordinate units to form autonomous models of the world but make them coherent through a centrally defined organizational model. In fact, to exploit a regularly changing environment, a large amount of knowledge about the environment is required: the organizational knowledge basis must distinguish between the states of the world and connect them diachronically. By partly decentralizing the acquisition of knowledge about the environment, it is possible to achieve higher levels of sophistication in the organizational model of the world, provided the coordination mechanisms—which are centralized—are powerful enough to enable the organization to solve conflicts of representations.

On the other hand, this very decentralization of the acquisition of knowledge can be a source of loss when it is more profitable for the organization to cling to a robust, stable set of routines. Therefore, when environmental changes are unpredictable but within predictable limits, decentralization of the accumulation of knowledge can only disrupt organizational coherence around a robust set of routines. This situation requires strong coordination in order to make the entire organization implement coherently such a set of robust routines and favors structures that centralize the accumulation of knowledge and emphasize horizontal coordination around a unique central body of knowledge.

Ultimately there appears to be a tension between the necessity of "keeping together" the organization and allowing diversity of experimentation. This topic will be further examined in the next section.

Exploitation vs. Exploration in Organizational Learning

We have already hinted at the fact that one of the crucial problems in organizational learning is the trade-off between exploitation of the available knowledge and exploration of new possibilities. Exploitation of the available knowledge involves refinement of the available technology, learning by doing, improvement of the division of labor, and all the activities oriented toward the search for higher efficiency. Exploration involves innovation, search for novelty, risk-taking, and all the activities oriented toward the discovery of new opportunities.

Successful organizations must combine exploitation and exploration, since both of them are vital. As March (1990, 1) puts it: "[Organizations] that engage in exploration to the exclusion of exploitation are likely to find that they suffer the costs of experimentation without gaining many of its benefits. They exhibit too many undeveloped new ideas and too little distinctive competence. Conversely, . . . [organizations] that engage in exploitation to the exclusion of exploration are likely to find themselves trapped in suboptimal stable equilibria."

Exploration and exploitation activities compete for scarce resources, and only in a few circumstances is it possible to discern clearly which organizational functions are oriented toward the exploitation of existing knowledge and which are instead oriented toward the generation of new competences. The problem has been tackled by statistical decision theory by means of such models as the "two-armed bandit" problem. Suppose we have a slot machine with two arms, A and B, and suppose that we know that one of the two arms—but we do not know which one—gives a higher average reward. The player therefore faces the problem of collecting information in order to infer which arm is associated with the higher payoff. Two possible sources of loss can merge: on the one hand the collection of information involves the allocation of some trials to the inferior arm, and on the other hand, there is always the risk of choosing as the most profitable arm the one that is actually inferior. If the decision maker tries to reduce the first source of loss by decreasing the number of experiments and clinging to the best observed arm, he will inevitably increase the chances of selecting the inferior arm. Vice versa, the chances of selecting the inferior arm can be reduced only by collecting more information about both arms and thus increasing the loss that derives from the trials allocated to the inferior arm.

Statistical decision theory has approached this trade-off by dichotomizing exploration and exploitation: the agent first performs a series of trials whose purpose is to collect information and then sticks irreversibly to the arm that appears to be the best one according to collected information. There exist several problems with this decision-theoretic approach. First of all, it assumes that the decision maker knows the alternatives among which the choice has to be made. In most real-life situations the problem of exploration is not just one of computing the statistics that characterize the distribution of some variables known as relevant, but rather one of discovery and definition of the alternatives themselves. Furthermore, the probability distributions may themselves depend on the actions of the decision makers: positive feedbacks, network externalities, and learning by doing make the profitability of the various alternatives depend on the decision maker's and other agents' actions. Finally, in most economic decisions there exist strong irreversibilities: the resources committed to an alternative cannot be cheaply redeployed.

All these complications make the maximization approach inadequate to give an account of most actual economic decisions. Another approach is instead based on bounded rationality and explains the balance between exploitation and exploration by referring to targets and aspiration levels. This approach is at the heart of the evolutionary theory of the firm presented in

Nelson and Winter (1982): firms stick to the present routine whenever the economic result remains above a certain target level. Only when the payoff falls below the target do firms engage in exploration for better alternatives. Targets and aspiration levels may in turn be subject to adaptation and change according to experience and imitation of other agents (March 1988a).

Actually, the separation between routine and search behavior can be somewhat misleading, especially when we consider organizational learning. Ultimately, the problem of the balance between exploitation and exploration becomes one of balance between the process of *selection* and the process of *mutation* in an evolutionary system. Within organizations, these two processes normally coexist and interact at different levels: one of the strengths of organizations is their capability of flexibly combining procedures for selection and procedures for innovation. Fast-learning and slow-learning individuals and departments can coexist. Innovation itself can become a largely routinized process, though uncertain in its outcome. Learning by doing can add exploratory value to normally exploitive activities.

March (1990, 7–8) stresses the importance of the social context in which organizational learning takes place. A "distinctive feature of the social context . . . is the mutual learning of an organization and the individuals in it. Organizations store knowledge in their procedures, norms, rules, and forms. They accumulate such knowledge over time, learning from their members. At the same time, individuals in an organization are socialized to organizational beliefs."

Such mutual learning is fundamental for the trade-off between exploration and exploitation in organizations. A high degree of differentiation of knowledge among the members of an organization increases the total amount of knowledge possessed by the organization. But differentiation makes coordination more difficult and ultimately can inhibit the social exploitation of this knowledge basis. On the contrary, a widely held body of organizational knowledge facilitates coordination and specialization but reduces the scope for decentralized experimentation, which could prove a vital source of organizational learning.

The framework outlined so far can help cast some light on the relevance of this trade-off. Consider an organizational structure where subordinate units receive and interpret two kinds of messages: one from the environment, which allows them to build their own independent knowledge about the world in which the firm operates, and one from the management, which instead defines the organizational state on which they should coordinate their actions. The weights with which these two types of messages enter the shops' decision processes define the organizational balance between differentiation and commonality of knowledge. Simulations show (Marengo 1992) that flexible adaptation to a slowly and regularly changing environment requires local experimentation and differentiation of learning processes, provided that a minimum coordination is guaranteed by a simple set of commonly known rules. On the contrary, when environments are unpredictably changing within predictable limits, organizational performance increases with the increase of the degree of attention to the managerial messages, while it decreases with the degree of decentralized experimentation.

Hence, there exists a tension between centralization and decentralization in the organizational learning process. Firms require both centralization and decentralization to operate successfully in changing environments. Decentralization in the acquisition of knowledge is a source of variety and experimentation and, ultimately, a fundamental source of learning. But, eventually, knowledge has to be made available for exploitation to the entire organization. When agents differ with regard to their representations of the environment and their cognitive capabilities, there must exist an organizational body of knowledge that guarantees the coherence of the various learning processes. In order to cope with changing environments, the process of generation and modification of such a body of knowledge, although fed by the decentralized learning processes, has to undergo some form of centralization. Thus, a tension inevitably arises between the forces that keep the coherence of the organization and the forces that promote decentralized learning.

Some examples may help illustrate this point. Consider the development of the M-form corporate organization, especially in Anglo-Saxon countries, analyzed by Chandler (1962). Clearly, the "divisionalization" of activities grouped according to product/market characteristics implies decentralization of decision making and learning. However, note also that one requires a parallel centralization of strategic activities—and of the related learning process—in order to reproduce the long-term coherence of the firm and its ability to discover and exploit new opportunities for innovation and growth. In turn, as argued at greater length in Aoki and Dosi (1991), this involves a fundamental informational and competence dilemma. The ability to develop innovation with some bearing on the general organization and strategies of the firm differs from and indeed is likely to be separated from the ability to conduct "business as usual."

Thus, in the Anglo-Saxon M-form organization, with its high degrees of functional hierarchy and specialization, decisions concerning the direction of innovation search must be placed quite high in the ranks of strategic management. But, if this is so, where should one place, for example, R&D activities, given the relative *nonspecificity* that some innovative knowledge implies? Should one set them within divisions, making them more responsive to product/market learning, but possibly missing broader innovative opportunities? Or should one centralize them in corporate laboratories, which depend directly on strategic management? And in turn, how do strategic managers learn the required "special skills" of detecting and selecting technological and organizational innovations? In this respect, Pavitt (1990b) has argued that the very rigidity of Anglo-Saxon divisionalized profit centers and the lack of technical competence of most strategic managers in the Anglo-Saxon countries help to explain the weak performance of British and U.S. industries. However, even if this is the case, no easy alternative prescription can be suggested without having a more general model that connects changes in organization, innovative competences, and corporate performance.

Ideally, one would like to see this dynamics of competences and organizational forms explicitly embedded in an evolutionary model wherein firms both interact with each other and change their internal structures and behaviors. Admittedly, no one has fully done it yet. We can, however, put forward some conjectures and preliminary results.

Conclusions: Patterns of Learning and Selection

Let us recall three major "stylized facts." First, in cross-national comparisons, one observes significant differences in the typical patterns of corporate organization with respect to information flows, the structure of the incentives to the members of the organization, and, ultimately, the rates and directions of learning.

However, and second, individual sectors of economic activities seem to display rather typical forms of organization of production and learning, which appear to be rather invariant across countries.[9] So, for example, the organization of innovation and production in, say, machine tools is different from that in textiles and seems to proceed along patterns that seem to hold in Europe as well as in Japan and the United States. Third, firms show persistent differences in their internal organization and competences even within the same countries and the same production activities.

We suggest that the above analysis of the nature of competences and their relationships with organizational forms helps us to interpret all three sets of phenomena. Firms are behavioral entities whose competences, decision rules, and internal governance structures coevolve with the environment in which they are embedded. Nonetheless, organizational change, as well as technological learning, is highly path-dependent. The strength of norms, routines, and "corporate cultures" resides precisely in their persistence and reproduction over time. As sociologists and organizational theorists tell us, this inertia provides some degree of consistency among individual behaviors and motivation to action even if incentive compatibilities are much weaker than those prescribed by economic theory, and even if information partitions border

---

9. For evidence and taxonomical exercises, see Pavitt (1984) and Patel and Pavitt (1991).

complete ignorance. But precisely that same inertia makes organizational arrangements quite differentiated and often highly suboptimal in their ability to seize technological and market opportunities.

Environmental selection, in the form of differential economic performances, together with technological and organizational imitation, tend to reduce the variety of both technological and organizational innovations that emerge. However, the locality of learning, the "opaqueness" of the environment, and the positive feedbacks linking particular directions of technological learning with particular organizational setups all imply the persistence of different forms of corporate and industrial organization, even when, ex post, they yield different competitive performances. In a jargon more familiar to economists: as one can easily generate multiple equilibria stemming from nonconvexities and increasing returns in the space of technologies, so one can also easily conjecture multiple "organizational trajectories" stemming from organizational learning about norms, competences, and corporate structures.

These properties, of course, are consistent with the earlier observation on persistent diversity among firms. However, the observed variations in organizational and behavioral traits are not unbounded: the institutional and market environment in which each firm operates is likely to set some viability constraint on such a variety. In this respect, for instance, Aoki's interpretation of the differences between the "American" and the "Japanese" firm is nested in the conditions under which the incentive structure and information flows occurring within the firm appropriately match the incentives and information flows stemming from the relations between the firm and the markets for labor, products, and finance. In turn, the properties of the latter depend on their institutional design. Hence, as Aoki (1988) shows, the viability of each organizational form is determined by the incentive compatibility of the various notional combinations between internal governance structures and industry-finance links, mechanisms of labor mobility, and user-producer links. So, for example, decentralized learning within the firm in order to be incentive-compatible, as in the Japanese archetype, has to be matched by rank hierarchies in internal labor mobility and a relatively lower reliance on labor market mobility as compared to firms that rely on more centralized forms of information processing and decision making, as in the American archetype.

Our analysis of competence building and innovative exploration—as distinguished from sheer information processing—adds a new dimension to these viability requirements. In fact, in an innovative world, evolutionary viability[10] ought to imply also some incentives either within the firm or, more generally, in the economic system to "break the rules" and explore new

---

10. A somewhat similar notion of "viability" is used in a sequential neo-Austrian model by Amendola and Gaffard (1988).

technologies and forms of organization. In fact, in contemporary Western economies this is done by various combinations between specific provisions for innovative efforts within incumbent firms and via the birth of new firms (Aoki and Dosi 1991; Dosi 1990).

Note that the foregoing analysis of competence-building implies at a normative level a strong argument in favor of pluralism and variety of organizations. Since there is not and *there cannot be* a simple invariant "one best way of doing things," only institutional setups of production and innovation allowing for diverse organizational and technological trajectories are likely to allow any one system to navigate that permanent tension between exploitation and exploration.

Moreover, at both descriptive and normative levels, our competence-based description of firms allows us in principle to analyze the limits of the set of "possible worlds," that is, of organizational structures and market dynamics that are evolutionary viable. Dosi, Teece, and Winter (1991) attempt to map the fundamental characteristics of possible *learning regimes* and possible *selection regimes* into particular modes of corporate organizations and strategies. It is argued that the mechanisms and speed by which product markets select among different products and different firms, coupled with the characteristics of the learning regimes (such as levels of technological opportunities, emulativeness, nature and applicability of knowledge bases, etc.), combine to determine the organizational features (e.g., specialization, horizontal diversification, etc.) that can be effectively selected.

Still a lot of work has to be done in this direction, but it seems a promising avenue to link a competence-based theory of the firm with a positive theory accounting for: (1) why firms differ; (2) why, despite these differences, they tend to show some organizational regularities, conditional on their principal activities and knowledge base; and (3) why sectors differ in their typical modes of corporate organization.

From a normative point of view, this may be a sound basis from which to derive prescriptions on R&D organization, intersectoral diversification, organizational change, and vertical integration/disintegration. It may be also a good starting point for sectoral industrial policies and, more generally, for the sort of "institutional engineering" that former centrally planned economies are undertaking in order to build viable market mechanisms.

Entrepreneurial Imagination, Information, and the Evolution of the Firm

Randall Bausor

Governing any enterprise requires information. Those responsible for an organization's activities must be both apprised of its endeavors and able to communicate their instructions. Since even the simplest institutions expire without systematic handling of information, most businesses dedicate nontrivial resources to constructing and implementing systems for accumulating, processing, and distributing information.

All institutions (including business firms) possess structures, procedures, and personnel dedicated to processing information. These systems, however, must have been previously planned and assembled. They must have been designed. The firm itself cannot be taken for granted or as being parametrically given, but must be engineered, built, and constructed.

Indeed, the doing of business lies not in simply producing outputs and collecting sales receipts, but arises from deliberate acts by which the business itself is fabricated. Among these strategies constitutive of the firm are those that construct and maintain the information systems essential to managing operations and controlling financial structure. These broader entrepreneurial issues of governance vitally determine a firm's economic viability.

In particular, the firm itself must initially have been imagined by the entrepreneur before it could have been subjected to the creative design processes leading from abstraction to actuality. These processes clearly extend past the initial phases of contemplating the founding—in terms of its organization, its finances, its manufacturing technologies, and its information systems—and proceed throughout its existence to prompt adaptations and adjustments until its possible ultimate dissolution and bankruptcy.

Thus, "tending to business" is a more broadly construed entrepreneurial process than just managing an already existing firm. Moreover, these constitutive entrepreneurial tasks are fundamental to a firm's survival and prosperity. Indeed, failure to successfully accomplish them necessarily jeopardizes the firm's operations and financial viability. As such, they deserve greater scrutiny from economists than they usually receive. The neoclassical theory of the firm, for example, analyzes a business's behavior given its structure and technology rather than investigating the activities and processes that generate that structure and technology in the first place.

This chapter addresses this weakness in economic analysis by investigating the dynamics of the design, construction, and adaptation of a fundamental component of any business organization: its information system. It argues that the creative activities by which such systems are engineered and implemented involve mental activities that transcend optimizing mathematics.

Consequently, the traditional analysis of the firm as a special application of the calculus of choice is inadequate and misleadingly specifies the role of entrepreneur as only that of one who minds the store. Those activities by which the firm is founded and sustained are shown to be analytically distinct from the management of its operations given its resources, structure, and technology.

Information Systems and the Creative Self-Constitution of the Firm

No business, from a child's lemonade stand to the grandest globe-girdling industrial giant, can conduct its affairs unless those in authority over and responsible for its activities have some idea of what is going on.

Incomplete and imperfect as such knowledge frequently is, it must be compiled from evidence collected both within the firm and from external sources. Since the behavior of those responsible for the firm depends upon their expectations and, further, since their expectations arise from the information available to them, the systematic acquisition, compilation, and distribution of *information* within the firm emerges as vitally important. Broadly construed, "information" includes the complete array of signals—from casual language acts such as gossip to formally processed numerical data—by which the state of the institution and of its environment can be articulated, assessed, and communicated. To be of value to decision makers, such information (which is distinct from the phenomena the information represents) must be cast within some cognitive (typically lingual) apparatus accessible to its recipient. Such information includes financial records; engineering and strictly technical aspects of commodity design and manufacturing control; personnel records; and the ocean of gossip, reports, memoranda, and internal correspondence that most organizations tend to generate.

Business organizations establish elaborate institutional mechanisms to facilitate and control the formulation and transmission of information. These systems include the formal mechanisms by which financial records are maintained, the bureaucracy by which personnel records of employees are collected and processed, the office mail room, computer networks, every file clerk, and every file. Informal information systems include fleeting opportunities for conversation (such as the company picnic) and the office of the office busybody. Although the informal information networks may be facilitated (or thwarted) by those controlling the firm, the formal information systems (some of which may be legally mandated, such as those regarding its financial or environmental affairs) must be deliberately fabricated. Survival, not to mention success, of the firm depends vitally on the quality of information such systems generate, the timing of their activities, and control over the distribution of their output. Consequently, most enterprises dedicate considerable effort and resources to their design, construction, implementation, and adaptation. The full reported extent of the true economic costs of these activities is difficult to surmise, but includes at least the full reported expense of accounting, personnel record-keeping, and inventory-control information systems.

Any enterprise's first product is itself. Before the configuring of the firm can long proceed, however, its entrepreneur must concoct an abstract plan for the business. Such a plan might contain ideas regarding the firm's products and technologies, mechanisms for managing the firm, and views on the information required to competently and coherently govern the enterprise. Compilation of such a plan requires *imagination*. Here "imagination" is understood to comprise those innovative psychological practices by which concepts arise and can be combined into the new cognitive structures by which plans and strategies emerge into the mind. Imagination in this sense contains, but is not limited to, cognition. Rather, it incorporates creative mental feats that apparently transcend "knowledge." Further, imagination of a possibility is independent of the appraised value of that possibility once it has been formulated, and both are quite distinct from the phenomenal manifestation of the imagined possibility per se. That is, the processes of imagining possible firms and possible organizations of firms are strictly mental and psychological. They provide new patterns within the entrepreneur's mind, patterns that he or she may or may not then choose to implement in constructing the business. We must now consider how these innovating intellectual and psychological imaginings contribute to the design and construction of the firm, especially to its information systems.

Such systems can be complex and subtle. Building them involves designing abstract channels through which information flows, acquiring the equipment and personnel through which such abstractions can be tangibly manifested, and constructing the information network according to plan. In addition, security of information is vitally important. Misplaced trust in a dishonest bookkeeper who subsequently proves to be an embezzler could prove lethal to the firm's profitability, for example, and hence security must also be engineered into the system itself. No enterprise can innocently trust that its affairs could be honestly and honorably known to its managers and no one else. Safety, security, and reliability of the information—financial as well as operational—cannot be presumed and cannot be neglected. Rather, in establishing the firm, its owner(s) must deliberately design into its structure and implement information systems conducive to managerial competence. Thus, neglecting such design challenges endangers the firm's profitability and easily proves inimical to its success.

Key to any serviceable information system, however, are creative acts of imaginative design and engineering. These systems do not spontaneously arise but must be constructed, and, before their construction can proceed, plans for their implementation must have been formulated. Such plans emerge only as the result of considerable abstract effort and require the imagination of their designer.

Imagination, understood as mental acts of innovation, is a concept familiar to many economists. Shackle's many contributions (1961, 1968, 1979) to the economics of uncertainty develop an argument for the central epistemic position of imagination in decision making. Similarly, Vickers (1978, 1986, 1987) has extensively explored the significance of imaginative acts for the construction of a theory of choice, especially as it relates to the theory of the firm and to financial considerations. Earl (1983, 1984) stresses the psychological importance of imagination in determining the wisdom of decisions, from which he builds a theory of the firm. In addition, Bausor pursues the economic dynamics of imagination and choice (1982-83, 1984, 1986). Each of these authors emphasizes the pivotal importance of the mental processes by which individuals form images of their economic situations and opportunities. These images, not the ontological phenomena they may reflect, govern behavior. In the current context, it is these entrepreneurial images (the product of imagination) that form the plan from which an enterprise emerges. In particular, someone must imagine, and then imaginatively plan, how a firm can collect, process, and distribute information before that firm's information systems and structures can be set in motion.

The process of designing information systems builds an image of what the final edifice will be. Just as one does not build a cathedral simply by piling rocks together, but first imagines what the finished cathedral will be, a business edifice cannot arise without an initial creative act of imagining what the firm might be. An entrepreneur's initial productive act is to imagine what a productive firm, including the information systems that will constitute its nerves, might be. Imagination remains through the design process as challenges must be faced in the self-constitution of the firm. Moreover, imaginative adaptations continue throughout the firm's existence as it responds to changing circumstances. That is, those responsible for the firm's performance must be able not only to imagine the opportunities available to it, but they must imaginatively anticipate what sort of firm is best suited to meet those opportunities.

Opportunities are imagined future possibilities, and an expectation necessarily manifests its possessor's current mental state. Imagination, however, is incomplete and fallible. An individual may fail to imagine what might truly be, and thus cannot in general be said to have imagined a complete set of all possible outcomes. Like all mental processes, imagination is bounded and threatened with ineptitude.[1] It requires fantasy, skill, luck, and fortune. Since no one is gifted with boundlessly thorough imaginings, however, our expectations cannot be said to be complete in the sense that they produce sample spaces over which all "belief" can be distributed by probability distribution functions. If, for example, you have not imagined the outcome that will ultimately ontologically prevail, then you cannot have formed any probability — zero, one, or any number between—regarding it. Thus, your set of imagined possible outcomes does not contain the "true" outcome and must therefore be incomplete. Something that has not been imagined might happen, and probability must surrender to authentic uncertainty.[2]

Similar imaginative powers generate an entrepreneur's design possibilities as he or she engineers a firm and its information systems. Just as with opportunities, design possibilities must first be imagined before they can be realized. Before one can construct an information system, one must choose from possible design options, and those options must have been imagined. For example, before one can decide which desktop computer to acquire, one must first imagine what a desktop computer might be, not to mention a need and use for such hardware. Similarly, before one can decide whether or not certain financial information should be generally available within the firm, one must imagine the consequences of restricting or not restricting access to it. Moreover, before one can responsibly decide what configuration of hardware to acquire, he or she ought to have imagined possible information-systemic applications of it.

As with any decision, you cannot make a choice until you have done the work of creating imagined possible outcomes. With the explicitly innovative

---

1. The issue here is not the same as Simon's "bounded rationality" since the concern is not with satisficing decisions (as opposed to optimal decisions) but with the reliability of the mental apparatus from which occasions for choice arise in the first place.

2. These problems transcend concern with "Bayesian" adjustment rules to describe learning since any such algorithm rests upon a given, phenomenally "objectively" defined sample space. The sample space is "given" and logically antecedent to learning. Lamentably, however, agents are not magically endowed with "sample spaces" but must imaginatively construct their own sets of possible future outcomes, each element of which is itself the product of a mental act: imagination.

design decisions by which the firm is constituted, the crucial dependence on imaginative creativity emerges as profoundly fundamental. Consequently, insight into the microeconomic processes by which firms are constituted (and reconstituted through adaptive responses to an unendingly uncertain destiny) requires analysis encompassing several typically neglected features.

First, no business exists as a simple "given." Neither it nor its technology, nor its financial structure, nor the information systems—not to mention the consequent information—have any existence, either conceptual or corporeal, without the active, deliberate creative tending of some interested human agent. Businesses do not just "happen," and microeconomists should not take their existence as axiomatic. Their genesis must be an indispensable component of the theory of the firm.

Second, before an enterprise commences operations, it must be constructed. Moreover, planning its fabrication requires designs for production processes, marketing networks, sales operations, financial organization and control, and the information systems by which the whole can be governed. Planning each of these aspects, none of which proceeds in isolation, requires powers of imaginative design and creative inspiration.

Third, assembling the firm and its information systems requires a psychological talent for imagining what the firm might be. One cannot even project an image of the firm, much less a detailed plan for what the firm will be, unless one has previously engaged powers of imagination.

Fourth, human imagination is incomplete and imperfect. It taxes the mind and drains psychological energy. The psyche's finite capacities limit the scope for imaginative creativity, producing finite and constricted sets of design options from which the firm's plans can be selected and the business built.

Fifth, we must ask whether or not the formation and reformation of enterprises can be reduced to the familiar calculus of optimization. In particular, is the neoclassical theory of choice, with its metaphor of decision, sufficiently rich to encompass a role for innovative imagination and intellectual creativity in the constitution of the firm? Alternatively, must economists escape the bounds of orthodox methods with analytical innovations of their own?

Optimization and the Informational Constitution of the Firm

Microeconomics presumes that all behavior can be analyzed as logically isomorphic to the mathematics of optimization. Since all actions are construed as the outcome of motivated decisions, the economic analysis of behavior reduces to the calculus of choice. Now we examine the capacity of mathematical optimization, as embodied in the microeconomics of choice, to replicate analytically the processes by which enterprises are informationally constituted.

All optimization problems consist of two parts: an opportunity set and an objective function. The opportunity set, O, contains all of the possible phenomena over which the agent is to choose. In the static analysis of the firm it is typically taken as a subset of an n-dimensional Euclidean space. The dynamic analysis of the firm requires a more complex structure for the opportunity set, in which it is usually a subset of a function space. Risk enters by probabilistically transforming the opportunity set, and game theory presents opportunities as strategies recognizing the possible responses of other agents to one's decision. The choice criteria by which an agent selects elements of O are mathematically represented by a function, $f(x)$, defined over a set X containing O, which maps X into the real line. This "objective function" is intended to yield a numerical ranking consonant with the agent's criteria for choosing from among the members of the opportunity set. When well-known algebraic, topological, and convexity properties are imposed on O, and continuity and differential properties attributed to $f(x)$, then the logic of decision reduces to the mathematics of extrema, from which the differential properties of optima can be derived. This is the mathematical foundation of the neoclassical theory of the firm.

Can this same logical structure—the theory of optimization as articulated in the mathematics of extrema—capture the subtlety of the imaginative acts by which information systems are designed and firms self-constituted? Doing so would require that all entrepreneurial behaviors constitutive and reconstitutive of the firm be capable of intellectual reduction to nothing but choice. This would require that the generation and regeneration of the business enterprise could be reduced to acts of choosing from phenomenally antecedent sets of opportunities. Such a view contradicts the view that managers creatively build the firm, including both its "opportunity set" and "objective function."

The recognition that every organization must have been planned to some extent and that all plans emerge from a cognitive broth laced with creativity and imagination fundamentally modifies one's understanding of an "opportunity" set's structure. If one is to choose a design for the firm's information systems, then alternative designs must have been imaginatively contrived. Only when this creative work—the true intellectual challenge of designing— has been undertaken can options be said to exist and can a nontrivial opportunity set be said to confront the entrepreneur. These constructive tasks by which the plans of the firm come into being prove to be the true test of entrepreneurial expertise. In practice, such possibilities might involve the selection of computational hardware and software, the compilation of accounting systems for financial and other purposes, the assembly of a work force to staff such systems, and even filling the bookkeeper's position. Although the number of possibilities, even for relatively small operations, can be huge, they are not beyond number.

Typically, such opportunity sets are finite and their members distinct and separate from each other. There may be, that is, no reasonable sense in which one can describe any two alternative imagined plans as arbitrarily close to one another. Indeed, the topological properties by which "closeness" can be precisely defined in sets of possible information systems have never been established.[3] Even if they had been, neither metrizability of the resulting space nor compactness of the resulting "opportunity" set necessarily follows.[4] This depends upon the whim of imagination's fancy and upon technologically imposed design constraints. (One might, for example, need to decide whether to hire one or two bookkeepers, but the prospect of hiring a number of bookkeepers equal to the square root of two is impossible.)

Moreover, nothing guarantees that spaces of "possible information systems" exhibit the additional algebraic properties necessary to define and establish convexity of sets. In general, addition and multiplication of elements of such a space have no natural intuitive meaning. Moreover, even if such algebraic structure is attained, nothing guarantees that an "opportunity set" compiled from the entrepreneur's imagination achieves the compactness and convexity properties necessary for the employment of the differential mathematics of extrema to the problem of optimization. Without an algebra defined over "all possible designs of information systems," however, convex sets of such systems necessarily cannot be constructed, and the "opportunity set of imagined possible information systems" that would be necessary to render these activities in choice theoretic terms cannot be fabricated. The very incompleteness of imagination assures that the resulting opportunity sets contain nonconvex and frequently disconnected regions.

One cannot choose to implement a design for an information system unless that design has emerged into consciousness and has been constructively

---

3. Opportunity sets are usually conceived as subsets of Euclidean spaces, such as commodity space in the theory of the household. Here, the spatial properties of the set, including its density, derive from the properties of the real numbers that form its foundation. An opportunity set of "planned" information systems or of "possible business firms," however, cannot generally be constructed as the subset of the Cartesian product of the real line. Consequently, the properties of Euclidean spaces cannot blithely be attributed to them. Natural spatial properties of sets of plans can be constructed from families of equivalence classes of them constructed from qualitative attributes they exhibit. This technique has been developed by Katzner (1983) and used by Bausor (1986) to build spaces of expectations.

4. Compactness of opportunity sets is vital to optimization since the fundamental theorem of mathematical optimization asserts that a continuous real-valued function on a compact set achieves an extremum. Recall also that continuity of the objective function is topologically contingent.

engineered into an operational possibility. Sets of such imagined possibilities, however, are likely to be porous and are unlikely to possess the mathematical properties of compactness and convexity traditionally imputed to sets of "all possibilities" from which rational choice is said to be made. Thus, although decisions must be made as a component of the processes by which firms are constituted, they will not necessarily obey the mathematical characterization of choice familiar in optimizing mechanics. Consequently, the self-constitutive activities by which information systems are engineered into firms cannot be reduced to a problem in the theory of optimal choice.

Similar difficulties confront attempts to identify an objective function governing the constitutive activities of the firm. An objective function is a device by which the various criteria for appraising options are condensed into a numerical ranking. If the "selection" of an information system is to be construed as the outcome of optimization, the familiar conditions by which preferences yield continuous objective functions must be satisfied. Indeed, if the Weierstrass theorem (that an extremum of a continuous mapping of a convex set exists) is to be employed, then continuity of the objective function proves indispensable. Continuity of such a function, however, is determinable only once the topological structure on its domain has been established. Since the domain in this case consists of the set of imagined possible information systems, its topological properties are unestablished and themselves depend upon the imaginative processes by which the opportunity set itself arises. Obviously, as the vagaries of imagination alter the opportunity set, so they also impact the consequent spatial properties imputed to that set. Therefore, the topological structure of the opportunity set over which design decisions are made is contingent upon the fanciful psychology generating that set. Thus, the continuity properties of an objective function defined over such a space also logically depend upon those acts of imagination, as must the very definition of the objective function. Consequently, the objective function itself varies with the imaginative acts constituting the firm, as must its continuity properties. Since the objective function by which an information system could be said to be "chosen" changes with the constitution of the firm, however, the self-generating behaviors by which the firm is fabricated cannot be reduced to the optimizing theory of choice.

Now we face the crux of the matter. The intellectual and psychological activities by which an entrepreneur imagines, creates, designs, engineers, forms, and reforms an enterprise cannot faithfully be construed in terms of an opportunity set and an objective function themselves independent of that behavior. Rather than obeying the outcome of an optimization problem, the entrepreneur constructs such a "problem." His or her behavior cannot be understood as the outcome of a process of merely "choosing" the desired firm. Rather, he or she must first imagine what the firm might be and subsequently attempt to fabricate it. Moreover, the issue affects not only the establishment of an enterprise, but persists throughout its existence, for the firm as an entity must be constantly tended, adjusted, adapted, and reconstituted as it responds to its environment and the creative imaginative powers of its managers. Its informational structure is not unalterable once established, but it is prone to revision at any time.[5] These acts of construction and reconstruction cannot be reduced to acts of choice. They begin with imagining what might be possible, and navigating flights of fancy requires activities transcending the making of rational decisions. Before rational decisions can possibly be committed, the context for those decisions must be constructed and the business of building that context requires talents greater than those necessary only for choosing. Economic "rationality" enters only once the material with which it can work has been provided. Abilities to make wise choices are vital to the welfare of any institution, but they are not the only talents necessary for success.

Prelude to a Theory of the Informational Constitution of the Firm

Analysis based solely on the metaphor of the firm as optimizing agent rationally choosing over complete opportunity sets neglects behavior basic to entrepreneurial activities. Thus it cannot provide the logical foundation for a comprehensive theory of the firm. Any general model of the firm must contain components in addition to those specifying the making of decisions.

Clearly, a bona fide analysis of entrepreneurial activity must accommodate imagination's vital place in behavior. The enterprising soul must be seen as one whose cleverness transcends calculation to encompass creativity, and whose confidence enables imagined possibilities to become actualities. The full scope of skills that combine to enable the tending to business cannot be reduced simply to minding the store. Before the store can be efficiently managed, it must be built.

Furthermore, an authentically rich theory of the firm must be dynamic. Not only must it encompass the procedures by which businesses are initially formed, but it must also encompass the cybernetic interaction between the constitutional and operational functions of governing an enterprise. Otherwise it cannot account for the ongoing reformulation of the firm in response to the uncertain outcomes of its own and other people's actions. Firms are not formed once and then left to live or die given that initial structure. Instead, they must be constantly rebuilt, replanned, and reconceived throughout their lives. Failure to do so surely breeds mortality and bankruptcy. Consequently,

---

5. Indeed, some occasions, such as discovery of an embezzler or receipt of unfavorable reports from an external auditor, may explicitly provoke systemic adaptations (e.g., fire the embezzler).

economists cannot understand the business of business until they gain insight into the feedback linkages between operational performance and the construction of the information systems necessary to those operations. Only a truly dynamic theory of the firm, one capable of modeling that interdependence between a firm's operations and its design, can lead to a valid microeconomics.

Moreover, such dynamic modeling must be cast in "historical" time. That is, time must not simply enter the analysis as yet another dimension. Plans, expectations, and action must precede their own consequences. In addition, expected outcomes and actual outcomes must not be definitionally identical since that logically obliterates the capacity of surprising outcomes to provoke reformulation of the firm. Further, the firm must not necessarily prove to have been the most lucrative institution possible for its entrepreneur. Only through models in which there is the capacity to blunder, to fail, to generate cumbersome and unhelpful information systems, to be inefficient, in short, to be out of equilibrium, can insight into the dynamic and strategic behavior of firms enter microeconomics. The firm itself must not be viewed as a steady state from which optimizing decisions emerge. Rather, economic models must reflect the realization that doing business is uncertain, that operational results may provoke reconstitution of the firm, just as reformulation of the firm provokes operational responses.

The dynamics of the informational constitution of the firm could be modeled as a cybernetic structure in which the business's information systems generate information, the receipt of which can provoke responses in either its operations or basic constitution. That is, those governing the firm could respond to "news" by adjusting its current operations or by reformulating the firm itself. They could, for example, redeploy resources to acquire updated software or to enhance security. Alternatively, they could hire a new external auditor. Such a feedback loop would link the firm's organization to its operations and then back to its future structure (and thence to further rounds of operations, information about those operations, and adaptive responses to those signals). Historical equilibrium would consist of a steady-state of the information system and would connote structural continuity of the firm's information processing (a desirable attribute if intertemporal comparisons of its actions are to be possible). More interesting than equilibrium, however, is historical evolution of the informational constitution of the firm—in which it is historically out of equilibrium. Many fascinating aspects of business behavior could be explored out of equilibrium. Is the firm evolving through small steps or is its alteration revolutionary? Is it converging onto a new steady-state? Is its behavior predictable or chaotic? Such questions can be formally formulated, much less answered, only within a historically dynamic model of the firm. They have no meaning within the traditional optimizing mechanics of microeconomics.

Part 5
Nature and Economic Evolution

Biological evolution proceeds on the whole by unconscious interaction. . . .
With the human race, conscious interaction becomes of great importance
and the niches for human artifacts are determined in part by . . . human
images of the future.

—Kenneth E. Boulding (1981)

On Economic Growth and Resource Scarcity: Lessons from Nonequilibrium Thermodynamics

Richard W. England

It is hardly controversial to observe that economics and physics are similar in some respects and that modern economics reflects the influence of certain methods and concepts employed by physical scientists. Several authors, for example, have alluded to the "mechanical" character of contemporary economic theory. In his *Foundations*, Samuelson (1947, 311) noted that "many economists have . . . become bogged down in the search for economic concepts corresponding to mass, energy, inertia, momentum, force, and space." A quarter century later, Samuelson (1972, 249) paid "credit to the followers of Galileo and Newton for taking the mathematical approach" and urged economists to continue emulating the method, if not the content, of their research.[1]

But what, exactly, does it mean to claim that economics is mechanical? Prigogine and his colleagues have written extensively on recent developments within physical science, and their writings can provide a useful summary of the mechanical approach to physical reality. According to Prigogine and Stengers (1984, 57), the central concern of classical mechanics since Galileo has been to explain and predict the trajectories of physical masses accelerating through space.

I would like to thank Robert Ayres, Herman Daly, Nicholas Georgescu-Roegen, Richard Norgaard, Martin O'Connor, Warren Samuels, and Robert Solow for their helpful comments. Despite their wise advice, the propositions that remain in this chapter are still open to close inspection and lively debate.

1. This passage is taken from the revised text of Samuelson's Nobel Prize lecture, delivered on December 11, 1970. In that text, he mentions "Newton" and "quantum mechanics" three times each, "thermodynamics" five times, "classical mechanics" once, and "physics" or "physicist" *fourteen* times. Interestingly, "biology" and "biologist" do not appear in his text. Another eminent economist who has repeatedly pointed to the mechanical nature of modern economics is Georgescu-Roegen (1971, 1–2; 1977, 267; 1982a, 10). Both Samuelson and Georgescu-Roegen were anticipated by Marshall (1956, 318), who remarked that in its "earlier stages . . . economics . . . [portrayed] demand and supply as crude forces pressing against one another, and tending towards a mechanical equilibrium."

In pursuit of that scientific goal, mechanics has embraced a particular ontology, or set of premises about the reality that it studies. First, it supposes that the physical world is fundamentally *simple*: "The main drive of classical science over a long period was directed toward the reduction of our vision of the complex world to the study of simple basic objects. This perspective . . . has led to . . . a description of physical systems in terms of atoms and molecules" (Prigogine and Allen 1982, 3). At first glance, this premise of essential simplicity seems highly plausible as one looks at physical systems like a pendulum or the solar system.[2]

Another ontological premise of classical mechanics is its belief in the *reversible* character of trajectories (Prigogine and Stengers 1984, 60–61). If the load attached to a pulley system can be lifted given application of sufficient force, then that load can also be lowered once that force ceases to operate. In addition, mechanics supposes that motion is *lawful* and *deterministic*. That is, "in order to calculate a trajectory we need, in addition to our knowledge of the laws of motion, an empirical definition of a single instantaneous state of the system. The general law then deduces from this 'initial state' the series of states the system passes through as time progresses" (Prigogine and Stengers 1984, 60). Thus, for example, knowledge of the laws of gravitation and of planetary positions relative to the sun allows one to predict the earth's future orbit with precision.

Still another premise about physical reality, one dating back to Plato, which Newton and Leibniz later adopted, is that mechanical systems are *conservative* (Nicolis and Prigogine 1989, 46). That is, despite trajectories of potentially cosmic scale, these systems are thought to be qualitatively unaffected and some key magnitudes unchanged by the motions of their components.[3] A final premise of Newtonian science is its claim that mechanical laws of motion are *universal* in scope (Prigogine and Stengers 1984, 213). For instance, mechanics presupposes that the period of a pendulum's swing is independent of the continent on which it is located and of the century during which it vibrates.

On Physics and Economics

Is there evidence that modern economics shares this set of ontological premises with classical mechanics? Space is too limited to offer a definitive answer,

---

2. Samuelson (1983, 11) is apparently committed to this ontological belief in simplicity: "I still . . . [believe that] Einstein was right to suspect that simple systems will be found to explain much of physics." This commitment echoes that of Leibniz several centuries earlier: "In all instances, Leibniz stringently applied the precept that simplicity prevailed in the world" (Mirowski 1989, 18).

3. Mirowski (1984, 1988) has written eloquently on the role of conservation principles in twentieth-century economic theory.

but examples do exist that suggest that economics has been deeply influenced by a mechanistic conception of reality.[4] A prime example is the neoclassical model of economic growth proposed by Solow (1956), a model that has been the benchmark for modern growth theories for more than three decades.

The simplicity of Solow's conception of economic growth is evident in the structure of his mathematical model. The entire economy is characterized by a single aggregate production function with two inputs, labor and capital. A single composite output with two uses, consumption and capital accumulation, is produced under conditions of full employment of existing labor and capital and of constant returns to scale.

The resulting process of economic growth is both lawful and deterministic. Changes through time in the labor force and capital stock are depicted by differential equations that represent the economy's "laws of motion." These economic dynamics, together with specification of the economy's technology and initial levels of labor and capital, determine a unique set of trajectories for net output, consumption, saving, and investment into the indefinite future.[5] Solow's model also permits reversibility of macroeconomic phenomena since exogenous shifts in the average propensity to save, population growth rate, and technological change parameters from positive to negative values imply, not immediate economic collapse, but, rather, a smooth contraction of the aggregate economy.

This account of macroeconomic dynamics is also conservative in several respects. Once exogenous propensities to save and to procreate have imparted an impetus to the economic system, it starts to expand in a "frictionless" sort of way. Growth, however, does not alter the structure of the economy in any fashion: no changes in market structure occur, product innovation is not recognized, and technological change (should it occur) is purely quantitative in character. The capacity of nature to deliver energy and materials to the production process and to absorb effluents generated by economic activity is also unimpaired by economic growth, which is equivalent to assuming that the environment is "simultaneously a horn of plenty and a bottomless sink" (Perrings 1987, 5). In addition to this continuing reproduction of the economy in qualitative terms, a fundamental numerical constant along the balanced growth path is the capital-labor ratio, which remains unchanged in the absence of exogenous shifts in system parameters.

Finally, Solow's model is (almost) universal in scope since the social context within which population growth, accumulation of capital goods, and innovation occur is barely specified. Corporations, families, and government

---

4. For an extensive comparison of the logical structures of classical mechanics and neoclassical economics, see Neuberg (1989).

5. Samuels (1989b, 531) argues that the quest for models with determinate solutions is an "overriding emphasis" of modern economics.

are not treated as an institutional framework that is required for economic expansion. Competitive input markets are indeed introduced in order to provide a mechanism that could guarantee full employment of productive inputs, but those factor markets are not essential to the model's specification (Solow 1956, 78).[6] Although economic growth theory has advanced since Solow's seminal contribution, it is probably the case that much of the subsequent literature has been influenced, and even formed, by his mechanical perspective on growth analysis.[7]

This is not to argue, of course, that modern economics is a slavish imitation of eighteenth-century Newtonian physics. The painstaking research of Mirowski (1984, 1986, 1988, 1989) has revealed, for example, that the fathers of neoclassical economic thought consciously appropriated the physical metaphor and mathematical technique of nineteenth-century energetics as they constructed their theoretical alternative to Smith, Ricardo, and Marx.[8] Energeticists had used the constrained optimization methods of Lagrange and Hamilton to describe motions of mass-points within closed physical systems with a fixed total of energy allocated between potential and kinetic forms. In the hands of Walras, Jevons, et al., "energy became transmuted into 'utility'. . . . Constrained optimization became the hallmark of neoclassical theory, its hard core being the postulation of a psychological field which behaved, for all intents and purposes, just like potential energy" (Mirowski 1986, 5).[9]

This conclusion about the origins of neoclassical economics leads us next to a more problematic issue, namely the relationship of modern economics to thermodynamics. This branch of physics, which originated in the practical engineering research of Carnot (1796–1832), had its genesis in classical

---

6. For a critique of modern growth models, see Georgescu-Roegen (1976, chap. 9).

7. This is not to say, however, that other points of view did not exist during the 1950s. Koopmans (1951, 48–49), for example, discussed the *irreversibility* of the production process. By analogy to physical relaxation phenomena, Georgescu-Roegen (1951) argued that different dynamic equations might be required to describe macroeconomic behavior at different stages of the business cycle. Nevertheless, Arrow (1988, 275) is correct in concluding that the "last thirty years have seen a steady development of dynamic analysis in economics. . . . The theoretical analysis of dynamic systems was largely devoted to the determination of their steady states or solutions which exhibited steady (exponential) growth."

8. According to Atkins (1984, 8–9), "[A] major achievement of nineteenth-century science . . . [was that energy] displaced from centrality the apparently more tangible concept of 'force,' which had been regarded as the unifying concept [of physics] ever since Newton."

9. Mirowski points to a number of conceptual difficulties that neoclassical theory faces because of its imitation of nineteenth-century energetics. One is the limited range of mathematical tools available to most modern economists because of their devotion to Lagrange and Hamilton (Mirowski 1986, 202). Another is the tough time deciding *what* within an economic system is conserved that is comparable to the energy of a physical system. Answering that question is imperative since the use of constrained optimization techniques implies that *something* is being conserved (Mirowski 1988, 19–20, 41).

mechanics but developed thereafter along a radically different path. As Samuelson (1983, 12) has recognized:

> Implicit in Galileo's analysis of freely falling bodies, and made explicit by Leibniz, is the law of conservation of (mechanical) energy for a (frictionless) system. . . . No observed system [however] is completely without friction. As actual systems lose mechanical energy, a rise in 'temperature' occurs. . . . Classical thermodynamics is the subject that deals with such interactions of mechanics and "temperatures."[10]

What, exactly, are the core principles of classical thermodynamics? I shall focus here on its first and second laws, which seem most relevant to economic affairs. The first law of thermodynamics states that:

> *matter* (*mass/energy*) *is neither created nor destroyed by any physical process.* . . . [I]t was [formerly] assumed that the law of conservation of mass and energy applied *separately* to each chemical species, and to energy. This is now known to be strictly incorrect, since mass can be converted into energy by fusion or by fission. The inverse process is also possible. . . . However, disregarding these exceptional cases, the first law does hold separately for each species, as well as to aggregates. (Ayres 1978, 38)

The second law has been offered in a diverse set of formulations. A modern formulation is that of Georgescu-Roegen (1986, 3): "[I]n an isolated system, . . . the available energy continuously and irrevocably degrades into unavailable states. . . . [A]n isolated system can exchange neither energy nor matter with its 'outside.'"[11] As Atkins (1984, 48, 62) discusses, "There are two modes of motion for the particles of a composite system: the motion may be coherent, when all the particles are in step, or the motion may be incoherent, when the particles are moving chaotically." Thus, the irrevocable degradation of energy predicted by the second law includes "not only its spatial dispersal over the atoms of the universe but the destruction of coherence too."

---

10. In light of the origin of thermodynamics in practical engineering problems, it is curious that Samuelson (1947, 21) conceives of the field as "a purely deductive science based upon certain postulates (notably the First and Second Laws of Thermodynamics)." Wicken (1987, 57) is closer to the mark when he asserts that "thermodynamics is the most empirical of sciences." Atkins (1984, 8) supports the latter position in arguing that thermodynamics "is based on a few statements that constitute succinct summaries of people's experiences with the way energy behaves in the course of its transformations."

11. The global economy is obviously not an isolated system. It is an open system, which exchanges both energy and mass with its terrestrial environment, and energy with its extraterrestrial environment.

It is this irreversible tendency of the physical universe towards disorder, or greater entropy, that has earned the second law its popular label, the Entropy Law (Ayres 1978, 44–45).

If modern economics reflects the influence of mechanical notions, can we also say that it has incorporated thermodynamic concepts into its theoretical scheme? The answer appears to be affirmative, but just barely. In a brief note, Lisman (1949) noted certain formal similarities between thermodynamic relations and mathematical economics, although he did not suggest that thermodynamic laws are relevant to the actual functioning of economic processes. More recently, however, Boulding (1976), Faber and Proops (1985), and Perrings (1987) have all argued that economic systems do, indeed, entail thermodynamic phenomena. The two authors who have tried in the most determined fashion to introduce economists to the lessons of thermodynamics are, however, Ayres and Georgescu-Roegen.[12]

What, precisely, are the lessons that economists might learn from the study of thermodynamics? Perhaps the most fundamental one is that the global economy cannot be theorized as an isolated system with a circular flow of money and commodities. Rather, it is an open system that continuously exchanges energy and matter with its physical environment (Georgescu-Roegen 1977, 267).[13] That this point is not yet fully appreciated within the economics profession is suggested by the unqualified exposition of circular-flow diagrams in many economic textbooks.

This openness of the global economy and the first law of thermodynamics, taken together, have several significant implications. One is the pervasiveness of waste-disposal and pollution problems in the modern economy (Kneese, Ayres, and d'Arge 1970, 4–5). A second is the need to view particular air pollution, water contamination, and solid-waste disposal problems as interconnected manifestations of the more general need to dispose of waste matter and energy (Kneese, Ayres, and d'Arge 1970, 6). Finally, since waste residuals must be returned to the environment in some form and since productivity of labor and capital depends on environmental conditions, there

---

12. See, for example, Kneese, Ayres, and d'Arge (1970), Ayres (1978), Ayres and Miller (1980), and Ayres and Nair (1984). For the works of Georgescu-Roegen, see his citations for the years 1971, 1976, 1977, 1982, and 1986. It is interesting to note that Georgescu-Roegen received his doctorate in statistics, not economics, and that Ayres was trained as a mathematical physicist (Tang, Westfield, and Worley, 1976, ix; Ayres 1978, v). Perhaps these intellectual backgrounds contributed to a less mechanically inclined approach to economic reasoning.

13. To date, not enough theoretical work has been done to distinguish the "economy" from its "environment." As Georgescu-Roegen (1971, 316–17) has remarked, the boundary between the two is not a distinct border but rather a "dialectical penumbra." Perrings (1987, 4) identifies social control of the physical agents governing production as the dividing line between economy and environment.

is "the necessity for any system generating residuals in the process of production to change over time, to evolve . . . ," not merely grow quantitatively (Perrings 1987, 8).

Thermodynamics and Resource Scarcity

Thermodynamics also has a number of important lessons to teach about the precise nature of resource scarcity and about the physical limits on technical improvement. As Ayres and Miller (1980, 359–60) acknowledge, there are

definite and well-known limits on physical performance in almost every field. . . . For instance, there is a definite lower limit to the amount of electricity required to produce a horsepower of mechanical work. There is a lower limit, similarly, to the amount of electricity required to produce a given amount of illumination. And, of course, there is a lower limit to the amount of available work derived from fossil fuels that is needed to generate a given amount of electricity. . . . There are [also] upper limits to the strength of materials.

Hence, even though electrical power generators, nuclear reactors, automobile engines, and other devices presently achieve only a fraction of their potential efficiency in thermodynamic terms, there are still physical ceilings on the ability of human ingenuity to raise actual efficiencies via technological innovation (Atkins 1984, 40).

This conclusion relates, in turn, to the proper conceptualization of scarcity, arguably the cornerstone concept of modern economics.[14] According to Levine (1977, 175, 181), "The central unifying principle of all [modern] economic thought . . . [is] the efficient allocation of scarce resources among competing ends. . . . [S]carcity is defined as the relation of given individual desires to the available world of objects which are capable of fulfilling those desires. Such objects are 'scarce' when the available supply is inadequate to completely satisfy the desires of individuals."

Scarcity becomes a much more complicated notion, however, once one recognizes that economic activity is subject to the laws of thermodynamics. As Georgescu-Roegen (1971, 20) points out, humanity's natural endowment "consists of two essentially distinct elements: (1) the *stock* of low entropy on

---

14. Walsh and Gram (1980, 3) observe, for example: "A sharp distinction can be drawn in the theory of general equilibrium between the classical theme of the accumulation and allocation of surplus output, and the neoclassical theme of the allocation of given resources among alternative uses."

or within the globe, and (2) the *flow* of solar energy."[15] Land in the Ricardian sense is limited in quantity but, because of gravitation and the first law of thermodynamics, that magnitude does not decline with economic use. Hence, although ecosystems can be degraded and biological diversity reduced, the surface of the globe does provide a nondepreciating space for human activity and a durable collector with which to gather a small portion of the sun's continuous emission of energy.

The second law of thermodynamics dictates, however, that terrestrial sources of matter and energy are scarce in a very different sense of the word. "[B]ecause no conversion of energy is achieved without material support, friction dissipates not only energy but also matter. . . . All around us there is oxidation, chipping, blowing, and washing away, *etc.*" (Georgescu-Roegen 1977, 268). In the absence of the entropy law, "we could use the energy of a piece of coal over and over again. . . . Also, engines, homes, and even living organisms . . . would never wear out. There would be no economic difference between material goods and Ricardian land" (Georgescu-Roegen 1976, 9). Unfortunately, however, the available energy extracted from fossil fuels is irrevocably transformed into waste heat, which, in turn, radiates into outer space, and a substantial portion of the materials obtained from high-grade mineral deposits are dissipated throughout the global environment during the economic processes of production and consumption.[16]

Whether physical dissipation of materials prevents their recovery and reuse at some future date is a matter of some controversy. Georgescu-Roegen (1977, 269) argues adamantly that *"dissipated matter is not recyclable."* Goeller and Weinberg (1978) and Ayres and Miller (1980), on the other hand, have argued that substantial opportunities exist to substitute among specific materials and that even extremely low physical concentrations of materials can be mined for human use. Although additional research into the physics of this question is desirable, I am inclined to agree with Aage (1984, 111), who speculates, "[Some authors] conclude that catastrophes of depletion are unlikely, provided that an inexhaustible, nonpolluting source of energy is at hand. . . . But of course such a source of energy is not at hand. . . . Therefore, the power of modern technology to exploit very thin concentrations of raw materials cannot reasonably sustain the extreme optimism [of those authors]."[17] In other words, the somber message of the second law (that

---

15. The earthly stock of "low entropy" consists of accessible physical concentrations of fossil fuels, metal ores, other minerals, etc. For a similar argument, see Georgescu-Roegen (1986, 8).

16. Faber, Stephan, and Niemes (1987) have analyzed the formal relationship between low entropy and economically useful spatial concentrations of the material elements used in production.

17. Both Goeller and Weinberg (1978, 9) and Ayres and Miller (1980, 354) concede that

dissipation of matter and energy are unavoidable consequences of their use) mutes the seemingly optimistic message of the first law (that matter and energy are not literally consumed during their use).

Has the economics profession as a whole acknowledged these lessons from thermodynamics? The first law has received a degree of recognition, as measured by economists' frequent citations of Kneese, Ayres, and d'Arge (1970). Recognition of the second law, on the other hand, has been more limited—if one measures that recognition by frequency of citation of Georgescu-Roegen (1971).[18] The attitude of many economists about the entropy law, if they have an opinion at all, could perhaps be summarized by the following remark of Samuelson (1972, 254) in his Nobel Prize lecture: "There is really nothing more pathetic than to have an economist . . . try to force analogies between the concepts of physics and the concepts of economics. How many dreary papers have I had to referee in which the author is looking for something that corresponds to entropy."

This indifference, and even hostility, to the entropy law within contemporary economics is somewhat surprising in light of its broad acceptance among modern scientists. Atkins (1984, vii) recalls "C. P. Snow's test of general literacy, in which not knowing the Second Law is equivalent to not having read a work of Shakespeare." A. S. Eddington, the eminent astronomer and physicist, once remarked, "The law that entropy always increases . . . holds, I think, the supreme position among the laws of Nature. . . . [I]f your theory is found to be against the second law of thermodynamics I can give you no hope." (Prigogine and Stengers 1984, 233). More recently, Wicken (1987, 6) has claimed that since "the Second Law governs all irreversible processes, a materialistically coherent cosmos requires their connection. To be causally compelling as science, evolution needs to make its ties with thermodynamics explicit."

This final remark may help to shed some light on the failure of the

---

their optimistic conclusions about the future availability of materials hinge on the use of unspecified, but presumably huge, amounts of tolerably inexpensive energy to "sift" through the earth's crust. Georgescu-Roegen (1982a, 13) argues that not only huge quantities of energy but also an inordinate amount of time would be required to concentrate dissipated materials to useful levels of concentration.

18. There is additional evidence to support this point. In their early survey of environmental economics, Fisher and Peterson (1976) mention the first law explicitly and cite Kneese, Ayres, and d'Arge (1970) but ignore the entropy law and Georgescu-Roegen (1971). It is also revealing that the editors of the *Journal of Economic Literature* and *Economic Journal* did not assign prominent economists to review his *Entropy Law* book (Adelman 1972; Green 1973). Faber, Stephan, and Niemes (1987, 6) have concluded, "It is well known that [modern] economics has been strongly influenced by classical mechanics. . . . The development of thermodynamics since the beginning of the nineteenth century, however, has remained largely unnoticed by economists."

entropy law to gain legitimacy within the court of contemporary economic reasoning. As Mirowski (1989, 390) has correctly asserted, "[T]here is the disturbing technical consideration that the entropy law induces a distinct orientation for time's arrow, formalizing the irreversibility of experience . . . . [N]eoclassical economics has always championed the existence of an economic rationality independent of historical situation." Hence, recognition of the second law would force modern economics to eschew its ahistorical, mechanical approach to economic affairs and take history rather more seriously than it has in the past.[19]

Another reason for the neglect of the entropy law by most economists is that it cannot yield precise, quantitative predictions about the future course of events. Rather, it "determines neither *when* (by clock-time) the entropy of a closed system will reach a certain level nor exactly *what* will happen. . . . The thermodynamic principles, therefore, leave some substantial freedom to the actual path and the time schedule of an entropic process" (Georgescu-Roegen 1971, 12). Since "the trend over the last century has been toward ever greater mathematical sophistication as part and parcel of the professionalization of economics" (Mirowski 1986, 180), this incapacity of the second law to generate determinate quantitative predictions seems to cast doubt on its scientific validity.[20]

A third reason for the failure of the entropy law to gain recognition within contemporary economics is that it appears to contradict the optimistic belief in economic progress held by most modern economists. Recall, for example, that despite their theoretical differences over the *stability* of the macroeconomic growth path, the models of Domar (1948) and Harrod (1939), on the one side, and those of Solow (1956) and Swan (1956), on the other, imply the *possibility* of exponential economic growth into the indefinite future. Such a conception of the economic process is hard to reconcile with the classical version of thermodynamics, which anticipates "a universe . . . heading for an inevitable 'heat death' at an indeterminate rate" (Mirowski 1989, 389).

A particularly vivid version of this pessimistic image of "heat death" has been offered to the economics profession by Georgescu-Roegen (1971, 20; 1976, 22–23) during the past two decades. He claims that entropic dissipation of matter and energy precludes continued economic growth and even implies the impossibility of a stationary-state economy of indefinite duration. This, in turn, implies the impossibility of continued population growth or even of a

---

19. The reversible, ahistorical character of modern economic theory has been noted by a number of authors, e.g., Dasgupta (1985, 78), Robinson (1978, 126), and Bausor (1986, 98). It is extremely significant that Solow (1985) in his scholarly maturity has called for recognition of both historical evolution and cultural diversity within economic theory.

20. Note, however, that research on finite-time thermodynamics has begun to pin down how much time is required for thermodynamic processes to unfold. See Andresen (1989).

maximum sustainable population. Rather, according to Georgescu-Roegen, the proper question for economic demography is the maximum quantity of person-years that the global economy can support prior to human extinction.[21]

These are gloomy claims, indeed, and their exposition has no doubt triggered psychological defenses of various sorts in the minds of numerous economists. It is crucial to point out, however, that Georgescu-Roegen (1976, 22) has *not* predicted the imminent demise of humanity as an unavoidable consequence of the unfolding of the entropy law. Rather, the "human species, of all species, is not likely to go suddenly into a short coma. Its end is not even in distant sight." Despite this qualification, the metaphor of eventual "heat death" for the universe and its corollary of human extinction are not palatable notions, especially for economists reared on the cool, sweet milk of technical progress and capital investment.

Dissipative Structures and Evolution

Is there another metaphor and associated theoretical paradigm that would induce economists to face the entropy law squarely and to seriously explore its implications for economic life? It is my belief that the recent writings of Prigogine can provide just such an intellectual impetus.[22] As Nicolis and Prigogine (1989, 51, 63) point out, modern research in physics and chemistry suggests that irreversible events and systemic instabilities are quite common in nature. Examples include chemical reactions, heat conduction and diffusion, viscous dissipation, and relaxation phenomena in electrically or magnetically polarized systems.

From empirical findings such as these, Prigogine has drawn the theoretical conclusion that there are several distinct varieties of thermodynamics (Prigogine and Stengers 1984, 137). Equilibrium thermodynamics, the classical version developed during the nineteenth century, focuses its attention on the final state of maximum entropy of isolated physical systems. However, equilibrium thermodynamics does not describe "what we know of social or biological evolution, which is marked by increasing diversification and complexity . . . . [T]he earth is not in thermodynamic equilibrium . . . but rather . . . far from equilibrium" (Prigogine and Allen 1982, 6).

What characterizes large-scale systems that are "far from" thermo-

---

21. Despite the cold shoulder that his views have received within the economics profession, Georgescu-Roegen (1986) has not recanted those views. For those younger economists unfamiliar with his impressive scholarly achievements, it is important to point out that he has been a Distinguished Fellow of the American Economic Association and has been described by Samuelson (1966, vii) as "a pioneer in mathematical economics . . . a scholar's scholar, an economist's economist."

22. Born in Russia in 1917, Prigogine received the Nobel Prize in 1977 for his research on the thermodynamics of nonequilibrium systems.

dynamic equilibrium? One feature is that they are best described by macroscopic variables and by boundary conditions linking them to their environments, e.g., temperature and pressure averages, not by the properties of their individual components (Nicolis and Prigogine 1989, 51).[23] Another characteristic of far-from-equilibrium systems is that they commonly display nonlinear relationships among these macroscopic variables (Prigogine and Stengers 1984, 137). Still another facet of such systems is that perturbations or random fluctuations "can force the system to leave a given macroscopic state and lead it on to a new state which has a different spatiotemporal structure" (Prigogine 1976, 93).

These characteristics, in turn, imply that such systems display instabilities and a tendency toward historical evolution. As Nicolis and Prigogine (1989, 14) have expressed the matter, "Far from equilibrium, *several solutions* are possible for the *same parameter values*. Chance alone will decide which of these solutions will be realized. The fact that only one among many possibilities occurred gives the system a historical dimension." Hence, at critical junctures in their histories, such systems may face alternative paths of future development and chance may play a role in determining which irreversible path is actually followed.[24]

Prigogine has employed the concept of *dissipative structures* to synthesize all of these points about far-from-equilibrium systems:

> We have introduced the notion of "dissipative structures," to emphasize the close association between structure and order on the one side, and dissipation or waste on the other. . . . The interaction of a system with the outside world, its embedding in nonequilibrium conditions, may become . . . the starting point for the formation of new dynamic states of matter. . . . We have called these structures *dissipative structures* to emphasize the constructive role of dissipative processes in their formation. (Prigogine and Stengers 1984, 12, 143)

Whether recent research on dissipative structures in the physical domain is pertinent to the analysis of economic phenomena can and should be debated. However, there is already some evidence that this theoretical notion

---

23. As Jantsch (1980, 23–24) observes, modern physics and chemistry have had to struggle against the earlier scientific view that all phenomena can be reduced to a single microscopic level of explanation—a level that physics used to seek in the atomic structure of matter. Interestingly, Samuelson (1947, 345) remarked more than four decades ago that successful analysis of systems with nonlinearities would require adoption of a macroscopic perspective.

24. Nicolis and Prigogine (1989, 13–14) illustrate this theoretical point nicely with their example of the Bénard cell experiment. Application of heat to a contained fluid will eventually induce convection cells within the fluid at a particular temperature, but the direction of rotation of those cells is purely a matter of chance. "We thus arrive at a remarkable cooperation between chance and determinism."

will become attractive and useful to economists in the years to come. Echoing Samuelson (1947, 288) on the presence of nonlinearities in social processes, Arrow (1988, 278) has argued that "many empirical phenomena are not covered well by either the theoretical or the empirical analyses based on linear stochastic systems. . . . These empirical results have given impetus to the closer study of . . . nonlinear dynamic models."[25]

More specifically, Arthur (1988, 1990a) has pointed to a number of concrete examples of "positive feedbacks," or nonlinearities, embedded in market systems. Those positive feedbacks often result from large fixed costs, learning effects, coordination effects, and adaptive expectations held by economic agents.

> Dynamical systems . . . with local positive feedbacks . . . tend to possess a multiplicity of asymptotic states or possible "emergent structures." The initial starting state combined with early random events or fluctuations acts to push the dynamics into the domain of one of these asymptotic states and thus to "select" the structure that the system eventually "locks into." (Arthur 1988, 9)

Similar conclusions have been advanced by Radzicki (1990b). This mode of economic reasoning is clearly compatible with the dissipative-structures approach of Prigogine.

What impact would acceptance of the dissipative-structures paradigm have on the conduct and performance of the economics profession? On the ontological front, its adoption would lead economic research along a more pluralistic path since some economic phenomena might prove to be deterministic and reversible in a mechanistic fashion whereas others might turn out to be probabilistic and irreversible in the thermodynamic sense.[26] As Prigogine himself has framed the issue: "Apparently there are two conflicting worlds, a world of [mechanistic] trajectories and a world of [evolutionary] processes, and there is no way of denying one by asserting the other" (Prigogine and Stengers 1984, 252).

Another ontological premise entailed by the dissipative-structures para-

---

25. Boldrin (1988, 49) states that nonlinear dynamics has not had a major impact on the development of modern economic theory up to this point. For a pioneering effort to develop a nonlinear macrodynamics, however, see Goodwin (1967), which contains a model formally similar to the ecological predator-prey model of Lotka and Volterra.

26. According to Allen and McGlade (1989, 7), the ecosystems that form the biological foundation for economic activity are fundamentally nonmechanical: "If a set of mechanical equations is set up which try to represent a real ecosystem, then, when they are run forward in time on a computer, most of the species present are eliminated. . . . Since the natural systems which surround us do in reality maintain their complexity, we may conclude that the mechanical equations which are used . . . do not capture the real interactions and adaptability of the natural system!"

digm is recognition of complexity, not simplicity, in many real domains. That is, we must "explore *complexity*, be it at the level of molecules . . . or even of social systems" (Nicolis and Prigogine 1989, ix). This obligation has already been accepted by Simon (1981, xi), who argues that the artificial phenomena of human society are "inextricably interwoven" with issues of complexity.[27]

Acknowledgment of complexity, in turn, entails the ontological view that reality is a hierarchy of autonomous but interacting processes, each with its own specific set of causal relations.[28] As Simon (1981, 196) poses the issue, "[C]omplexity frequently takes the form of hierarchy . . . [which] is one of the central structural schemes that the architect of complexity uses." Hence, just as most biologists would admit that ecosystems, species, and individual organisms are all significant levels of natural reality, economists need to face the fact that social classes, corporate organizations, and the state are levels of economic reality that cannot be reduced to sets of atomistic, optimizing individuals.

A final ontological premise awaiting those economists who embrace a nonequilibrium thermodynamic perspective is the central role of chance and novelty in the real world.[29] Dissipative structures, according to Prigogine, display "a delicate interplay between chance and necessity, between fluctuations and deterministic laws. We expect that near a bifurcation, . . . random elements would play an important role, while between bifurcations the deterministic aspects would become dominant" (Prigogine and Stengers 1984, 176).[30]

What practical precepts do these ontological premises suggest to the contemporary economist? One is the need for accelerated transfer of scientific

---

27. "Roughly, by a complex system I mean one made up of a large number of parts that interact in a nonsimple way. In such systems . . . . , given the properties of the parts and the laws of their interaction, it is not a trivial matter to infer the properties of the whole" (Simon 1981, 195). For similar ideas, see Hodgson (1987).

28. For more on this point, see Danchin (1983), Jantsch (1980), and Wolff and Resnick (1987).

29. The notion that free will and human creativity are important when one applies the dissipative-structures paradigm to human society is explored by Artigiani (1987) in his analysis of eighteenth-century political revolutions. In his discussion of technological change, Clark (1990) pursues a similar line of argument.

30. A bifurcation point for a nonequilibrium system is a critical value of its control parameter beyond which there is not a single solution state for the system corresponding to each parameter value. Once that crucial point has been exceeded, several solution states are associated with any particular parameter value, and random perturbations decide which state is actually realized. Note that this is quite different from chaotic behavior, which can be generated by relatively simple dynamic systems and which, although apparently random to the observer, has a deterministic basis (Baumol and Quandt 1985; Kamminga 1990). A thorny methodological problem facing economists is how to distinguish among aperiodic behaviors generated by exogenous shocks, complex endogenous interactions, and chaos within simple systems (Ruelle 1988).

capital between the natural and social sciences.[31] Another is the need for greater intellectual humility in the face of systemic complexity and evolutionary change driven in part by random chance.[32] Still another is the need for professional tolerance so that issues of social class and corporate organization can take their rightful place alongside individual decision making as legitimate topics for economic research.[33] A final methodological dictum implied by these premises is the need to expand the range of analytical tools used in economic research. Since models of complex nonlinear systems often defy formal mathematical solution, computer simulations will have to be gleaned for scientific insights into the dynamics of those systems (Thompson and Stewart 1986, ix; Forrester 1987b, 136). Since economic systems frequently take the form of adaptive nonlinear networks, in which large numbers of evolving agents displaying bounded rationality interact, combinatorics could prove to be a useful analytical tool (Holland 1988).

Evolutionary Futures: A Simple Model

This is not to say, of course, that conventional mathematical models are useless as we seek to grasp nonlinearities, complexity, dissipation, chance, etc. Although formal mathematical representations inevitably fail to grasp the actual richness of economic phenomena, they may nonetheless possess some heuristic value.[34]

Consider, for example, a simple dynamic model that aims to mimic some of the historical features of the global economy. Two facts of modern economic history that beg for recognition are the accelerating expansion of world population and the sustained increase in global product per capita, which have occurred for several centuries (Kuznets 1966, chap. 2).[35] Another notable trend is the demographic transition to low fertility, which began in the indus-

31. Tribe (1989) has drawn the similar conclusion that research on constitutional law would benefit from an infusion of insights from modern physics.

32. In a similar but distinct vein, Baumol and Quandt (1985) argue that chaotic behavior in economic systems may severely limit the efficacy of macroeconomic forecasting models.

33. Norgaard (1989) has argued vigorously and persuasively for methodological and theoretical pluralism within economics.

34. How much heuristic value they can possess is debatable. O'Connor (1990, C-16) stresses the epistemological limits of formal economic theorizing: "One never starts in a vacuum when it comes to problem-solving. On the contrary there are always too many opinions and not enough consensus, too many uncertainties and contradictory certainties."

35. Two caveats need to be mentioned at this point. One is that the measured increase in *gross output* per capita has greatly exceeded the rise in *net income* per head because the expansion of commodity production has entailed natural resource depletion and ecosystem degradation, two forms of depreciation not recognized by national income accounts (Daly 1991, 31–39). The second is that the growth of global output per head masks social inequality within nations and uneven development among regions and nations (United Nations 1991, chap. 2).

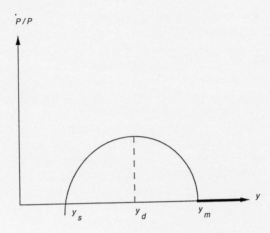

Fig. 1. Stylized effect of economic development on demographics

trial nations a century ago and which has apparently begun to spread to a number of developing countries (Jacobson 1988, 153). Still another crucial fact is that economic development of the modern world has been fueled, to a great extent, by the combustion of fossil hydrocarbons (see Norgaard's chapter in this volume).

These stylized facts are represented in the following elementary model of economic and demographic growth. Let the impact of world economic development on global fertility and mortality be given by:

$$\dot{P}/P = \alpha_0 y^2 + \alpha_1 y + \alpha_2 \text{ when } y \le y_m, \text{ and} \qquad (1a)$$

$$\dot{P}/P = 0 \text{ when } y > y_m, \qquad (1b)$$

where P is total population, y is output per capita, and where $\alpha_0 < 0$, $\alpha_1 > 0$, $\alpha_2 < 0$. This specification implies, as depicted in figure 1, that total population is stable at a subsistence level of per capita output (y_s), grows at an accelerating rate as modest levels of affluence are achieved, enters a demographic transition once per capita income exceeds y_d, and ultimately stabilizes at a high level of affluence.

Simultaneously, as Blanchet (1991) and others have noted, demographic considerations affect income growth and wealth accumulation. Let us suppose that:

$$\dot{y} = \beta P^2 - (y - y_s), \ \beta > 0, \text{ when } 0 < P \le P_c, \text{ and} \qquad (2a)$$

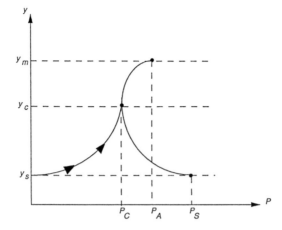

Fig. 2. Two stages of economic development

$$\dot{y} = - \gamma_1 \cdot (y - y_c)^3 + \gamma_2 \cdot (y - y_c)(P - P_c), \text{ with } \gamma_1 \text{ and } \gamma_2 > 0,$$

when $P > P_c$.[36] \hfill (2b)

The specification of equations (1) and (2) imagines a two-stage process of economic development and population growth. Suppose that human society started its economic adventure with an initial population approximately equal to zero and a subsistence standard of living. Then suppose some innovation raised output per head above its subsistence level, thereby triggering a dual process of accelerating population growth and rising affluence. As depicted in figure 2, the stable expansion path during this earlier historical stage would extend in a nonlinear fashion from $(0, y_s)$ to (P_c, y_c).

However, at the historical moment when population and affluence reached the bifurcation point (P_c, y_c), "business as usual" would no longer be possible. The growing annual flow of fossil fuels required to support a large population at an unprecedented level of affluence would result in regional and global changes in atmospheric chemistry. Extensive conversion of land surface to human use would result in loss of biodiversity and of the essential services

---

36. The specification of equation (2a) is not meant to argue that growing population has been the *essential cause* of rising affluence. Growing affluence during recent centuries has been the outcome of a complex set of interacting processes including mechanization of production, emergence of new forms of property ownership and new social classes, the marriage of science and technology, the development of new ideologies and personality traits, etc. Thus, (2a) is simply a way to describe the *historical correlation* of income and population growth that we have observed.

of ecosystems. Uneven development among the members of human society would contribute to warfare, tropical deforestation, and other environment-degrading activities.[37]

Thus, at the critical moment of social bifurcation, human society faces two historic possibilities. Along one path of economic development, the "tragedy of the commons" could be played out on a global scale as a combination of unrestrained environmental degradation and natural-resource depletion leading to falling average productivity and a reversal of the demographic transition. At the extreme, this path would result in a Malthusian trap with an enormous population (P_s) living at subsistence. Since business competition and employment insecurity foster a myopic perspective, and since ethnic and nationalist rivalries discourage international management of common property, this scenario is a real historic option.[38]

If, on the other hand, the world's population were to enact a set of national laws and international treaties governing emission of toxic materials and greenhouse gases, encouraging energy conservation and use of renewable energy supplies, reducing Third World indebtedness, etc., then a more benign path of economic development might proceed, albeit at a decelerating rate.[39] This historic option (represented by the upper-right branch in figure 2) would also eventually result in a stable population (P_A), but at a much higher level of affluence.[40] Such an outcome would reflect the replacement of today's short-term particularistic perspective by a longer-term global point of view.[41]

How to inspire and internalize that broader focus on human affairs is perhaps the most pressing task we face as a species. The future path of the world economy has not been predetermined by history and "unpredictability of the future [is] the essence of [the] human adventure" (Nicolis and Prigogine 1989, 238). At this moment, we need the social and political equivalent of Schumpeter's business entrepreneur, individuals who can imagine and construct novel ways of husbanding the global economy instead of mechanically

---

37. The growing impact of human society on the global environment is surveyed in Goudie (1986).

38. For two analyses of social inequality and its negative impact on environmental protection, see England (1986, 1990).

39. For a discussion of what institutional and moral changes might be required to "lock onto" this path, see Daly and Cobb (1989).

40. The inequality $P_A < P_S$ depicted in figure 2 is a consequence of the parabolic shape of the bifurcation graph implied by equation $(2b)$ and of the assumption that the demographic transition begins at a level of per capita income lower than that which signals the onset of the second stage of economic development, i.e., $y_d < y_c$. Both of those assumptions are, of course, empirically debatable. The mathematical details of this model are available in an appendix from the author.

41. For a compelling critique of the myopic viewpoint implied by present-value calculations using positive discount rates, see Howarth and Norgaard (1990).

following established routines. Innovative efforts of this sort would have a decisive influence on the future trajectory of human society.[42]

To sum up, it is clear that acceptance of nonequilibrium thermodynamics as a cornerstone of economic inquiry leads one to a certain kind of metaphorical vision. Not the vision of a lukewarm cup of coffee that has settled at the temperature of the surrounding room, nor that of a sugar lump uniformly dissolved in a beaker of water. The proper metaphor is that of a rosebush in an English garden—an organism that requires pruning, sunshine, and watering; a plant whose fallen leaves and petals rot on the ground; but also a living thing of beauty that continuously seeks to maintain and reproduce itself through history. That organic metaphor is the appropriate starting point for a dialogue between natural and economic science, a dialogue that can, it is hoped, help us to construct a sustainable future.

---

42. Locking onto a benign path of economic development will require a new technological regime that can replace the fossil-fuel-dependent technologies of the past two centuries (Georgescu-Roegen 1982a, 28–33). Perhaps small nations and nongovernmental organizations will play a key role as social and technical innovators in the decades to come.

The Coevolution of Economic and Environmental Systems and the Emergence of Unsustainability

Richard B. Norgaard

. . . we may recall the comment on social and political affairs made by that humane, grumpy, but normally clearheaded commentator, Walter Lippmann, which distills much of what has come to light in our own inquiry. "To every human problem," he said, "there is a solution that is simple, neat, and *wrong*"; and that is as true of intellectual as it is of practical problems. The seduction of High Modernity lay in its abstract neatness and theoretical simplicity: both of these features blinded the successors of Descartes to the unavoidable complexities of concrete human experience.

—Final words to Stephen Toulmin's *Cosmopolis* (1975)

Economic understanding of development has drawn on diverse metaphors of change. Economies have been portrayed to develop as embryos grow; to unfold through stages like the morphogenesis of caterpillars into butterflies; to gradually evolve through selective pressures; to progressively improve through better knowledge, social organization, and technology; and to go through revolutions. These disparate metaphors, many of them biological, have enriched our understanding and empowered our explanations. Nevertheless, capital accumulation has been the principal explanation of change in neoclassical, Marxist, and popular thought, the most important in formal economic models, and a basis for the design of powerful development institutions. The accumulation explanation is so seductive, simple, and neat that the complexities of changes in understanding, technologies, and ways of organizing are typically reduced to additions to human, physical, and organizational capital.

Yet as the century comes to a close, the fate of the "modern project" in the North, and its extension as development in the South, is unclear. While capitalism has become the triumphant economic form, the sustainability of development is in doubt because of environmental degradation. Amidst economic globalization, both cultural homogenization and cultural resistance have intensified. Meanwhile, new understandings of change as chaotic, unpredictable processes and as periodic, rapid coevolution of parts to whole new forms are becoming a part of our consciousness. These unfoldings in our environmental knowledge, cultural behavior, and ways of perceiving change do not append neatly to the dominant formal model of economic development. Given the novelty of the times, the number of ways economists formally understand processes of change might better match the richness of our metaphors and rhetoric.

Dominant Premises of Western Thought

To avoid being selected out as misfits in Western intellectual evolution, economists have been obliged to adopt the widely held, modernist premises of Western thought: atomism, mechanism, objectivism, universalism, and monism (fig. 1). Atomism posits that parts can be understood apart from the systems in which they are embedded and that systems are simply the sum of their parts. Mechanism posits that relations between parts of a system do not change, a condition necessary for pre-diction and control. Universalism states that the heterogeneous and complex world around us can be explained by the interaction of a relatively small number of universal principles. Objectivism posits that our values, ways of knowing, and actions can be kept apart from the systems we are trying to understand. Monism posits that our separate disciplinary ways of knowing are merging into a coherent whole. The history of economic thought, especially its increasing formalization and separation from the other social science understandings during the latter half of this century, reflects the dominating selective, as well as seductive, influence of these premises.

In fact these "isms" poorly characterize the diverse and contradictory ways people, whether as lay-people or as scientists, actually think about the complexities of the world around them. They are, however, the "official" premises, the ones reinforced by explanations of how science is supposed to work. Being solidly held among scientists and their admirers in the last century, they became embedded in institutions linking science to public decision making, and they remain the premises to which scientists implicitly appeal when defending a prediction or prescription. Thus these premises still determine the bounds of acceptable political discourse and structure the processes of public fact gathering, policy making, and implementation (Norgaard 1992).

These five philosophical premises have been perfectly good suppositions from which to reason. They facilitated a level of prediction and control beyond that ever known before. At the same time, intervention in environmental

Dominant Modernist Premises	Emerging Additional Premises
Atomism: Systems consist of unchanging parts and are simply the sum of their parts.	Holism: Parts cannot be understood apart from their wholes and wholes are different from the sum of their parts.
Mechanism: Relationships between parts are fixed, systems move smoothly from one equilibria to another, and changes are reversible.	Multimodelism: Systems might be mechanical, but they might also be deterministic yet not predictable or smooth because they are chaotic or simply very discontinuous. Systems can also be evolutionary.
Universalism: Diverse, complex phenomena are the result of underlying universal principles that are few in number and unchanging over time and space.	Contextualism: Phenomena are contingent upon a large number of factors particular to the time and place. Similar phenomena might well occur in different times and places due to widely different factors.
Objectivism: How we value, perceive, and understand systems are apart from the systems we are trying to understand and act upon, even social systems.	Subjectivism: Systems cannot be understood apart from our current values and means of perceiving, or apart from how we have known, valued, and hence acted upon systems in the past.
Monism: Our separate individual ways of understanding complex systems are merging into a coherent whole.	Pluralism: Complex systems can only be known through alternate patterns of thinking that are necessarily simplifications of reality. Different patterns are inherently incongruent.

Fig. 1. Premises of Western thought

and economic systems using reasoning based solely on these premises has resulted in longer-term, broader consequences that were not foreseen. The problem now is that these premises have been so embedded in our institutions and so controlling of public discourse about science and policy that they have excluded the use of patterns of thinking dependent upon other premises. Other patterns of thinking are needed to understand the numerous unforeseen changes in environmental and economic systems that the use of the dominant patterns has wrought (Roth 1987; Norgaard 1989). It has been the unpredicted unsustainability of the interactions between economic and environmental systems that, along with reculturization driven by the vacuity of materialism, have made the future of modernity so tenuous.

These dominant beliefs about science are no longer maintained by philosophers as self-evident (Grene 1985; Rorty 1979; Toulmin 1972, 1982). Parts need not have well-defined, constant, and atomic existences. Systems need not be mechanical. Knowledge can be context specific. Different models employ necessarily different simplifications and are thereby necessarily incomparable and quite likely incompatible (Feyerabend 1975; Quine 1953). Perhaps most importantly for economics, social philosophers are acknowledging that how we have understood social systems historically affects both our actions within those systems and our efforts to redesign them (Unger 1975; Toulmin 1975). Similarly, agricultural systems are now being interpreted as artifacts of human intervention around earlier understandings of agriculture (Altieri 1987). A coevolutionary explanation of change readily incorporates these new metaphysical and epistemological perspectives. Given the atomistic-mechanistic nature of the dominant formal models in economics, coevolutionary models ought therefore to be especially advantageous.

Development as a Coevolutionary Process

Consider development as a process of coevolution between knowledge, values, organization, technology, and the environment (fig. 2). Each of these subsystems is related to each of the others; yet each is also changing and effecting change in the others. Deliberate innovations, chance discoveries, and random changes occur in each subsystem thereby selecting on the distribution of the qualities of components in each of the other subsystems. Whether new components prove fit depends on the characteristics of each of the subsystems at the time. With each subsystem putting selective pressure on each of the others, they coevolve in a manner whereby each reflects the other. Thus, everything is coupled, yet everything is changing (Norgaard 1988).

To further elaborate the process, imagine that the subsystems' values, knowledge, social organization, and technology of figure 2 are made up of different "types" of ways of valuing, knowing, organizing, and doing things. Similarly the environmental subsystem consists of numerous types of species, environmental factors, and relationships between them. The survival and relative dominance, or frequency, of each particular type in each subsystem is explained by its historical fitness with respect to the types of things in the other subsystems. The relative importance, or frequency distribution, of different types results from selection processes.

Imagine that a new type is introduced into one of the subsystems. For example, imagine that a new way of understanding, let us call it N for Newtonian, is introduced into the knowledge subsystem of Western culture. The survival and relative importance of N will depend on the selective pressures from the other subsystems. If N does not fit, it will not survive. If N "fits," it will survive. If N fits better than other ways of knowing, it will replace them, or at least reduce their relative importance, and thereby increase its own dominance relative to others. If N survives, it begins to put selective pressure on the components of the other subsystems, and if N is increasing in

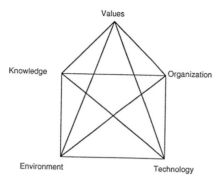

Fig. 2. Development as coevolution

dominance, it will exert more and more selective pressure on the relative dominance, or frequency distribution, of components within the other subsystems. This process, with introductions, experiments, and mutations occurring within each subsystem, is occurring across all of the subsystems simultaneously. With each subsystem applying selective pressure on each of the other subsystems, they all reflect each other.

Environmental subsystems are treated symmetrically with the subsystems of values, knowledge, social organization, and technology in this coevolutionary explanation of development. New technologies, for example, exert new selective pressures on species, while newly evolved characteristics of species, in turn, select for different technologies. Similarly, transformations in the biosphere select for new ways of understanding the biosphere. For example, the use of pesticides induces resistance and secondary pest resurgence, selecting both for new pesticides and for more systematic ways of thinking about pest control. Pests, pesticides, pesticide production, pesticide institutions and policy, how we understand pest control, and how we value chemicals in the environment all demonstrate an incredibly tight coevolution that took place during the second half of this century (Brown 1991, chap. 2).

This is an unusual way to think about how people interact with environmental systems. Our dominant way of thinking about environmental issues portrays people as degrading environments rather than as affecting a complex evolutionary feedback process of selective pressures between economic and environmental systems. There need not, however, be a contradiction in these ways of thinking. In the short run, people interact in accordance with the atomistic-mechanistic worldview, physically influencing parts and relations within environmental systems. The coevolutionary model, however, incorporates longer-term evolutionary feedbacks. To emphasize coevolutionary processes is not to deny that people directly intervene in and change the characteristics of environments. The coevolutionary perspective puts its emphasis on the chain of events thereafter—how different interventions alter the selective pressure and hence the relative dominance of environmental traits, which, in turn, select for particular values, knowledge, organization, and technology, leading to the subsequent interventions in the environment.

The coevolutionary vantage also provides an unusual perspective on the environment-economy relationship with respect to economic thinking. It neither assumes that economies destroy the environment because of the myopic greed of powerful capitalists who must be overthrown nor assumes that environmental failure stems from externalities that can be corrected through creation of new markets. Rather, the coevolutionary perspective presents an alternative to the picture of the development process that is shared by both Marxists and neoclassicals. Development in the modern worldview stems from the conscious accumulation of human capital, its rational application to the design and accumulation of technological and organizational capital, and the accumulation of physical capital. In this vision, the accumulation of human-produced capital hopefully more than offsets an inevitable, though manageable, degradation in natural capital. A dichotomy is established wherein economic development, a "good," is compensated by environmental deterioration, a "bad."

This overly general characterization of human-produced capital and natural capital as offsetting substitutes sustains the more particular discussion on the extent to which key types of natural capital are complements to human-produced capital (Ehrlich 1989). Portraying resources and environmental systems with fixed attributes that become used up or not sufficiently offset has required economists to try to measure natural capital (Repetto et al. 1989), find indicators of whether natural capital has become scarce relative to human-produced capital (Barbier 1989, for a summary; Norgaard 1990, for a logical refutation), determine the limits of renewable systems (Vitousek et al. 1986), and incorporate this information into the economic planning process (Ahmad, El-Serafy, and Lutz 1989). These efforts have been extremely productive, but the epistemological ideas behind conceptual pluralism indicate that pursuing other paradigms will increase the robustness of our understanding.

In the coevolutionary explanation of change, on the other hand, knowledge, technologies, and social organization merely change, rather than advance, and the "betterness" of each is only relative to how well each fits with everything else in a coevolving whole. Coevolutionary change, rather than a process of rational design and improvement, occurs through experimentation, only partly conscious, and through selection. The qualities of economic and environmental systems are constantly redefining each other within the process of the coevolving whole. Development as accumulation assumes a constant metric, which the coevolutionary vision adamantly denies. And yet from the values of any culture at any point in time, the past can still be described and valued in the coevolutionary paradigm, whereas the future can only be vaguely foreseen and weighed.

From the coevolutionary vantage, the distribution of power or control, interpreted from both the neoclassical and the Marxist perspective, is visibly affecting the choice of technologies, the construction of knowledge, the selection of dominant values, the reproduction of social structure, and the transformation of the environment. The coevolutionary vantage, however, does not offer as good a view of these workings as either the neoclassical or the Marxist perspective; but neither does it deny these understandings. Rather, it frames them more broadly, over longer periods, and helps us see how these perspectives themselves are evolving constructions of the larger process of modernization.

The modernist explanation of history links development to (1) an accumulation of knowledge and capital facilitating control over nature and (2) environmental interventions that necessarily reduce the naturalness of the environment. The coevolutionary explanation recognizes that many aspects of environmental systems are the result of human intervention over millennia. It emphasizes how nature is social, in effect how environments are economic, by incorporating how people have put selective pressure on the biosphere. Similarly, it emphasizes how societies are natural in that their ways of valuing, knowing, organizing, and doing things have been selected by environmental conditions. This inherent reflection, or mutual fitness, of components does not imply that we live in the best of all possible worlds, however. Current fitness, for example, does not mean that extinction is not around the corner. Nor does the coevolutionary perspective excuse us from the responsibility to strive for improvements. By comparing the two worldviews, however, we see more clearly how the division between natural and unnatural, or social and unsocial, is a modern construction of nature and development.

One of its striking differences from the conventional interpretation of people's relationship to the environment is that, in the coevolutionary explanation, environmental transformations can both benefit people and improve upon "nature" by existing standards of value. In the conventional interpretation, for example, "natural" systems are portrayed as never having been disturbed by people, and disturbance inevitably decreases naturalness. Decreases in biodiversity are among the current portrayals of human disturbance. But few terrestrial systems have not been affected by people. There is evidence now that the diversity of potatoes in Peru was increased through human activities (Brush 1982). Furthermore, the diversity of the Amazon tropical rainforest may have been positively influenced by new evolutionary opportunities created in the patches of jungle temporarily cleared by indigenous peoples. While these phenomena can certainly be explained as exceptions through conventional reasoning, they fit better into the coevolutionary depiction of people's relationship with nature. By helping us to see when and how economic activities have stimulated favorable coevolution, the portrayal could give us new direction.

The Coevolution of Unsustainability

From the coevolutionary vantage, let me elaborate two complementary explanations of the appearance of unsustainability. First, from this new position we can see more clearly how economies have transformed during recent centuries—from coevolving with their ecosystems to coevolving around the combustion of fossil hydrocarbons. In this transformation, people have been freed from environmental feedbacks on their economic activities, which they experience relatively quickly and generally as individuals and communities. The feedbacks that remain occur over longer periods and are experienced collectively, even globally, making them more difficult to perceive and counteract (Norgaard 1984). Second, the coevolutionary paradigm helps us interpret how the spatial structure of economies grew and merged into a global economy, coevolving with economic arguments rooted in modernist premises of science. This coevolution of economic organization with economic patterns of explanation has increased the "distance" between consumption and production, and between economic action and environmental effects, inducing the environmental "externalities" that economic theory itself treats as an exception. While each of these interconnected transformations has been elaborated in other literatures, the coevolutionary framework helps us see how Western understanding has affected the transformation of environmental systems, how economic thinking has affected the nature of economies, and how unsustainability appears to have emerged.

When agriculture began some five to ten thousand years ago, there were probably about 5 million people in the world. Population doubled eight times, increasing to about 1.6 billion people by the middle of the nineteenth century. These eight doublings in world population occurred through diverse coevolutions of values, knowledge, ways of organizing, technologies, and environmental systems that favored the expansion of the human population, an increase in longevity, and cultural change. Economic and environmental systems coevolved in different ways, creating a patchwork quilt of cultures around the globe. The process was contextual and historically contingent. Life improved through a myriad of agricultural innovations and environmental transformations that facilitated the capture of energy from the sun matched by social transformations to provide sustaining feedbacks with the environment. Trade occurred between the patches and became increasingly important with improvements in ships, and vast but weak empires, as well as later systems of colonial rule, were imposed over the patchwork of different cultures. Trade, empires, and colonization affected the coevolution within patches through the exchange of ideas, materials, technology, and ways of organizing (not infrequently by force), yet the patches remained quite distinct well into the nineteenth century.

Beginning in Europe and North America in the nineteenth century, values, knowledge, institutions, and technology began to coevolve with fossil hydrocarbons rather than ecosystems. Western social systems coevolved with the selective pressures of a new fossil hydrocarbon economy rather than the historic environmental economy, resulting in new ways of working and living. New transportation infrastructure, larger firms and bigger cities, new emphases in education, and new ways of organizing people coevolved. Ecological systems were also transformed, but the process of transformation changed from the artful manipulation undertaken during the rise of agriculture to the overriding and controlling of ecosystem functions through energy imported into the agricultural system. Fossil hydrocarbons drove a wedge between the immediate and longer-term interactions people had with ecosystems, and the knowledges, technologies, and institutions for managing these interactions selectively decayed. To the extent that social systems responded to environmental transformations, they were reactionary, belated efforts to prevent excessive damage rather than to enhance new opportunities.

By tapping into fossil hydrocarbons, Western societies freed themselves, at least for a time, from many of the complexities of interacting with environmental systems. With an energy source other than the sun, tractors replaced animal power, fertilizers replaced the complexities of interplanting crops that were good hosts of nitrogen-fixing bacteria with those that were not, and pesticides replaced the biological controls provided by more complex agroecosystems. Furthermore, inexpensive commercial energy meant crops could be stored for longer periods and transported over greater distances. Each of these accomplishments was based on the partial (atomized) understanding of separate sciences and separate technologies. At least in the short run, separate adjustments of the parts seemed to fit into a coherent, stable whole. Agriculture transformed from an agroecosystem culture of relatively self-sufficient communities to an agroindustrial culture of many separate, distant actors linked by global markets. These massive changes in technology and organization gave people the sense of having control over nature and being able to consciously design their future. The coevolutions in mining, industry, and transportation added to this sense of control.

The first explanation of the unsustainability of development then is simply that reliance on fossil hydrocarbons freed individuals from immediate environmental interactions while it shifted environmental impacts (in ways that have proven difficult to comprehend) to broader and broader publics, indeed the global polity, and onto future generations. Working with these collective, longer-term, and more uncertain interrelationships is at least as challenging as environmental management has ever been historically.

The coevolutionary perspective, however, helps us see that the problem is not simply a matter of establishing market incentives to adjust how we interact with nature. Our values, knowledge, and social organization have coevolved around the fossil hydrocarbon economy. Our fossil-fuel-driven economy has not simply transformed the environment. In addition, it has selected for individualist, materialist values; favored the development of reductionist understanding at the expense of systemic understanding; and preferred a bureaucratic, centralized form of control that works better for electric utilities and other types of industrial enterprises than for ecosystem management. Our ability to perceive and resolve environmental problems within the dominant modes of valuing, thinking, and organizing is severely constrained as a consequence of these coevolutionary trends. It is not an accident that neoclassical economics addresses the *piecemeal correction* of resource and environmental inefficiencies through improved markets, largely ignoring the historical role of markets within a broader vision of viable relations between economies and the environment.

Economic thought, as part of Western knowledge, has itself also influenced the coevolutionary process. International trade theorists, for example, have long known that the basic market model has no spatial dimensions. It implicitly assumes that all the world's economies could fit on the head of a pin, a premise that denies the need for a subdiscipline on trade. Transport costs, of course, can be added into the model, but they only complicate the reasoning without much affecting the policy conclusions, and hence are still typically ignored. The complications of domestic market structures, multinational corporations, technological change, employment policy, and other factors, however, do affect policy conclusions (Krugman 1990).

The situation is similar in the case of environmental economics. The basic market model assumes away the impediments of information costs, the existence of diverse forms of collective ownership and obligations, and the costs of enforcing private rules and collective agreements. Economists then acknowledge that environmental problems exist because, in "exceptional" circumstances, these factors can be important. The increasing prevalence and severity of environmental problems suggest that addressing them with models that treat them as exceptions is dubious at best. Yet, as in the case of international trade, the environmental policy conclusion has been the same: markets are good and should be made to work as well as possible. These conclusions can be modified to account for the peculiarities of economic and social organization beyond the market, but again, since these are not included in the amended model, they are treated as exceptions (Bromley 1989). How

Western societies trade and interact with the environment has coevolved for two centuries with the understanding, and hence policy conclusions, associated with the basic market model, with only recent and belated attention to the exceptions to the premises of the model. Furthermore, the trade and environmental problems associated with the exceptions to the dominant view have been multiplicative. Had our policies been driven by analyses that stressed the very factors that are treated as exceptions in the market model, we would neither have the type of global economy nor the types of environmental problems we have today.

The global economy has coevolved around the assumption of individualism as much as the logic of trade. The logic states that when two agents who are free to choose actually do choose to enter into an exchange, it is because the transaction makes each of them better off. The assumption has always been that it is human and corporate individuals who should be free to choose. Had the atomistic premise of natural philosophy not so readily translated into the individualism of Western social thought, we might today presume that communities, bioregions, nations, or even spatially overlapping cultural groups should be free to choose.

The difference between individual and community interest, of course, is intimately tied to the systemic character of environmental systems. Nature cannot readily be divided up and assigned to individuals. For this reason, collective management is often necessary. Adopting "Free to choose" as individualist ideology and using it to justify the expansion of exchange across communities thus opens up new opportunities for market failures. Spatial economic expansion increases the social phenomena labeled "distancing" by sociologists (Giddens 1990), the increased separation of individual action from its social and environmental consequences, thereby increasing the difficulty of establishing the monitoring, contracts, and enforcement that sustainable interactions require. The expansion of markets across communities and space, in short, needs to be coupled both with new environmental management systems at the community level and new management systems across more communities. Exchange theory kept "simple and neat" assumes away both distance and community. To the extent that environmental problems are more easily perceived and controlled at local and community levels (Dryzek 1987), unsustainable interactions between the economy and environment are a coevolutionary outcome of contemporary economic thinking.

Conclusions

The coevolutionary framing of the interrelationship between economic and environmental systems pursued here contrasts sharply with the dominant separate framings of economists and environmentalists. In the coevolutionary view, environments and economies reflect each other: society's ways of valuing, knowing, organizing, and doing coevolve with the environment, each exerting selective pressure on the other. At the same time, the coevolutionary model is useless for the sorts of predictions that Newtonian thinking does so precisely, but it helps explain why precise mechanistic predictions do not come true. And yet the coevolutionary view does have design value. It highlights that the evolutionary process will have more potential, and will be likely to continue longer into the future, the greater the diversity of its parts and relations, including diversity in how we understand. The neoclassical and coevolutionary frameworks thus highlight each other's nature, strengths, weaknesses, and appropriateness of use.

Environmental economics, in keeping with the discipline as a whole, has been ahistorical. Market failures have been analyzed and solutions prescribed without reference to how externalities arose through the evolutionary processes of development. The coevolutionary explanation helps us see how development selects for externalities as well as selects for forms of social organization that make externalities difficult to internalize. Environmental externalities have arisen, in part, because fossil hydrocarbon economies override environmental systems rather than work with them. But externalities have also arisen and persisted because we tend to view economies and environments atomistically, presuming the whole to be simply the sum of separate parts. Interrelations leading to market failure are presumed not to exist until a problem is publicly recognized because the dominant premises of science treat complexity as an exception in much the same way as the neoclassical market model treats externalities as exceptions. Economic and environmental institutions have coevolved with atomistic premises about the nature of environmental and economic systems, leading to the unsustainable relations between economy and environment appearing today.

The two complementary coevolutionary explanations presented in this chapter are but part of the story. Values, for example, have also coevolved in a way that contributes to unsustainability. The idea of progress, originally concerned with moral development, coevolved with the material concerns of Western science and the modern project, the extension of atomism to individualism in social thought, and the development of economic thought to the individual materialism we have today (Bellah et al. 1991; Nelson 1991; Howarth and Norgaard 1992). The coevolutionary potential of environmental systems themselves, furthermore, is no longer what it was or could be, contributing further to unsustainability. Hence, the interactions between environment and economy and their unsustainability are a product of many complementary processes.

The contemporary clash between the secular religions of economism and environmentalism is a battle over conflicting, historic portrayals of economic and environmental systems and what they imply about our options for the future. These conflicting portrayals, however, are rooted in the same dominant premises of Western thought that are now so embedded in Western institutions. Thus, new visions and strategies to improve the sustainability of development from within formal institutions are proving difficult to discern. At the same time, nongovernmental environmental and social groups are busily questioning conventions, exploring new approaches, and testing alternatives. Some groups are finding ways to work with formal institutions, changing them from within. Others are pushing from without for whole new visions of environment and development. As individuals, many of us find ourselves positioned within the formal structure while consciously, administratively, and financially supporting newer, more informal social organizations. And yet over the past decade, nongovernmental organizations, with their heretical ways of characterizing problems and assaulting issues, have acquired unexpected roles and status, formalities of their own, while older institutions have been conceptually and strategically gridlocked. The coevolutionary process goes on. Indeed, the times appear especially interesting from this new vantage.

Bibliography

Aage, H. 1984. "Economic Arguments on the Sufficiency of Natural Resources." *Cambridge Journal of Economics* 8 (March): 105–13.

Abernathy, W., and J. Utterback. 1978. "Patterns of Industrial Innovation." *Technology Review* 80 (June/July): 41–47.

Abreu, D., and A. Rubinstein. 1988. "The Structure of Nash Equilibrium in Repeated Games with Finite Automata." *Econometrica* 56 (November): 1259–81.

Adelman, F. 1972. "Review." *Journal of Economic Literature* 10 (June): 458–60.

Ahmad, Y., S. El-Serafy, and E. Lutz, eds. 1989. *Environmental Accounting for Sustainable Development.* Washington, D.C.: World Bank.

Alchian, A. 1950. "Uncertainty, Evolution, and Economic Theory." *Journal of Political Economy* 58 (June): 211–21.

Allen, P. M. 1988. "Dynamic Models of Evolving Systems." *System Dynamics Review* 4:109–30.

Allen, P. M., and J. M. McGlade. 1987. "Modeling Complex Human Systems: A Fisheries Example." *European Journal of Operational Research* 24:147–67.

———. 1989. "Optimality, Adequacy and the Evolution of Complexity." In Christiansen and Parmentier, 3–21.

Althusser, L. 1969. *For Marx.* New York: Pantheon Books.

Altieri, M. 1987. *Agroecology: The Scientific Basis of Alternative Agriculture.* Boulder: Westview.

Amariglio, J. 1990. "Economics as a Postmodern Discourse." In W. Samuels, ed., *Economics as Discourse*, 15–46. Boston: Kluwer.

Amariglio, J., S. Resnick, and R. Wolff. 1990. "Division and Difference in the 'Discipline' of Economics." *Critical Inquiry* 17 (Autumn): 108–37.

Amendola, M., and J. Gaffard. 1988. *The Innovative Choice.* Oxford: Basil Blackwell.

Andersen, D., and J. Sturis. 1988. "Chaotic Structures in Generic Management Models: Pedagogical Principles and Examples." *System Dynamics Review* 4 (Summer): 218–45.

Anderson, P., K. Arrow, and D. Pines, eds. 1988. *The Economy as an Evolving Complex System.* Redwood City, Calif.: Addison-Wesley.

Andreassen, P. 1990. "Judgmental Extrapolation and the Salience of Change." *Journal of Forecasting* 9:347–72.

Andresen, B. 1989. "Finite-Time Thermodynamics." In Christiansen and Parmentier, 529–34.

227

Aoki, M. 1986. "Horizontal vs. Vertical Information Structure of the Firm." *American Economic Review* 76 (December): 971–83.

———. 1988. *Information, Incentives and Bargaining in the Japanese Economy.* Cambridge: Cambridge University Press.

Aoki, M., and G. Dosi. 1991. "Corporate Organization, Finance and Innovation." In V. Zamagni, ed., *Finance and the Enterprise.* New York: Academic Press.

Arrow, K. 1962. "The Economic Implications of Learning by Doing." *Review of Economic Studies* 29:155–73.

———. 1974a. *The Limits of Organization.* New York: W.W. Norton.

———. 1974b. "On the Agenda of Organizations." In R. Marris, ed., *The Corporate Society.* London: Macmillan.

———. 1986. "Rationality of Self and Others in an Economic System." *Journal of Business* 59 (October): S385–S399.

———. 1988. "Workshop on the Economy as an Evolving Complex System: Summary." In Anderson, Arrow, and Pines, 275–81.

Arthur, W. B. 1988. "Self-Reinforcing Mechanisms in Economics." In Anderson, Arrow, and Pines, 9–31.

———. 1989. "Competing Technologies, Increasing Returns, and Lock-in by Historical Events." *The Economic Journal* 99 (March): 116–31.

———. 1990a. "Positive Feedbacks in the Economy." *Scientific American* 262 (February): 92–99.

———. 1990b. "'Silicon Valley' Locational Clusters: When Do Increasing Returns Imply Monopoly?" *Mathematical Social Sciences* 19:235–51.

Arthur, W. B., Y. Ermoliev, and Y. Kaniovski. 1987. "Path-Dependent Processes and the Emergence of Macro-Structure." *European Journal of Operational Research* 30:294–303.

Artigiani, R. 1987. "Revolution and Evolution: Applying Prigogine's Dissipative Structures Model." *Journal of Social and Biological Structures* 10:249–64.

Atkins, P. 1984. *The Second Law.* New York: W. H. Freeman.

Axelrod, R. 1976. *The Structure of Decision: The Cognitive Maps of Political Elites.* Princeton: Princeton University Press.

Ayres, R. 1978. *Resources, Environment, & Economics: Applications of the Materials/Energy Balance Principle.* New York: John Wiley.

Ayres, R., and S. Miller. 1980. "The Role of Technological Change." *Journal of Environmental Economics and Management* 7 (December): 353–71.

Ayres, R., and I. Nair. 1984. "Thermodynamics and Economics." *Physics Today* 37 (November): 62–71.

Babbage, C. 1846. *On the Economy of Machinery and Manufactures.* 4th ed. London: John Murray.

Bakhtin, M. 1981. *The Dialogic Imagination.* Austin: University of Texas Press.

Balmuth, M. 1973. "Origins of Coinage." In P. Naster, ed., *A Survey of Numismatic Research 1966–1971,* 27–34. New York: International Numismatic Commission.

Barbier, E. 1989. *Economics, Natural-Resource Scarcity and Development: Conventional and Alternative Views.* London: Earthscan.

Bateson, G. 1972. *Steps to an Ecology of Mind*. New York: Ballantine.

Batten, D., J. Casti, and B. Johansson, eds. 1987. *Economic Evolution and Structural Adjustment*. Berlin: Springer-Verlag.

Baumol, W., and R. Quandt. 1985. "Chaos Models and Their Implications for Forecasting." *Eastern Economic Journal* 11 (January-March): 3–15.

Bausor, R. 1982–83. "Time and the Structure of Economic Analysis." *Journal of Post Keynesian Economics* 5 (Winter): 163–79.

———. 1984. "Toward a Historically Dynamic Economics: Examples and Illustrations." *Journal of Post Keynesian Economics* 6:360–76.

———. 1986. "Time and Equilibrium." In Mirowski.

Becker, G. 1976. *The Economic Approach to Human Behavior*. Chicago: University of Chicago Press.

Beinhocker, E., R. Henderson, L. Newman, and J. Sterman. 1993. "A Behavioral Model of Learning Curve Strategy." Cambridge: Sloan School of Management, MIT. Mimeo.

Bellah, R., R. Madsen, W. Sullivan, A. Swidler, and S. Tipton. 1991. *The Good Society*. New York: Alfred A. Knopf.

Bergson, H. 1944. *Creative Evolution*. New York: Random House.

Bertrand, J. 1883. "Théorie mathématique de la richesse sociale, par L. Walras." *Journal des savants*, 499–508.

Blanchard, O., and L. Summers. 1986. "Hysteresis and the European Unemployment Problem." In S. Fisher, ed., *NBER Macroeconomics Annual 1986*, 15–77. Cambridge: National Bureau of Economic Research.

Blanchet, D. 1991. "On Interpreting Observed Relationships between Population Growth and Economic Growth: A Graphical Exposition." *Population and Development Review* 17 (March): 105–13.

Boehm, S. 1990. "The Austrian Tradition: Schumpeter and Mises." In K. Hennings and W. J. Samuels, eds., *Neoclassical Economic Theory, 1870 to 1930*, 201–41. Boston: Kluwer.

Bohm, D. 1988. "Postmodern Science and a Postmodern World." In D. R. Griffen, ed., *The Reenchantment of Science*, 57–68. Albany: State University of New York Press.

Boldrin, M. 1988. "Persistent Oscillations and Chaos in Dynamic Economic Models: Notes for a Survey." In Anderson, Arrow, and Pines, 49–75.

Boulding, K. 1962. *Conflict and Defense*. New York: Harper and Row.

———. 1968. *Beyond Economics*. Ann Arbor: University of Michigan Press.

———. 1976. "The Great Laws of Change." In A. M. Tang et al., eds., *Evolution, Welfare, and Time in Economics*, 3–14. Lexington, Mass.: Lexington Books.

———. 1981. *Evolutionary Economics*. Beverly Hills: Sage.

———. 1991. "What Is Evolutionary Economics?" *Journal of Evolutionary Economics* 1 (January): 9–17.

Bowler, P. 1988. *The Non-Darwinian Revolution: Reinterpreting a Historical Myth*. Baltimore: Johns Hopkins University Press.

Bowles, S., and H. Gintis. 1986. *Democracy and Capitalism*. New York: Basic Books.

———. 1990. "Contested Exchange: New Microfoundations of the Political Economy of Capitalism." *Politics and Society* 18, no. 2:165–220.

Bromley, D. 1989. *Economic Interests and Institutions: The Conceptual Foundations of Public Policy.* Oxford: Blackwell.

Brøns, M., and J. Sturis. 1991. "Local and Global Bifurcations in a Model of the Economic Long Wave." *System Dynamics Review* 7 (Winter): 41–60.

Brown, T. 1991. *The Effects of Consumer Demand on Pesticide Regulation in the Market for Apples.* Ph.D. diss. in Agricultural and Resource Economics, University of California, Berkeley.

Brunner, K., and A. Meltzer. 1971. "The Uses of Money: Money in the Theory of an Exchange Economy." *American Economic Review* 61:784–805.

Brush, S. 1982. "The Natural and Human Environment of the Central Andes." *Mountain Research and Development* 2:14–38.

Buchanan, J., and G. Tullock. 1962. *Calculus of Consent.* Ann Arbor: University of Michigan Press.

Burkhardt, R., Jr. 1977. *The Spirit of the System: Lamarck and Evolutionary Biology.* Cambridge: Harvard University Press.

Caldwell, B. 1986. *Beyond Positivism: Economic Methodology in the Twentieth Century.* London: George Allen and Unwin.

Cantwell, J. 1991. "Historical Trends in International Patterns of Technological Innovation." In J. Foreman-Peck, ed., *New Perspectives on the Late Victorian Economy.* New York: Cambridge University Press.

Chandler, A., Jr. 1962. *Strategy and Structure: Chapters in the History of Industrial Enterprise.* Cambridge: MIT Press.

———. 1990. *Scale and Scope: The Dynamics of Industrial Capitalism.* Cambridge: Harvard University Press.

Chase, R. 1985. "A Theory of Socioeconomic Change: Entropic Processes, Technology, and Evolutionary Development." *Journal of Economic Issues* 19 (December): 797–823.

Chasse, J. 1984. "Marshall, the Human Agent and Economic Growth: Wants and Activities Revisited." *History of Political Economy* 16 (Fall): 381–404.

Checkland, P. 1981. *Systems Thinking, Systems Practice.* Chichester: Wiley.

Christiansen, P., and R. Parmentier, eds. 1989. *Structure, Coherence and Chaos in Dynamical Systems.* Manchester: Manchester University Press.

Clark, N. 1990. "Evolution, Complex Systems and Technological Change." *Review of Political Economy* 2 (March): 26–42.

Clark, N., and C. Juma. 1987. *Long-Run Economics: An Evolutionary Approach to Economic Growth.* London: Pinter.

Clement, C. 1983. *The Lives and Legends of Jacques Lacan.* New York: Columbia University Press.

Coase, R. 1960. "The Problem of Social Cost." *Journal of Law and Economics* 3 (October): 1–44.

Cohen, L., and R. Noll. 1991. *The Technology Pork Barrel.* Washington, D.C.: Brookings.

Cohen, M. 1984. "Conflict and Complexity: Goal Diversity and Organizational Search Effectiveness." *American Political Science Review* 78 (June): 435–54.

———. 1987. *Adaptation of Organizational Routines*. Ann Arbor: University of Michigan Institute of Public Policy Studies. Mimeo.

Colander, D., and R. Brenner, eds. 1992. *Educating Economists*. Ann Arbor: University of Michigan Press.

Coleman, J. 1988. "Social Capital in the Creation of Human Capital." *American Journal of Sociology* 94:95–120 (supplement).

Colp, R. 1982. "The Myth of the Marx-Darwin Letter." *History of Political Economy* 14 (Winter): 416–82.

Commons, J. R. 1924. *The Legal Foundations of Capitalism*. New York: Macmillan.

Copeland, M. 1958. "On the Scope and Method of Economics." In D. Dowd, ed., *Thorstein Veblen: A Critical Appraisal*, 57–75. Ithaca: Cornell University Press.

Coveney, P., and R. Highfield. 1990. *The Arrow of Time*. New York: Ballantine.

Coward, R., and J. Ellis. 1977. *Language and Materialism: Developments in Semiology and the Theory of the Subject*. London: Routledge and Kegan Paul.

Crémer, J. 1980. "A Partial Theory of Optimal Organization of a Bureaucracy." *Bell Journal of Economics* 11 (Autumn): 683–93.

———. 1990. "Common Knowledge and the Co-Ordination of Economic Activities." In M. Aoki, B. Gustafsson, and O. E. Williamson, eds., *The Firm as a Nexus of Treaties*. London: Sage.

Cross, R., and A. Allan. 1988. "On the History of Hysteresis." In R. Cross, ed., *Unemployment, Hysteresis, and the Natural Rate Hypothesis*, 26–38. Oxford: Basil Blackwell.

Crump, T. 1981. *The Phenomenon of Money*. London: Routledge and Kegan Paul.

Cullenberg, S. 1988. "Theories of Social Totality, the Okishio Theorem and the Marxian Tendency for the Rate of Profit to Fall." Ph.D. thesis, University of Massachusetts, Amherst.

Currie, M., and I. Steedman. 1990. *Wrestling with Time: Problems in Economic Theory*. Ann Arbor: University of Michigan Press.

Cutland, N. 1980. *Computability: An Introduction to Recursive Function Theory*. Cambridge: Cambridge University Press.

Cyert, R., and J. March. 1963. *A Behavioral Theory of the Firm*. Englewood Cliffs, N.J.: Prentice-Hall.

Daly, H. 1991. *Steady-State Economics*. Washington, D.C.: Island Press.

Daly, H., and J. Cobb. 1989. *For the Common Good*. Boston: Beacon Press.

Danchin, A. 1983. "Permanence and Change." *SubStance* 12:61–71.

Darwin, C. 1904. *The Descent of Man*. 2d ed. New York: Hill and Co.

Dasgupta, A. K. 1985. *Epochs of Economic Theory*. Oxford: Basil Blackwell.

David, P. 1975. *Technical Choice, Innovation and Economic Growth*. Cambridge: Cambridge University Press.

———. 1985. "CLIO and the Economics of QWERTY." *American Economic Review* 75 (May): 332–37.

———. 1991. "Computer and Dynamo: The Modern Productivity Paradox in a Not-

Too-Distant Mirror." In Organization for Economic Cooperation and Development, *Technology and Productivity*. Paris: OECD.

———. 1992. "Heroes, Herds, and Hysteresis in Technological History: Thomas Edison and the Battle of the Systems Reconsidered." *Industrial and Corporate Change* 9.

Davis, N. 1967. *Greek Coins and Cities*. London: Spink.

Davisson, W., and J. Uhran. 1979. *A Primer for NDTRAN: A System Dynamics Interpreter*. Notre Dame: University of Notre Dame.

Day, R. H. 1975. "Adaptive Processes and Economic Theory." In Day and Groves, 1–38.

———. 1983. "Dynamical Systems Theory and Complicated Economic Behavior." In Morecroft, Andersen, and Sterman, 1–30.

———. 1984. "Disequilibrium Economic Dynamics: A Post-Schumpeterian Approach." *Journal of Economic Behavior and Organization* 5:57–76.

———. 1987. "The General Theory of Disequilibrium Economics and of Economic Evolution." In Batten, Casti, and Johansson, 46–63.

Day, R. H., and T. Groves, eds. 1975. *Adaptive Economic Models*. New York: Academic Press.

Day, R. H., and W. Shafer. 1986. "Keynesian Chaos." *Journal of Macroeconomics* 7:277–95.

Debreu, G. 1959. *Theory of Value: An Axiomatic Analysis of General Equilibrium*. New Haven: Yale University Press.

Derrida, J. 1981. *Positions*. Chicago: University of Chicago Press.

Dewey, J. 1910. *How We Think*. New York: D. C. Heath.

———. 1938. *Logic: The Theory of Inquiry*. New York: Holt, Rinehart and Winston.

Diamond, P. 1987. "Multiple Equilibria in Models of Credit." *American Economic Review* 77:82–86.

Diehl, E. 1990. *MicroWorld Creator User Manual*. Cambridge: MicroWorlds, Inc.

Dixit, A. 1992. "Investment and Hysteresis." *Journal of Economic Perspectives* 6: 107–32.

Dobb, M. 1937. *Political Economy and Capitalism*. New York: International Publishers.

Domar, E. 1948. "The Problem of Capital Accumulation." *American Economic Review* 38 (December): 777–94.

Dosi, G. 1982. "Technological Paradigms and Technological Trajectories: A Suggested Interpretation of the Determinants and Directions of Technical Change." *Research Policy*.

———. 1988. "Sources, Procedures and Microeconomic Effects of Innovation." *Journal of Economic Literature* 26 (September): 1120–71.

———. 1990. "Finance, Innovation and Industrial Change." *Journal of Economic Behavior and Organization* 13 (June): 299–319.

———. 1991. *Information, Competences and the Firm*. Paper presented at the conference on "Fundamental Issues in Strategy: A Research Agenda for the 1990s." Napa, California.

Dosi, G., and M. Egidi. 1991. "Substantive and Procedural Uncertainty. An Exploration of Economic Behaviours in Complex and Changing Environments." *Journal of Evolutionary Economics* 1 (April): 145–68.

Dosi, G., C. Freeman, R. R. Nelson, G. Silverberg, and L. Soete, eds. 1988. *Technical Change and Economic Theory*. London: Pinter.

Dosi, G., D. Teece, and S. Winter. 1991. "Toward a Theory of Corporate Coherence." In G. Dosi, R. Giannetti, and P. A. Toninelli, eds., *Technology and the Enterprise in a Historical Perspective*. Oxford: Oxford University Press.

Dryzek, J. 1987. *Rational Ecology: Environment and Political Economy*. Oxford: Basil Blackwell.

Dubois, D., and H. Prade. 1987. *Defense et illustration des approaches non-probabilistes de l'imprecis et de l'incertain*. Université Paul Sabatier, Toulouse. Rapport L.S.I. No. 269.

Dyer, A. 1984. "The Habit of Work: A Theoretical Exploration." *Journal of Economic Issues* 18 (June): 557–64.

———. 1986. "Veblen on Scientific Creativity." *Journal of Economic Issues* 20 (March): 21–41.

DYSMAP2. 1992. Department of Business and Management Studies, University of Salford, Salford M5 4WT, United Kingdom.

Earl, P. 1983. *The Economic Imagination: Towards a Behavioural Analysis of Choice*. Armonk, N.Y.: M. E. Sharpe.

———. 1984. *The Corporate Imagination: How Big Companies Make Mistakes*. Armonk, N.Y.: M. E. Sharpe.

Eberlein, R. 1991. *Vensim: The Ventana Simulation Environment*. Arlington, Va.: Ventana Systems, Inc.

Eddington, A. 1943. *The Nature of the Physical World*. New York: Macmillan.

Edgell, S. 1975. "Thorstein Veblen's Theory of Evolutionary Change." *American Journal of Economics and Sociology* 34 (July): 267–80.

Edgell, S., and R. Tilman. 1989. "The Intellectual Antecedents of Thorstein Veblen: A Reappraisal." *Journal of Economic Issues* 23 (December): 1003–26.

Eggertsson, T. 1990. *Economic Behavior and Institutions*. New York: Cambridge University Press.

Ehrlich, P. 1989. "The Limits to Substitution: Meta-resource Depletion and a New Economic-Ecological Paradigm." *Ecological Economics* 1:9–16.

Elster, J. 1983. *Explaining Technical Change*. New York: Cambridge University Press.

Engels, F. 1964. *Dialectics of Nature*. London: Lawrence and Wishart.

England, R. 1986. "Production, Distribution, and Environmental Quality: Mr. Sraffa Reinterpreted as an Ecologist." *Kyklos* 39:230–44.

———. 1990. "Marx and the Environment: A Preliminary Model." *Review of Political Economy* 2 (July): 221–33.

Ergas, H. 1989. "Does Technology Policy Matter?" In B. Guile and H. Brooks, eds., *Technology and Global Competition*. Washington, D.C.: National Academy Press.

Evans, G., and G. Ramey. 1992. "Expectation Calculation and Macroeconomic Dynamics." *American Economic Review* 82:207–24.

Faber, M., and J. Proops. 1985. "Interdisciplinary Research between Economists and Physical Scientists: Retrospect and Prospect." *Kyklos* 38:599–616.

———. 1990. *Evolution, Time, Production and the Environment*. Berlin: Springer-Verlag.

Faber, M., G. Stephan, and H. Niemes. 1987. *Entropy, Environment and Resources: An Essay in Physico-Economics*. Berlin: Springer-Verlag.

Feyerabend, P. 1975. *Against Method*. London: Verso.

Fisher, A. C., and F. Peterson. 1976. "The Environment in Economics: A Survey." *Journal of Economic Literature* 14 (March): 1–33.

Fisher, F. M. 1983. *Disequilibrium Foundations of Equilibrium Economics*. Cambridge: Cambridge University Press.

Florida, R., and M. Kenney. 1989. *The Breakthrough Illusion*. New York: Basic Books.

Forrest, S. 1990. "Emergent Computation: Self-Organizing Collective and Cooperative Phenomena in Natural and Artificial Computing Networks." *Physica D* 42 (June): 1–11.

Forrester, J. 1961. *Industrial Dynamics*. Cambridge: MIT Press.

———. 1968. *Principles of Systems*. Cambridge, Mass.: Productivity Press.

———. 1969. *Urban Dynamics*. Cambridge, Mass.: Productivity Press.

———. 1972. *World Dynamics*. Cambridge, Mass.: Productivity Press.

———. 1975. "Market Growth as Influenced by Capital Investment." In J. Forrester, ed., *Collected Papers of Jay W. Forrester*, 111–32. Cambridge, Mass.: Productivity Press.

———. 1985. " 'The' Model versus a Modeling 'Process.' " *System Dynamics Review* 1:133–34.

———. 1987a. "Nonlinearity in High-Order Models of Social Systems." *European Journal of Operational Research* 30:104–9.

———. 1987b. "Lessons from System Dynamics Modeling." *System Dynamics Review* 3 (Summer): 136–49.

Forrester J., and P. Senge. 1980. "Tests for Building Confidence in System Dynamics Models." In A. Legasto, Jr., J. Forrester, and J. Lyneis, eds., *System Dynamics*, 209–28. Amsterdam: North Holland.

Foss, N. 1991. "The Suppression of Evolutionary Approaches in Economics: The Case of Marshall and Monopolistic Competition." *Methodus* 3 (December): 65–72.

Foucault, M. 1976. *The Archaeology of Knowledge*. New York: Harper and Row.

Freeman, C. 1982. *The Economics of Industrial Innovation*. 2d ed. London: Pinter.

———. 1987. *Technology Policy and Economic Performance: Lessons from Japan*. London: Pinter.

———. 1990. "Schumpeter's Business Cycles Revisited." In Heertje and Perlman, 17–38.

———. 1991. "The Nature of Innovation and the Evolution of the Productive System." In Organization for Economic Cooperation and Development, *Technology and Productivity*. Paris: OECD.

Freud, S. 1950. *The Interpretation of Dreams*. New York: Modern Library.

Friedman, L. 1985. *A History of American Law*. 2d ed. New York: Simon and Schuster.

Friedman, M. 1953. "The Methodology of Positive Economics." In M. Friedman, *Essays in Positive Economics*, 4–14. Chicago: University of Chicago Press.

Futia, C. 1980. "Schumpeterian Competition." *Quarterly Journal of Economics* 94 (June): 677–95.

Galbraith, J. 1960. *The Affluent Society*. Boston: Houghton Mifflin.

Geanakoplos, J. 1990. *Game Theory without Partitions, and Applications to Speculation and Consensus*. Santa Fe Institute, Working paper no. 90-018.

Georgescu-Roegen, N. 1951. "Relaxation Phenomena in Linear Dynamic Models." In T. Koopmans, ed., *Activity Analysis of Production and Allocation*, 116–31. New York: John Wiley.

———. 1971. *The Entropy Law and the Economic Process*. Cambridge: Harvard University Press.

———. 1976. *Energy and Economic Myths*. New York: Pergamon.

———. 1977. "The Steady State and Ecological Salvation: A Thermodynamic Analysis." *Bioscience* 27 (April): 266–70.

———. 1980. "The Entropy Law and the Economic Problem." In H. Daly, ed., *Economics, Ecology, Ethics: Essays toward a Steady State Economy*, 49–81. San Francisco: W. H. Freeman.

———. 1982a. "Energetic Dogma, Energetic Economics, and Viable Technologies." In J. Moroney, ed., *Advances in Economics of Energy and Resources*, vol. 4, 1–39. Greenwich, Conn.: JAI Press.

———. 1982b. "Energy Analysis and Technology Assessment." In Schieve and Allen.

———. 1986. "The Entropy Law and the Economic Process in Retrospect." *Eastern Economic Journal* 12 (January-March): 3–25.

Geroski, P., and A. Jacquemin. 1984. "Dominant Firms and Their Alleged Decline." *International Journal of Industrial Organization* 2 (March): 1–27.

Giddens, A. 1984. *The Constitution of Society: Outline of the Theory of Structuration*. Cambridge: Polity Press.

———. 1990. *The Consequences of Modernity*. Stanford: Stanford University Press.

Gilboa, I. 1988. "Information and Meta Information." In M. Vardi, ed., *Theoretical Aspects of Reasoning about Knowledge*, 227–43. Los Altos, Calif.: Morgan Kaufmann.

Gintis, H. 1992. "The Analytical Foundations of Contemporary Political Economy." In Roberts and Feiner, 108–16.

Goeller, H., and A. Weinberg. 1978. "The Age of Substitutability." *American Economic Review* 68 (December): 1–11.

Goodman, M. 1977. *Study Notes in System Dynamics*. Cambridge, Mass.: Productivity Press.

Goodwin, R. 1967. "A Growth Cycle." In C. Feinstein, ed., *Socialism, Capitalism and Economic Growth*, 54–58. Cambridge: Cambridge University Press.

———. 1991. "Schumpeter, Keynes and the Theory of Economic Evolution." *Journal of Evolutionary Economics* 1:29–47.

Gort, M., and S. Klepper. 1982. "Time Paths in the Diffusion of Product Innovations." *The Economic Journal* 92 (September): 630–53.

Goudie, A. 1986. *The Human Impact on the Natural Environment*. Cambridge: MIT Press.

Gould, J. 1993. *System Dynamics Review: Special Issue on Pre-College Education* 9.

Gould, S. 1978. *Ever since Darwin: Reflections in Natural History*. London: Burnett Books.

———. 1986. "Evolution and the Triumph of Homology, or Why History Matters." *American Scientist* 74 (January): 60–69.

Granovetter, M. 1985. "Economic Action and Social Structure: The Problem of Embeddedness." *American Journal of Sociology* 91 (November): 481–510.

Green, M. 1973. "Review." *The Economic Journal* 83 (June): 551–53.

Grene, M. 1985. "Perception, Interpretation, and the Sciences: Towards a New Philosophy of Science." In D. Depew and B. Weber, eds., *Evolution at a Crossroads: The New Biology and the New Philosophy of Science*. Cambridge: MIT Press.

Groenewegen, P. 1990. "Marshall and Hegel." *Économie appliquée* 43: 63–84.

Gruber, H. 1974. *Darwin on Man: A Psychological Study of Scientific Creativity, Together with Darwin's Early and Unpublished Notebooks*. New York: E. P. Dutton.

Gruchy, A. 1972. *Contemporary Economic Thought: The Contribution of Neo-Institutional Economics*. Clifton, N.J.: Augustus M. Kelley.

Hahn, F. 1982. *Money and Inflation*. London: Basil Blackwell.

———. 1987. "Auctioneer." In J. Eatwell, M. Milgate, and P. Newman, eds., *The New Palgrave Dictionary of Economics*, 4 vols., 1:137. New York: W. W. Norton.

Hamilton, D. 1953. *Newtonian Classicism and Darwinian Institutionalism: A Study of Change in Economic Theory*. Albuquerque: University of New Mexico Press.

Hannan, M., and J. Freeman. 1989. *Organizational Ecology*. Cambridge: Harvard University Press.

Hanusch, H., ed. 1988. *Evolutionary Economics: Applications of Schumpeter's Ideas*. Cambridge: Cambridge University Press.

Harris, A. 1934. "Economic Evolution: Dialectical and Darwinian." *Journal of Political Economy* 42 (February): 34–79.

Harrod, R. 1939. "An Essay in Dynamic Theory." *The Economic Journal* 49 (March): 14–33.

Hayek, F. 1945. "The Use of Knowledge in Society." *American Economic Review* 35 (September): 519–30.

Heath, M. 1954. *The Role of the State in Economic Development in Georgia to 1860*. Cambridge: Harvard University Press.

Heertje, A. 1988. "Schumpeter and Technical Change." In Hanusch, 71–89.

Heertje, A., and M. Perlman, eds. 1990. *Evolving Technology and Market Structure: Studies in Schumpeterian Economics*. Ann Arbor: University of Michigan Press.

Heichelheim, F. 1931. "Die Ausbreitung der Münzgeldwirtschaft und der Wirtschaftsstil im archaischen Griechenland." *Schmollers Jahrbuch* 55:37–62.

———. 1938. *Wirtschaftsgeschichte des Altertums*. Leiden: Sjithoff.

———. 1956. "Geld- und Münzgeschichte: (I) Anfänge und Antike." *Handwörterbuch der Sozialwissenschaften*. Tübingen: Fischer.

Henderson, R. 1991. "Underinvestment and Incompetence as Responses to Radical Innovation: Evidence from the Photolithographic Alignment Equipment Industry." Cambridge: MIT. Mimeo.

Henderson, R., and K. Clark. 1990. "Architectural Innovation: The Reconfiguration of Existing Product Technologies and the Failure of Established Firms." *Administrative Sciences Quarterly* 35 (March): 9–30.

Hicks, J. 1969. *A Theory of Economic History*. New York: Oxford University Press.

———. 1981. *Wealth and Welfare*. Cambridge: Harvard University Press.

Hirschman, A. 1970. *Exit, Voice, and Loyalty*. Cambridge: Harvard University Press.

Hirshleifer, J. 1985. "The Expanding Domain of Economics." *American Economic Review* 75 (December): 53–70.

Ho, Mae-Wan, and P. Saunders. 1982. "The Epigenetic Approach to the Evolution of Organisms—With Notes on Its Relevance to Social and Cultural Evolution." In H. Plotkin, ed., *Learning, Development, and Culture*, 343–61. Chichester: John Wiley.

Hobson, J. 1914. *Work and Wealth*. London: Macmillan.

Hodgson, G. 1984. *The Democratic Economy: A New Look at Planning, Markets and Power*. Harmondsworth: Penguin.

———. 1987. "Economics and Systems Theory." *Journal of Economic Studies* 14: 65–86.

———. 1988. *Economics and Institutions: A Manifesto for a Modern Institutional Economics*. Cambridge and Philadelphia: Polity Press and University of Pennsylvania Press.

———. 1991a. "Hayek's Theory of Cultural Evolution: An Evaluation in the Light of Vanberg's Critique." *Economics and Philosophy* 7 (March): 67–82.

———. 1991b. "Economic Evolution: Intervention Contra Pangloss." *Journal of Economic Issues* 25 (June): 519–33.

———. 1993. *Economics and Evolution: Bringing Back Life into Economics*. Ann Arbor: University of Michigan Press.

Hodgson, G., W. Samuels, and M. Tool, eds. 1993. *Handbook of Institutional and Evolutionary Economics*. Aldershott: Edward Elgar.

Hodgson, G., and E. Screpanti, eds. 1991. *Rethinking Economics: Markets, Technology and Economic Evolution*. Aldershott: Edward Elgar.

Hofstadter, D. 1979. *Gödel, Escher, Bach: An Eternal Golden Braid*. New York: Basic Books.

Hogarth, R. 1987. *Judgement and Choice*. New York: Wiley.

Holland, J. 1986. "Escaping Brittleness: The Possibilities of General Purpose Learning Algorithms Applied to Parallel Rule-Based Systems." In R. Michalski, J. Carbonell, and T. Mitchell, eds., *Machine Learning II*, 593–623. Los Altos, Calif.: Morgan Kaufmann.

———. 1988. "The Global Economy as an Adaptive Process." In Anderson, Arrow, and Pines, 117–24.

Holland, J., K. Holyoak, R. Nisbett, and P. Thagard. 1986. *Induction: Processes of Inference, Learning and Discovery*. Cambridge: MIT Press.

Holmes, O. W., Jr. [1881] 1945. *The Common Law*. Boston: Little, Brown.

Homer, J. 1985. "Worker Burnout: A Dynamic Model with Implications for Prevention and Control." *System Dynamics Review* 1:42–62.

———. 1993. "A System Dynamics Model of National Cocaine Prevalence." *System Dynamics Review* 9:49–78.

Hopkins, P. 1992. "Simulating *Hamlet* in the Classroom." *System Dynamics Review* 8:91–98.

Horwitz, M. 1977. *The Transformation of American Law, 1780-1860*. Cambridge: Harvard University Press.

Howarth, R., and R. Norgaard. 1990. "Intergenerational Resource Rights, Efficiency, and Social Optimality." *Land Economics* 66 (February): 1–11.

———. 1992. "Environmental Valuation under Sustainability." *American Economic Review* 82 (May): 473–77.

Hughes, T. 1987. *Networks of Power: Electrification in Western Society 1880–1930*. Baltimore: Johns Hopkins University Press.

Huizinga, J. 1940. *Homo ludens*. Amsterdam: Pantheon.

Hutter, M. 1992. "Organism as a Metaphor in German Economic Thought." In P. Mirowski, ed., *Markets Read in Tooth and Claw*. Cambridge: Cambridge University Press.

Ingold, T. 1986. *Evolution and Social Life*. Cambridge: Cambridge University Press.

Iwai, K. 1984a. "Schumpeterian Dynamics [Part I]: An Evolutionary Model of Innovation and Imitation." *Journal of Economic Behavior and Organization* 5 (June): 159–90.

———. 1984b. "Schumpeterian Dynamics [Part II]: Technological Progress, Firm Growth and 'Economic Selection.'" *Journal of Economic Behavior and Organization* 5 (September-December): 321–51.

Jacobson, J. 1988. "Planning the Global Family." In Lester Brown et al., *State of the World 1988*, 151–69. New York: W. W. Norton.

Jantsch, E. 1980. *The Self-Organizing Universe*. Oxford: Pergamon.

Johansson, B., D. Batten, and J. Casti. 1987. "Economic Dynamics, Evolution and Structural Adjustment." In Batten, Casti, and Johansson, 1–23.

Jones, L. 1989. "Schumpeter versus Darwin: In re Malthus." *Southern Economic Journal* 56 (October): 410–22.

Jovanovic, B. 1982. "Selection and Evolution of Industry." *Econometrica* 50:649–70.

Kahneman, D., P. Slovic, and A. Tversky, eds. 1982. *Judgment under Uncertainty: Heuristics and Biases*. Cambridge: Cambridge University Press.

Kahneman, D., and A. Tversky. 1979. "Prospect Theory: An Analysis of Decision under Risk." *Econometrica* 47:263–91.

Kaldor, N. 1972. "The Irrelevance of Equilibrium Economics." *The Economic Journal* 82 (December): 1237–55.

Kamminga, H. 1990. "What Is This Thing Called Chaos?" *New Left Review*, no. 181 (May-June): 49–59.

Kapp, K. W. 1968. "In Defense of Institutional Economics." *Swedish Journal of Economics* 70:1–18.

———. 1976. "The Nature and Significance of Institutional Economics." *Kyklos* 29:209–32.

Katz, M., and C. Shapiro. 1985. "Network Externalities, Competition, and Compatibility." *American Economic Review* 75 (June): 424–40.

Katzner, D. 1983. *Analysis without Measurement*. New York: Cambridge University Press.

Kay, N. 1988. "The R&D Function: Corporate Strategy and Structure." In Dosi et al., 282–94.

Keynes, J. M. 1924. "Alfred Marshall." *Economic Journal* 34 (September): 311–72.

———. 1937. "The General Theory of Employment." *Quarterly Journal of Economics* 51, no. 2:209–23.

Kindleberger, C. 1978. *Manias, Panics, and Crashes*. New York: Basic Books.

Klepper, S., and E. Grady. 1990. "The Evolution of New Industries and the Determinants of Market Structure." *Rand Journal of Economics* 21 (Spring): 27–44.

Kneese, A., R. Ayres, and R. d'Arge. 1970. *Economics and the Environment: A Materials Balance Approach*. Washington, D.C.: Resources for the Future.

Kogut, B. 1991. "Country Capabilities and the Permeability of Borders." *Strategic Management Journal* 12 (Summer): 33–47.

Koopmans, T. 1951. "Analysis of Production as an Efficient Combination of Activities." In T. Koopmans, ed., *Activity Analysis of Production and Allocation*, 33–97. New York: John Wiley.

Kraay, C. 1976. *Archaic and Classical Greek Coins*. London: Methuen.

Kreps, D. 1990a. *A Course in Microeconomic Theory*. New York: Harvester Wheatsheaf.

———. 1990b. *Game Theory and Economic Modelling*. Oxford: Oxford University Press.

Krippendorf, K. 1984. "Paradox and Information." *Progress in Communication Sciences* 5:46–71.

Krugman, P. 1990. *Rethinking International Trade*. Cambridge: MIT Press.

———.1991. "History and Industry Location: The Case of the Manufacturing Belt." *American Economic Review* 81 (May): 80–83.

———. 1992. *The Age of Diminished Expectations*. Cambridge: MIT Press.

Kuznets, S. 1966. *Modern Economic Growth: Rate, Structure and Spread*. New Haven: Yale University Press.

Landau, R., and N. Rosenberg. 1992. *Technology and the Wealth of Nations*. Stanford: Stanford University Press.

Langlois, R. 1992. "Transaction Cost Economics in Real Time." *Industrial and Corporate Change*.

———, ed. 1986. *Economics as a Process: Essays in the New Institutional Economics*. Cambridge: Cambridge University Press.

Laszlo, E. 1987. *Evolution: The Grand Synthesis*. Boston: Shambhala.

Latour, B., and S. Woolgar. 1979. *Laboratory Life: The Social Construction of Scientific Fact*. Beverly Hills: Sage Publications.

Laum, B. 1924. *Heiliges Geld*. Tübingen: Mohr.

Lazonick, W. 1990. *Competitive Advantage on the Shop Floor*. Cambridge: Harvard University Press.

———. 1991. *Business Organization and the Myth of the Market Economy*. New York: Cambridge University Press.

Leathers, C. 1990. "Veblen and Hayek on Instincts and Evolution." *Journal of the History of Economic Thought* 12 (June): 162–78.

Levin, G., G. Hirsch, and E. Roberts. 1975. *The Persistent Poppy: A Computer Aided Search for Heroin Policy*. Cambridge, Mass.: Ballinger.

Levin, G., E. Roberts, G. Hirsch, D. Klingler, N. Roberts, and J. Wilder. 1976. *The Dynamics of Human Service Delivery*. Cambridge: Ballinger.

Levine, D. 1977. *Economic Studies: Contributions to the Critique of Economic Theory*. London: Routledge & Kegan Paul.

Levins, R., and R. Lewontin. 1985. *The Dialectical Biologist*. Cambridge: Harvard University Press.

Lewis, A. 1985. "On Effectively Computable Realization of Choice Functions." *Mathematical Social Sciences* 10.

———. 1986. *Structure and Complexity. The Use of Recursion Theory in the Foundations of Neoclassical Mathematical Economics and the Theory of Games*. Ithaca: Cornell University Department of Mathematics. Mimeo.

Lewontin, R. 1982. "Organism and Environment." In H. Plotkin, ed., *Learning, Development, and Culture*, 151–70. Chichester: John Wiley.

Lindblom, C. 1977. *Politics and Markets*. New York: Basic Books.

Lisman, J. 1949. "Econometrics and Thermodynamics: A Remark on Davis' Theory of Budgets." *Econometrica* 17 (January): 59–62.

Loasby, B. 1978. "Whatever Happened to Marshall's Theory of Value?" *Scottish Journal of Political Economy* 25 (February): 1–12.

Lorenz, H.-W. 1989. *Nonlinear Dynamical Economics and Chaotic Motion*. Berlin: Springer-Verlag.

Lucas, R. 1978. "On the Size Distribution of Business Firms." *Bell Journal of Economics* 9 (Autumn): 508–23.

Luhmann, N. 1984. *Soziale Systeme*. Frankfurt: Suhrkamp.

———. 1988. *Die Wirtschaft der Gesellschaft*. Frankfurt: Suhrkamp.

———. 1990a. *Die Wissenschaft der Gesellschaft*. Frankfurt: Suhrkamp.

———. 1990b. *Essays in Self-Reference*. New York: Columbia University Press.

Lyneis, J. 1980. *Corporate Planning and Policy Design*. Cambridge, Mass.: Productivity Press.

Lyotard, J.-F. 1984. *The Postmodern Condition: A Report on Knowledge*. Minneapolis: University of Minnesota Press.

McCloskey, D. 1985. *The Rhetoric of Economics*. Madison: University of Wisconsin Press.

McIntyre, R. 1989. "Theories of Economic Growth, Economic Decline, and Uneven Development in the U.S. Steel Industry." Ph.D. thesis, University of Massachusetts, Amherst.

Malthus, T. R. 1926. *An Essay on the Principle of Population, as It Affects the Future*

Improvement of Society, with Remarks on the Speculations of Mr. Godwin, M. Condorcet, and Other Writers. London: Macmillan.

March, J. 1988a. *Decisions and Organizations.* Oxford: Basil Blackwell.

———. 1988b. "Variable Risk Preferences and Adaptive Aspirations." *Journal of Economic Behavior and Organization* 9 (January): 5–24.

———. 1990. *Exploration and Exploitation in Organizational Learning.* Stanford, Calif.: Stanford University. Mimeo.

Marengo, L. 1992. *Structure, Competence and Learning in an Adaptive Model of the Firm.* Papers on Economics and Evolution, edited by the European Study Group for Evolutionary Economics. Freiburg.

Marshall, A. 1898. "Distribution and Exchange." *The Economic Journal* 8 (March): 37–59.

———. 1956. "Mechanical and Biological Analogies in Economics." In A. C. Pigou.

———. 1961. *The Principles of Economics.* 9th ed. London: Macmillan.

———. 1975. *The Early Economic Writings of Alfred Marshall, 1867–1890,* edited by J. K. Whitaker. London: Macmillan.

Marx, K. 1967. *Capital.* New York: International Publishers.

———. 1976. *Capital,* vol. 1. Harmondsworth: Pelican.

———. 1977. *Karl Marx: Selected Writings,* edited by D. McLellan. Oxford: Oxford University Press.

Marx, K., and F. Engels. 1953. *Marx and Engels on Malthus,* edited by R. L. Meek. London: Lawrence and Wishart.

März, E. 1991. *Joseph Schumpeter: Scholar, Teacher and Politician.* New Haven: Yale University Press.

Mass, N. 1975. *Economic Cycles: An Analysis of the Underlying Causes.* Cambridge, Mass.: Productivity Press.

May, R. 1976. "Simple Mathematical Models with Very Complicated Dynamics." *Nature* 261:459–67.

Mayr, E. 1982. *The Growth of Biological Thought.* Cambridge: Harvard University Press.

Meadows, D. 1982. "Whole Earth Models and Systems." *The CoEvolution Quarterly* 34:98–108.

Merten, P., R. Löffler, and K.-P. Wiedmann. 1987. "Portfolio Simulation: A Tool to Support Strategic Management." *System Dynamics Review* 3:81–101.

Merton, R. 1936. "The Unanticipated Consequences of Purposive Social Action." *American Sociological Review,* 894–904.

Metcalfe, J. 1988. "Evolution and Economic Change." In A. Silbertson, ed., *Technology and Economic Progress,* 54–85. Basingstoke: Macmillan.

Metcalfe, J., and M. Gibbons. 1986. "Technological Variety and the Process of Competition." *Économie appliquée* 39, no. 3:493–520.

Metcalfe, J., and P. Saviotti, eds. 1991. *Evolutionary Theories of Economic and Technological Change.* Reading, England: Harwood.

Mill, J. S. [1848] 1900. *Principles of Political Economy.* London: Colonial Press.

Mirowski, P. 1984. "The Role of Conservation Principles in Twentieth Century Economic Theory." *Philosophy of the Social Sciences* 14 (December): 461–73.

———. 1988. *Against Mechanism: Protecting Economics from Science.* Totowa: Rowman & Littlefield.

———. 1989. *More Heat than Light: Economics as Social Physics, Physics as Nature's Economics.* Cambridge: Cambridge University Press.

———. 1990. "Learning the Meaning of a Dollar: Conservation Principles and the Social Theory of Value in Economic Theory." *Social Research* 57:689–717.

———, ed. 1986. *The Reconstruction of Economic Theory.* Boston: Kluwer-Nijhoff.

Mises, L. von. 1978. *Notes and Recollections.* Spring Mills, Pa.: Libertarian Press.

Moñtano, M., and W. Ebeling. 1980. "A Stochastic Evolutionary Model of Technological Change." *Collective Phenomena* 3:107–14.

Morecroft, J. 1983. "System Dynamics: Portraying Bounded Rationality." *Omega* 11:131–42.

Morecroft, J., D. Andersen, and J. Sterman, eds. 1983. *Proceedings of the 1983 International System Dynamics Conference.* Pine Manor College, Massachusetts.

Morecroft, J., and J. Sterman, eds. 1992. *Modeling for Learning: Special Issue of the European Journal of Operational Research* 59.

Morishima, M., and G. Catephores. 1988. "Anti-Say's Law versus Say's Law: A Change in Paradigm." In Hanusch, 23–53.

Mosekilde, E., J. Aracil, and P. M. Allen. 1988. "Instabilities and Chaos in Nonlinear Dynamic Systems." *System Dynamics Review* 4 (Summer): 14–55.

Mosekilde, E., E. Larsen, J. Sterman, and J. Thomsen. 1992. "Nonlinear Mode-Interaction in the Macroeconomy." *Annals of Operations Research* 37:185–215.

Mosekilde, E., and S. Rasmussen. 1986. "Technical Economic Succession and the Economic Long Wave." *European Journal of Operational Research* 25:27–38.

Mosekilde, E., S. Rasmussen, and T. Sørensen. 1983. "Self-Organization and Stochastic Re-Causalization in System Dynamics Models." In Morecroft, Andersen, and Sterman, 128–60.

Moss, S. 1984. "The History of the Theory of the Firm from Marshall to Robinson and Chamberlin: The Source of Positivism in Economics." *Economica* 51 (August): 307–18.

Moxnes, E. 1992. "Positive Feedback Economics and the Competition between 'Hard' and 'Soft' Energy Supplies." *Journal of Scientific and Industrial Research* 51:257–65.

Mueller, D. 1986. *Profits in the Long Run.* Cambridge: Cambridge University Press.

Mueller, D., and J. Tilton. 1969. "Research and Development as Barriers to Entry." *Canadian Journal of Economics* 2 (November): 570–79.

Myrdal, G. 1939. *Monetary Equilibrium.* London: Hodge.

———. 1944. *An American Dilemma: The Negro Problem and Modern Democracy.* New York: Harper and Row.

———. 1957. *Economic Theory and Underdeveloped Regions.* London: Duckworth.

Nelson, R. H. 1991. *Reaching for Heaven on Earth: The Theological Meaning of Economics.* Savage, N.J.: Rowman and Littlefield.

Nelson, R. R. 1991. "Why Do Firms Differ and How Does It Matter?" *Strategic Management Journal* 12 (Winter): 61–74.

Nelson, R. R., and N. Rosenberg. 1993. "Technical Innovation and National Systems." In R. R. Nelson, ed., *National Innovation Systems: A Comparative Study*. New York: Oxford University Press.

Nelson, R. R., and S. Winter. 1974. "Neoclassical vs. Evolutionary Theories of Economic Growth: Critique and Prospectus." *Economic Journal* 84 (December): 886–905.

———. 1982. *An Evolutionary Theory of Economic Change*. Cambridge: Harvard University Press.

Nelson, W. E. 1975. *Americanization of the Common Law*. Cambridge: Harvard University Press.

Neuberg, L. 1989. *Conceptual Anomalies in Economics and Statistics*. Cambridge: Cambridge University Press.

Nicolis, G., and I. Prigogine. 1977. *Self-Organization in Non-Equilibrium Systems: From Dissipative Structures to Order through Fluctuations*. New York: John Wiley.

———. 1989. *Exploring Complexity: An Introduction*. New York: W. H. Freeman.

Niehans, J. 1971. "Money and Barter in General Equilibrium with Transaction Costs." *American Economic Review* 61:773–83.

Niman, N. 1991. "Biological Analogies in Marshall's Work." *Journal of the History of Economic Thought* 13 (Spring): 19–36.

Norgaard, R. 1984. "Coevolutionary Development Potential." *Land Economics* 60:160–73.

———. 1988. "Sustainable Development: A Co-Evolutionary View." *Futures* 20:606–20.

———. 1989. "The Case for Methodological Pluralism." *Ecological Economics* 1:37–57.

———. 1990. "Economic Indicators of Resource Scarcity: A Critical Essay." *Journal of Environmental Economics and Management* 18:19–25.

———. 1992. "Environmental Science as a Social Process." *Environmental Monitoring and Assessment* 20:95–110.

Norris, C. 1982. *Deconstruction Theory and Practice*. London: Methuen.

———. 1983. *The Deconstructive Turn*. London: Methuen.

North, D. 1981. *Structure and Change in Economic History*. New York: W. W. Norton.

———. 1990. *Institutions, Institutional Change, and Economic Performance*. Cambridge: Cambridge University Press.

Oakley, A. 1990. *Schumpeter's Theory of Capitalist Motion: A Critical Exposition and Reassessment*. Aldershott: Edward Elgar.

O'Connor, M. 1990. *Time and Environment*. Ph.D. thesis in economics, University of Auckland.

Oyama, S. 1985. *The Ontogeny of Information*. Cambridge: Cambridge University Press.

Paich, M., and J. Sterman. 1993. "Boom, Bust, and Failures to Learn in Experimental Markets." *Management Science* 39 (December).

Pareto, V. 1963. *The Mind and Society*. 2 vols. New York: Dover.

Parsons, T. 1932. "Economics and Sociology: Marshall in Relation to the Thought of His Time." *Quarterly Journal of Economics* 46:316–47.

———. 1937. *The Structure of Social Action*. 2 vols. New York: McGraw-Hill.

———. 1968. "Social Interaction." In *International Encyclopedia of the Social Sciences*, vol. 7, 429–41. New York: Macmillan.

Patel, P., and K. Pavitt. 1988. "The International Distribution and Determinants of Technological Activities." *Oxford Review of Economic Policy* 4.

———. 1991. "Large Firms in Western Europe's Technological Competitiveness." In L. G. Mattson and B. Stymme, eds., *Corporate and Industry Strategies for Europe*. Amsterdam: Elsevier.

Pavitt, K. 1984. "Sectoral Patterns of Technical Change: Towards a Taxonomy and a Theory." *Research Policy* 13:343–74.

———. 1988. "International Patterns of Technological Accumulation." In N. Hood and J. Vahine, eds., *Strategies in Global Competition*. London: Croom Helm.

———. 1990a. "What We Know about the Strategic Management of Technology." *California Management Review* 32 (Spring): 17–26.

———. 1990b. *Some Foundations for a Theory of the Large Innovating Firm*. Sussex, England: Science Policy Research Unit, University of Sussex. Mimeo.

Perelman, L. 1980. "Time in System Dynamics." In A. Legasto, Jr., J. Forrester, and J. Lyneis, eds., *System Dynamics*, 75–89. Amsterdam: North Holland.

Perez, C. 1985. "Micro-Electronics, Long Waves and World Structural Change." *World Development* 13 (March): 441–63.

Perrings, C. 1987. *Economy and Environment: A Theoretical Essay on the Interdependence of Economic and Environmental Systems*. Cambridge: Cambridge University Press.

Pigou, A. C. 1922. "Empty Economic Boxes: A Reply." *The Economic Journal* 32 (December): 458–65.

———. 1928. "An Analysis of Supply." *The Economic Journal* 38 (September): 238–57.

———, ed. 1956. *Memorials of Alfred Marshall*. New York: Kelley and Millman.

Piore, M., and C. Sabel. 1984. *The Second Industrial Divide*. New York: Basic Books.

Polanyi, M. 1968. "Life's Irreducible Structure." *Science* 160:1308–12.

Porter, M. 1990. *The Competitive Advantage of Nations*. New York: Free Press.

Posner, R. 1973. *Economic Analysis of Law*. Boston: Little, Brown.

Prahalad, C., and G. Hamel. 1990. "The Core Competence of the Corporation." *Harvard Business Review* 90 (May/June): 79–91.

Prigogine, I. 1976. "Order through Fluctuation: Self-Organization and Social System." In E. Jantsch and C. Waddington, eds., *Evolution and Consciousness: Human Systems in Transition*, 93–133. Reading, Mass.: Addison-Wesley.

———. 1990. "Foreword." In Coveney and Highfield, 15–17.

Prigogine, I., and P.M. Allen. 1982. "The Challenge of Complexity." In Schieve and Allen, 3–29.

Prigogine, I., and I. Stengers. 1984. *Order Out of Chaos: Man's New Dialogue with Nature*. New York: Bantam.

Primm, J. 1954. *Economic Policy in the Development of a Western State: Missouri, 1820–1860*. Cambridge: Harvard University Press.

Pugh, A. 1983. *DYNAMO User's Manual*. Cambridge: MIT Press.

Quine, W. 1953. *From a Logical Point of View*. Cambridge: Harvard University Press.

Radner, R. 1968. "Competitive Equilibrium under Uncertainty." *Econometrica* 36 (January): 31–58.

Radzicki, M. 1988a. "A Note on Kelsey's 'The Economics of Chaos or the Chaos of Economics.'" *Oxford Economic Papers* 40 (December): 692–93.

———. 1988b. "Institutional Dynamics: An Extension of the Institutionalist Approach to Socioeconomic Analysis." *Journal of Economic Issues* 22 (September): 633–66.

———. 1990a. "Methodologia Oeconomiae et Systematis Dynamis." *System Dynamics Review* 6 (Winter): 123–47.

———. 1990b. "Institutional Dynamics, Deterministic Chaos, and Self-Organizing Systems." *Journal of Economic Issues* 24 (March): 57–102.

Rahmeyer, F. 1989. "The Evolutionary Approach to Innovation Activity." *Journal of Institutional and Theoretical Economics* 145 (June): 275–97.

Reagan-Cirincione, P., S. Schuman, G. Richardson, and S. Dorf. 1991. "Decision Modeling: Tools for Strategic Thinking." *Interfaces* 21 (Nov.-Dec.): 52–65.

Reisman, D. 1987. *Alfred Marshall: Progress and Politics*. London: Macmillan.

Repetto, R., W. Magrath, C. Beer, and F. Rossini. 1989. *Wasting Assets: Natural Resources in the National Income Accounts*. Washington, D.C.: World Resources Institute.

Resnick, S., and R. Wolff. 1987. *Knowledge and Class: A Marxian Critique of Political Economy*. Chicago: University of Chicago Press.

———. 1988. "Marxian Theory and the Rhetorics of Economics." In A. Klamer, D. McCloskey, and R. Solow, eds., *The Consequences of Economic Rhetoric*, 47–63. Cambridge: Cambridge University Press.

———. 1992. "Radical Economics: A Tradition of Theoretical Differences." In Roberts and Feiner, 15–43.

Richardson, G. 1991. *Feedback Thought in Social Science*. Philadelphia: University of Pennsylvania Press.

Richardson, G., and A. Pugh. 1981. *Introduction to System Dynamics Modeling with DYNAMO*. Cambridge, Mass.: Productivity Press.

Richmond, B., and S. Peterson. 1992. *STELLA II: An Introduction to Systems Thinking*. Hanover, N.H.: High Performance Systems.

Richmond, B., S. Peterson, and D. Boyle. 1990. *STELLA II User's Guide*. Hanover, N. H.: High Performance Systems.

Roberts, B., and S. Feiner, eds. 1992. *Radical Economics*. Boston: Kluwer.

Roberts, E. 1978. *Managerial Applications of System Dynamics*. Cambridge, Mass.: Productivity Press.

Roberts, N. 1974. "A Computer System Simulation of Student Performance in the Elementary Classroom." *Simulation and Games* 5:265–90.

Roberts, N., D. Andersen, R. Deal, M. Garet, and W. Shaffer. 1983. *Introduction to Computer Simulation: The System Dynamics Approach.* Reading, Mass.: Addison-Wesley.

Robinson, E. 1956. "The Date of the Earliest Coins." *The Numismatic Chronicle and Journal of the Royal Numismatic Society* 16:1–8.

Robinson, J. 1962. *Essays in the Theory of Economic Growth.* London: Macmillan.

————. 1978. *Contributions to Modern Economics.* New York: Academic Press.

Roemer, J. 1986. "'Rational Choice' Marxism: Some Issues of Method and Substance." In J. Roemer, ed., *Analytical Marxism*, 191–201. Cambridge: Cambridge University Press.

————. 1988. *Free to Lose.* Cambridge: Harvard University Press.

Rorty, R. 1979. *Philosophy and the Mirror of Nature.* Princeton: Princeton University Press.

————. 1991. *Objectivity, Relativism, and Truth* and *Essays on Heidegger and Others.* In *Philosophical Papers*, vols. 1 and 2. Cambridge: Cambridge University Press.

Rosser, J., Jr. 1992. "The Dialogue between the Economic and the Ecologic Theories of Evolution." *Journal of Economic Behavior and Organization* 17:195–215.

Roth, G. 1986. "Selbstorganisation—Selbsterhaltung—Selbstreferentialität: Prinzipien der Organisation der Lebewesen und ihre Folgen für die Beziehung zwischen Organismus und Umwelt." In A. Dress, H. Henrichs, and G. Küppers, eds., *Selbstorganisation: die Entstehung von Ordnung in der Gesellschaft*, 149–80. Munich: Piper.

Roth, G., and H. Schwegler, eds. 1981. *Self-organizing Systems: An Interdisciplinary Approach.* Frankfurt: Campus.

Roth, P. 1987. *Meaning and Method in the Social Sciences: A Case for Methodological Pluralism.* Ithaca: Cornell University Press.

Rubinstein, A. 1986. "Finite Automata Play the Repeated Prisoner's Dilemma." *Journal of Economic Theory* 36 (June): 83–96.

Ruccio, D. 1991. "Postmodernism and Economics." *Journal of Post Keynesian Economics* 13 (Summer): 495–510.

Ruelle, D. 1988. "Can Nonlinear Dynamics Help Economists?" In Anderson, Arrow, and Pines, 195–204.

Rumelt, R. 1988. *How Much Does Industry Matter?* UCLA Anderson School of Management. Mimeo.

Rutherford, M. 1984. "Thorstein Veblen and the Processes of Institutional Change." *History of Political Economy* 16 (Fall): 331–48.

Sah, R., and J. Stiglitz. 1986. "The Architecture of Economic Systems: Hierarchies and Polyarchies." *American Economic Review* 76 (September): 716–27.

Samuels, W. 1974. *Pareto on Policy.* New York: Elsevier.

————. 1988. *Institutional Economics.* 3 vols. Aldershott: Edward Elgar.

————. 1989a. "The Legal-Economic Nexus." *George Washington Law Review* 57 (August): 1556–78.

———. 1989b. "Determinate Solutions and Valuational Processes: Overcoming the Foreclosure of Process." *Journal of Post Keynesian Economics* 11 (Summer): 531–46.

———. 1992. "The Pervasive Proposition, 'What Is, Is and Ought to Be': A Critique." In W. Milberg, ed., *The Megacorp and Macrodynamics: Essays in Memory of Alfred Eichner*. Armonk, N.Y.: M. E. Sharpe.

Samuels, W., and A. Miller, eds. 1987. *Corporations and Society: Power and Responsibility*. Westport, Ct.: Greenwood.

Samuelson, P. 1947. *Foundations of Economic Analysis*. Cambridge: Harvard University Press.

———. 1966. "Foreword." In N. Georgescu-Roegen, *Analytical Economics*, vii–ix. Cambridge: Harvard University Press.

———. 1972. "Maximum Principles in Analytical Economics." *American Economic Review* 62 (June): 249–62.

———. 1978. "Maximizing and Biology." *Economic Inquiry* 26 (April): 171–83.

———. 1983. "Rigorous Observational Positivism: Klein's Envelope Aggregation; Thermodynamics and Economic Isomorphisms." In F. Adams and B. Hickman, eds., *Global Econometrics: Essays in Honor of Lawrence R. Klein*. Cambridge: MIT Press.

Santarelli, E., and E. Pesciarelli. 1990. "The Emergence of a Vision: The Development of Schumpeter's Theory of Entrepreneurship." *History of Political Economy* 22 (Winter): 677–96.

Schefold, B. 1986. "Schumpeter as a Walrasian Austrian and Keynes as a Classical Marshallian." In H.-J. Wagener and J. Drukker, eds., *The Economic Law of Motion of Modern Society: A Marx-Keynes-Schumpeter Centennial*, 93–111. Cambridge: Cambridge University Press.

Schieve, W., and P. M. Allen, eds. 1982. *Self-organization and Dissipative Structures: Applications in the Physical and Social Sciences*. Austin: University of Texas Press.

Schmalensee, R. 1985. "Do Markets Differ Much?" *American Economic Review* 75 (March): 341–51.

Schumpeter, J. 1934. *The Theory of Economic Development*. Cambridge: Harvard University Press.

———. 1939. *Business Cycles*. 2 vols. New York: McGraw-Hill.

———. 1951. *Essays on Economic Topics*. Cambridge: Cambridge University Press.

———. 1952. *Ten Great Economists: From Marx to Keynes*. London: George Allen and Unwin.

———. 1954. *History of Economic Analysis*. New York: Oxford University Press.

———. 1976. *Capitalism, Socialism and Democracy*. 5th ed. London: George Allen and Unwin.

Schweber, S. 1977. "The Origin of the *Origin* Revisited." *Journal of the History of Biology* 10 (Fall): 229–316.

Senge, P. 1980. "A System Dynamics Approach to Investment Function Formulation and Testing." *Socioeconomic Planning Sciences* 14:269–80.

———. 1990. *The Fifth Discipline*. New York: Doubleday.

Shackle, G. 1961. *Decision, Order and Time in Human Affairs*. Cambridge: Cambridge University Press.

———. 1968. *Uncertainty in Economics and Other Reflections*. Cambridge: Cambridge University Press.

———. 1972. *Epistemics and Economics: A Critique of Economic Doctrines*. Cambridge: Cambridge University Press.

———. 1979. *Imagination and the Nature of Choice*. Edinburgh: Edinburgh University Press.

Shantzis, S., and W. Behrens. 1973. "Population Control Mechanisms in a Primitive Agricultural Society." In D. L. Meadows and D. H. Meadows, eds., *Toward Global Equilibrium: Collected Papers*, 257–88. Cambridge, Mass.: Productivity Press.

Shepsle, K., and B. Weingast. 1981. "Structure Induced Equilibrium and Legislative Choice." *Public Choice* 37 (Fall): 503–20.

Shionoya, Y. 1986. "The Science and Ideology of Schumpeter." *Revista internazionale di scienze economiche e commerciale* 33:729–62.

Silverberg, G. 1984. "Embodied Technical Progress in a Dynamic Economic Model: The Self-organization Paradigm." In R. Goodwin, M. Kruger, and A. Vercelli, eds., *Nonlinear Models of Fluctuating Growth*. Berlin: Springer-Verlag.

———. 1987. "Technical Progress, Capital Accumulation and Effective Demand: A Self-organization Model." In Batten, Casti, and Johansson.

———. 1988. "Modelling Economic Dynamics and Technical Change: Mathematical Approaches to Self-organisation and Evolution." In Dosi et al., 531–59.

Silverberg, G., G. Dosi, and L. Orsenigo. 1988. "Innovation, Diversity, and Diffusion: A Self-organizing Model." *Economic Journal* 98 (December): 1032–54.

Simon, H. 1947. *Administrative Behavior*. New York: Macmillan.

———. 1957. *Models of Man*. New York: John Wiley.

———. 1976. "From Substantive to Procedural Rationality." In S. J. Latsis, ed., *Method and Appraisal in Economics*, 129–48. Cambridge: Cambridge University Press.

———. 1979. "Rational Decision Making in Business Organizations." *American Economic Review* 69:493–513.

———. 1981. *The Sciences of the Artificial*. Cambridge: MIT Press.

———. 1982. *Models of Bounded Rationality*. Cambridge: MIT Press.

———. 1984. "On the Behavioral and Rational Foundations of Economic Dynamics." *Journal of Economic Behavior and Organization* 5:35–55.

Smith, B. 1988. *Contingencies of Value*. Cambridge: Harvard University Press.

Smith, P. 1988. *Discerning the Subject*. Minneapolis: University of Minnesota Press.

Sober, E. 1985. "Darwin on Natural Selection: A Philosophical Perspective." In D. Kohn, ed., *The Darwinian Heritage*. Princeton: Princeton University Press.

Solow, R. 1956. "A Contribution to the Theory of Economic Growth." *Quarterly Journal of Economics* 70 (February): 65–94.

———. 1985. "Economic History and Economics." *American Economic Review* 75 (May): 328–31.

Spencer, H. 1890. *First Principles*. 5th ed. London: Williams and Norgate.

———. 1892. *Essays Scientific, Political and Speculative*. New York: Appleton.

Sraffa, P. 1926. "The Laws of Returns under Competitive Conditions." *Economic Journal* 36 (December): 535–50.

Sterman, J. 1984. "Appropriate Summary Statistics for Evaluating the Historical Fit of System Dynamics Models." *Dynamica* 10:51–66.

———. 1985. "A Behavioral Model of the Economic Long Wave." *Journal of Economic Behavior and Organization* 6 (January): 17–53.

———. 1987. "Expectation Formation in Behavioral Simulation Models." *Behavioral Science* 32:190–211.

———. 1988a. "People Express Management Flight Simulator." Cambridge: Sloan School of Management, MIT. Software and documentation.

———. 1988b. "Deterministic Chaos in Models of Human Behavior: Methodological Issues and Experimental Results." *System Dynamics Review* 4 (Summer): 148–78.

———. 1988c. "Modeling Managerial Behavior: Misperceptions of Feedback in a Dynamic Decision Making Experiment." *Management Science* 35:321–39.

———. 1989a. "Misperceptions of Feedback in Dynamic Decision Making." *Organizational Behavior and Human Decision Processes* 43:301–35.

———. 1989b. "Deterministic Chaos in an Experimental Economic System." *Journal of Economic Behavior and Organization* 12:1–28.

Sturis, J., K. Polonsky, E. Mosekilde, and E. van Cauter. 1991. "Computer Model for Mechanisms Underlying Ultradian Oscillations of Insulin and Glucose." *American Journal of Physiology* 260:E801–E809.

Stutzer, M. 1980. "Chaotic Dynamics and Bifurcation in a Macro Model." *Journal of Economic Dynamics and Control* 2:353–76.

Swan, T. 1956. "Economic Growth and Capital Accumulation." *Economic Record* 32 (November): 334–61.

Swaney, J. 1985. "Economics, Ecology, and Entropy." *Journal of Economic Issues* 14 (December): 853–65.

Swedberg, R. 1991. *Joseph A. Schumpeter: His Life and Work*. Cambridge: Polity Press.

Tang, A., F. Westfield, and J. Worley. 1976. "Preface." In A. Tang et al., eds., *Evolution, Welfare, and Time in Economics*. Lexington, Mass.: Lexington Books.

Teece, D. 1986. "Profiting for Technological Innovation." *Research Policy*.

Teece, D., et al. 1990. *Firms' Capabilities, Resources and the Concept of Strategy*. University of California at Berkeley, Centre for Research in Management. Working paper no. 90-8.

Thomas, B. 1991. "Alfred Marshall on Economic Biology." *Review of Political Economy* 3 (January): 1–14.

Thompson, J., and H. Stewart. 1986. *Nonlinear Dynamics and Chaos*. Chichester, England: John Wiley.

Tool, M., ed. 1988. *Evolutionary Economics*. 2 vols. Armonk, N.Y.: M. E. Sharpe.

Toulmin, S. 1972. *Human Understanding: The Collective Use and Evolution of Concepts*. Princeton: Princeton University Press.

———. 1975. *Cosmopolis: The Hidden Agenda of Modernity*. New York: Free Press.

———. 1982. *The Return to Cosmology: Postmodern Science and the Theology of Nature*. Berkeley: University of California Press.

Tribe, L. 1989. "The Curvature of Constitutional Space: What Lawyers Can Learn from Modern Physics." *Harvard Law Review* 103 (November): 1–39.

Turner, J. 1985. *Herbert Spencer: A Renewed Appreciation*. Beverly Hills: Sage.

Tushman, M., and D. Anderson. 1986. "Technological Discontinuities and Organizational Environments." *Administrative Sciences Quarterly* 31 (September): 439–65.

Tushman, M., and E. Romanelli. 1985. "Organizational Evolution: A Metamorphosis Model of Convergence and Reorientation." In L. Cummings and B. Staw, eds., *Research in Organizational Behavior*, vol. 4. Greenwich, Ct.: JAI Press.

Tushman, M., and L. Rosenkopf. 1992. "Organizational Determinants of Technological Change: Towards a Sociology of Technological Evolution." In B. Staw and L. Cummings, eds., *Research in Organizational Behavior*, vol. 14, 311–47. Greenwich, Ct.: JAI Press.

Tversky, A., and D. Kahneman. 1974. "Judgement under Uncertainty: Heuristics and Biases." *Science* 185:1124–31.

Unger, R. 1975. *Knowledge and Politics*. New York: The Free Press.

United Nations Development Programme. 1991. *Human Development Report 1991*. New York: Oxford University Press.

Ure, P. 1922. *The Origin of Tyranny*. Cambridge: Cambridge University Press.

Utterback, J. 1974. "Innovation in Industry and the Diffusion of Technology." *Science* 183 (15 February): 620–26.

Utterback, J., and F. Suarez. 1993. "Innovation, Competition, and Industry Structure." *Research Policy* 22:1–21.

Vanberg, V. 1986. "Spontaneous Market Order and Social Rules: A Critique of F. A. Hayek's Theory of Cultural Evolution." *Economics and Philosophy* 2:75–100.

Varela, F. 1979. *Principles of Biological Autonomy*. New York: Elsevier North Holland.

Varian, H. 1979. "Catastrophe Theory and the Business Cycle." *Economic Inquiry* 17:14–28.

Veblen, T. 1898. "Why Is Economics Not an Evolutionary Science?" *Quarterly Journal of Economics* 12 (July): 373–97.

———. 1899. *The Theory of the Leisure Class: An Economic Study of Institutions*. New York: Macmillan.

———. 1914. *The Instinct of Workmanship, and the State of the Industrial Arts*. New York: Augustus Kelley.

———. 1915. *Imperial Germany and the Industrial Revolution*. New York: Macmillan.

———. 1919. *The Place of Science in Modern Civilisation and Other Essays*. New York: Huebsch.

———. 1934. *Essays on Our Changing Order*. New York: Viking Press.

Vennix, J., and J. Gubbels. 1992. "Knowledge Elicitation in Conceptual Model Building: A Case Study of Modeling a Regional Health-Care System." *European Journal of Operational Research* 59:85–101.

Vickers, D. 1978. *Financial Markets in the Capitalist Process*. Philadelphia: University of Pennsylvania Press.

———. 1986. "Time, Ignorance, Surprise, and Economic Decisions." *Journal of Post Keynesian Economics* 9 (Fall): 48–57.

———. 1987. *Money Capital in the Theory of the Firm*. New York: Cambridge University Press.

Vitousek, P., P. Ehrlich, A. Ehrlich, and P. Matson. 1986. "Human Appropriation of the Products of Photosynthesis." *Bioscience* 36:368–73.

von Hippel, E. 1988. *The Sources of Innovation*. New York: Oxford University Press.

Walker, D. 1986. "Walras's Theory of the Entrepreneur." *De Economist* 134:1–24.

Walras, L. 1954. *Elements of Pure Economics, or the Theory of Social Wealth*. New York: Augustus Kelley.

Walsh, V., and H. Gram. 1980. *Classical and Neoclassical Theories of General Equilibrium*. New York: Oxford University Press.

Warglien, M. 1991. "Exit, Voice and Learning." In N. Rasuch and M. Warglien, eds., *Artificial Intelligence in Organization and Management Theory*. Amsterdam: Elsevier.

Weidauer, L. 1975. *Probleme der frühen Elektronprägung*. Fribourg: Office du Livre.

Wesson, R. 1991. *Beyond Natural Selection*. Cambridge: MIT Press.

Whitaker, J. 1977. "Some Neglected Aspects of Alfred Marshall's Economic and Social Thought." *History of Political Economy* 9 (Summer): 161–97.

———. 1990. "What Happened to the Second Volume of the Principles? The Thorny Path to Marshall's Last Books." In J. K. Whitaker, ed., *Centenary Essays on Alfred Marshall*. Cambridge: Cambridge University Press.

Wicken, J. 1987. *Evolution, Thermodynamics, and Information*. New York: Oxford University Press.

Wilber, C., and R. Harrison. 1978. "The Methodological Basis of Institutional Economics: Pattern Model, Storytelling, and Holism." *Journal of Economic Issues* 12:61–89.

Williamson, O. 1975. *Markets and Hierarchies*. New York: Free Press.

———. 1985. *The Economic Institutions of Capitalism*. New York: Free Press.

———. 1990. *Strategizing, Economizing and Economic Organization*. Paper presented at the conference on "Fundamental Issues in Strategy: A Research Agenda for the 1990s." Napa, California.

Winter, S. 1964. "Economic Natural Selection and the Theory of the Firm." *Yale Economic Essays* 4:225–72.

———. 1982. "An Essay on the Theory of Production." In S. Hymans, ed., *Economics and the World Around It*, 55–93. Ann Arbor: University of Michigan Press.

———. 1984. "Schumpeterian Competition in Alternative Technological Regimes." *Journal of Economic Behavior and Organization* 5 (September): 287–320.

———. 1986. "The Research Program of the Behavioral Theory of the Firm." In B. Gilad and S. Kaish, eds., *Handbook of Behavioral Economics*. Greenwich, Ct.: JAI Press.

————. 1987. "Knowledge and Competence as Strategic Assets." In D. J. Teece, ed., *The Competitive Challenge*, 159–84. Cambridge, Mass.: Ballinger.

Witt, U., ed. 1991. *Explaining Process and Change. Approaches to Evolutionary Economics*. Ann Arbor: University of Michigan Press.

Wittenberg, J., and J. Sterman. 1992. "Modeling the Dynamics of Scientific Revolutions." In J. Vennix et al., eds., *Proceedings of the 1992 System Dynamics Conference*, 827–36. Utrecht: Utrecht University.

Wolff, R., and S. Resnick. 1987. *Economics: Marxian versus Neoclassical*. Baltimore: Johns Hopkins University Press.

Womack, J., D. Jones, and D. Roos. 1991. *The Machine That Changed the World*. Cambridge: MIT Press.

Young, A. A. 1928. "Increasing Returns and Economic Progress." *Economic Journal* 38 (December): 527–42.

Young, R. M. 1969. "Malthus and the Evolutionists: The Common Context of Biological and Social Theory." *Past and Present*, no. 43 (May): 109–41.

Zarnowitz, V. 1985. "Recent Work on Business Cycles in Historical Perspective: A Review of Theories and Evidence." *Journal of Economic Literature* 23:523–80.

Zukav, C. 1979. *The Dancing Wu Li Masters*. New York: William Morrow.

Contributors

Randall Bausor is currently Associate Professor of Economics at the University of Massachusetts at Amherst, U.S.A., and in the past has served on the faculties of Virginia Commonwealth University and the University of Colorado at Boulder. He was educated at Duke University and has written on the conceptual and philosophical difficulties arising from attempts to mathematically model dynamic economic phenomena.

Giovanni Dosi is Professor of Applied Economics, University of Rome "La Sapienza," Italy, having received his doctorate from the University of Sussex. He has been a visiting professor and scholar at several universities in the United Kingdom, United States, Brazil, and Mozambique.

Richard W. England is Associate Professor of Economics at the University of New Hampshire, U.S.A. He received his Ph.D. from the University of Michigan and remembers his days in Ann Arbor fondly. His published work includes an anthology entitled *Economic Processes and Political Conflicts: Contributions to Modern Political Economy*.

Geoffrey M. Hodgson is University Lecturer in Economics at the Judge Institute of Management Studies, University of Cambridge, United Kingdom. His published work includes *Economics and Evolution* and *Economics and Institutions*.

Michael Hutter received his doctorate in economics from the University of Munich, where he also served as Assistant Professor. He is presently Professor of Economics at the University of Witten/Herdecke, Germany. His research interests and publications cover law and economics, art economics, history of economic thought, monetary history, and social systems theory.

Luigi Marengo received his doctorate from the Science Policy Research Unit, University of Sussex, United Kingdom, and is presently a Research Fellow with the Department of Economics, University of Trento, Italy.

Richard R. Nelson is presently George Blumenthal Professor of International and Public Affairs, Business and Law at Columbia University, U.S.A. He has long had an interest in developing evolutionary economics and has written (along with Sidney Winter) one of the more important new works in this area.

Richard B. Norgaard is a Professor in the Energy and Resources Program at the University of California at Berkeley, U.S.A. He received his doctorate in economics from the University of Chicago in 1971 and went on to acquire his understanding of environmental and cultural coevolution through working with anthropologists and biologists in the Brazilian Amazon, with entomologists concerned about California agriculture, and with physicists studying energy and the environment. He has recently completed *Development Betrayed*.

Michael J. Radzicki is Associate Professor of Social Science and Policy Studies at Worcester Polytechnic Institute, U.S.A. He holds a Ph.D. in economics from the University of Notre Dame and serves on the editorial boards of the *Journal of Economics Issues* and *System Dynamics Review*. His published papers have appeared in those journals as well as the *Oxford Economic Papers* and *Economics Letters*.

Stephen A. Resnick, Professor of Economics at the University of Massachusetts at Amherst, is the coauthor (with Richard D. Wolff) of *Knowledge and Class: A Marxian Critique of Political Economy* and of *Economics: Marxian versus Neoclassical*. He produced along with Harriet Fraad and Richard Wolff a forthcoming book on class, gender, and power in U.S. households. Currently he is preparing a manuscript on a class analysis of the U.S.S.R. with Richard Wolff. He is an editorial board member of *Rethinking Marxism*.

Warren J. Samuels is Professor of Economics at Michigan State University, U.S.A. He specializes in the history of economic thought, law and economics, and methodology. He has written and edited extensively in institutional economics and is working on a major study on the use of the concept of the invisible hand. His *Essays on the History and Discourse of Economics* were published in 1993.

James D. Shaffer has been a member of the agricultural economics faculty at Michigan State University since 1949. His teaching has included institutional and behavioral economics and food systems economics. His research has focused on the problems of economic organization, coordination, and regulation in the United States and in many less-developed countries. He is a Fellow of the American Agricultural Economics Association and has received the Distinguished Faculty Award at MSU.

A. Allan Schmid is Professor of Agricultural Economics, Michigan State University. He works in the areas of law and economics, public choice, and benefit-cost analysis. He is the author of *Property, Power and Public Choice*, *Benefit-Cost Analysis: A Political Economy Approach*, and, with Warren J. Samuels, *Law and Economics: An Institutional Perspective*.

John D. Sterman is Associate Professor at MIT's Sloan School of Management and Director of its System Dynamics Group. His research includes the theory and practice of system dynamics, including simulation of organizational behavior and economic dynamics, experimental studies of decision making in complex dynamic environments, and the application of nonlinear dynamical theory to human systems. He has pioneered the development of "management flight simulators"—interactive simulations of corporate and economic systems to help decision makers gain deeper understanding of complex dynamics.

Richard D. Wolff, professor of economics at the University of Massachusetts at Amherst, is the coauthor (with Stephen A. Resnick) of *Knowledge and Class* and of *Economics: Marxian versus Neoclassical*. He has recently completed a forthcoming book, along with Harriet Fraad and Stephen Resnick, on class, gender, and power. He is a member of the editorial board of *Rethinking Marxism* and is preparing a manuscript on the U.S.S.R. with Stephen Resnick.